"For more than ten years, Marriott Hotels and Aaron Cushman made beautiful public relations music together. Cushman has one of the most creative minds I have ever seen. Together, we helped Marriott Hotels grow. PR people at all levels have got to pick up this book."
– *Tom McCarthy, Former Vice President of Advertising and Public Relations, Marriott Hotels, Inc.*

"Whether it's sports, show business, or Fortune 500 corporations, Cushman knows how to make news. He has helped me keep my column in the *Sun-Times* full of timely, topical, and meaningful stories. His book is filled with terrific anecdotes about famous people and familiar products."
– *Irv Kupcinet,* Chicago Sun-Times, *"Kup's Column"*

"In the field of marketing/public relations, Cushman has no peer. Without a doubt, his book is a must-read for PR professionals."
– *Asher Birnbaum, Publisher of* Tennis *magazine*

"Under Cushman's PR direction, Century 21 realized positive domestic and international media exposure beyond our expectations, and that meant increased sales. He is a great PR professional."
– *Richard Loughlin, President and CEO, Century 21 Real Estate Corporation (retired)*

"Cushman is a grand icon in the travel public relations field. Everything he writes has the touch of a professional."
– *Carl and Ann Purcell, photographic journalists*

"Aaron Cushman brings to the practice of public relations what his long-time partner, Bill Veeck, brought to baseball – innovation, integrity, and a love of the game. Aaron's aptly titled book takes us on a rollicking ride through his adventures in PR, representing famous people, companies, and places. A new generation of practitioners needs an infusion of his passion for the fascinating business of public relations, which his book provides."
– *Thomas L. Harris, Author, Professor, and Founding Partner of Golin Harris International*

A Passion for Winning

Fifty Years of Promoting Legendary People and Products

A Passion for Winning

Fifty Years of Promoting Legendary People and Products

by

Aaron D. Cushman

Lighthouse Point Press
Pittsburgh, Pennsylvania

A Passion for Winning
Fifty Years of Promoting Legendary People and Products
by Aaron D. Cushman

Published by:

Lighthouse Point Press
100 First Avenue, Suite 525
Pittsburgh, PA 15222

Copyright © 2004 by Aaron D. Cushman
Printed in the United States of America
Library of Congress Control Number: 2003113331

Publisher's Cataloging in Publication Data
Cushman, Aaron D.
A Passion for Winning: Fifty Years of Promoting Legendary People and Products
        p.   cm.

1.   Business
2.   Public Relations
3.   Autobiography
ISBN 0-9637966-1-5: $21.95 Hardcover

This book is printed on acid-free stock.
First Printing, January 2004

Dedication

This book is dedicated to the four women in my life who taught me love: my mother, Eva; my aunt, Teen; my sister, Charlotte; and my wife and best friend, Doris.

i

Table of Contents

Introduction

Over my fifty years in the public relations business, I have always felt that it was probably the most frustrating, maligned, misunderstood – and the most exciting – business imaginable. There wasn't a single day over all those years that I wasn't eager to get to the office. In the business that I had chosen to spend my life in, the greatest excitement – and challenges – were derived from the knowledge that, on any given day, I could be confronted with the opportunity to solve a new problem.

To recognize that you have the ability to mold public opinion for specific people, places, products, or services is almost mind-boggling. To see it happen over and over again as the years pass is both exhausting and genuinely thrilling. To know without any question that all the hard work, research, and skillful implementation applied to a public relations problem or opportunity will bring the desired result is heady and powerful. I have been on a fifty-year high without even taking more than an aspirin. I'm guilty! I love this business.

Now that the dust has settled and I look back on a half century of achievement, I realize that the changes that have occurred in the public relations business have been monumental. True, few things stay the same, but our industry has seen more than its share of transformation. Increased security now limits personal contact with the media. And, sadly, the lack of ethical conduct now involves members of the media, as well as those few less honorable public relations practitioners.

On the plus side, technology has revolutionized the way we write, research our material, and transmit written and oral communications. Most representatives of both print and broadcast media – at all levels – have accepted the fact that with the ever-increasing growth and globalization of American industry, the role played by professional public relations has become critical to the success of all involved parties.

This is based, in part, on the realization that it is economically and physically impossible for media to provide accurate and extensive coverage of the myriad interests of American business on a worldwide basis. Consequently, an almost grudging respect has developed by media for capable – and ethical – public relations practitioners. Similarly, the leaders of corporate America today show great respect for our industry, undoubtedly a direct result of years of meaningful counsel and guidance, combined with public relations' proven effectiveness. Corporate America's increased understanding of the machinations of public relations has helped to bring greater acceptance.

Despite the passage of time and the sweeping changes that have taken place within the public relations industry, there is one constant: Nothing can or will ever replace the need for *creativity*. New and better ideas will always be in demand and will continue to be the yardstick against which we are measured. In this, the age of spin, the public relations leaders of the future will continue to be those who have made *innovation* their hallmark.

To those of you who have chosen public relations as your career, I hope you will prosper and succeed on the roller coaster that symbolizes this exhilarating business. I hope, also, that you will have as much sheer fun as I did throughout the ride.

CHAPTER 1

Welcome to the PR Business _____

*There were no courses and no seminars (on public
relations) offered in local colleges. So it was fly by the seat
of your pants – trial and error – a method that is not likely
to work today.*

I had no idea what public relations was. Of course, no one else did
either in 1947. Standing on the corner of Randolph Street and Michigan
Avenue in downtown Chicago, the winter wind creeping inside my suit, I
was intent on becoming an advertising man. In my wildest imagination, I
could not foresee a scenario where Aaron D. Cushman & Associates, Inc.,
would one day be ranked among the twenty-five largest independent PR
agencies in the nation, and fifth or sixth largest in Chicago.

Having written letters to every ad firm I could find, it was time to
introduce myself in person. I knocked on each agency door along Michigan
Avenue, from Randolph Street north to the Drake Hotel, and didn't get
much further than the receptionist's desk.

I was ambitious, educated, and increasingly frustrated. My search went
on for weeks, and while I worried about my future, I remained committed
to a decision I made just two years before – a decision I came to in the skies
above a devastated Germany.

It was late April 1945, and World War II was winding down. For more
than four months, I was a member of the 351st Bomb Group. I was stationed
in the small English town of Polebrook, located just outside of Peterborough.

I remember the morning being typically English: dark clouds, some
fog and drizzling. I had the covers pulled up around my ears when I felt

someone shaking me. "Lieutenant, wake up, Lieutenant."

It was 3:45 a.m. Breakfast is 4:30, and briefing at five. I knew when I went to sleep we had a mission scheduled for the following day.

As I rubbed the sleep from my eyes, I could feel the familiar gnawing twirl in my stomach, the anxious and uncomfortable sensation that always crept in on mission days. I sat up on the edge of my cot as Sgt. Hanson leaned over and whispered, "Something is very strange this morning, Lieutenant."

"What's up, Hanson?" I grumbled.

"Sir, they've taken the ball turret out of the plane."

We flew B-17 four-engine bombers. Our group carried the red triangle insignia on the rudder fin. The ball turrets served as the only protection from ME-109 German fighter planes attacking at our underside. Because we'd be vulnerable as hell without those twin 50-caliber machine guns, I was sure Hanson was mistaken.

"C'mon, Sarge, they wouldn't do that," I assured him.

"Don't know, sir, but they sure are gone."

I asked Hanson if it was just our ship. "Hell no," he said, "it's every plane in the squadron."

I shook my head in disbelief. Then, almost casually, Hanson turned and over his shoulder added, "That's not all. Ready for this one? We're not loading bombs!"

Now, that really threw me. No ball turret. No bombs. Must be some kind of training mission, I figured, perhaps to work on our formation flying. Rather than try to sort it out, I decided to wait for the briefing to get it all firsthand.

At 5 a.m. on the button, there was a sudden end to the chatter as the Commanding Officer (CO) walked into the briefing room. Behind him was the target destination wall we regularly examined before each mission. The wall is typically draped in cloth until the CO is ready to outline our objectives. Today, with word of the missing ball turrets and no bombs having spread throughout the base, the crew was especially curious about the wall.

The CO began by telling us we were about to embark on the most unusual mission we had been on to this point. No factories, cities, or submarine pens to blast. Today, he explained, we are going to bring back French soldiers who had been prisoners of war since France was overrun by German forces in 1940.

The CO pulled back the drape covering the destination wall to reveal a detailed map of Europe. Every eye in the room traced the thin, black line that ran from Polebrook across Europe to Linz, Austria. That was our flight plan.

General George Patton's Third Army had just liberated this area of Austria and, although fighting continued south of Linz, thanks to the P-51s and P-47s of the 9th Air Force, the skies were cleared of most German fighters. Not only that, but since the American and British Armies had backed all opposition deep into Germany, the threat of serious anti-aircraft fire was practically nonexistent. This was far different than in '43, when the 8th Air Force was looking at thirty percent of its planes lost on most missions.

The old man, as we called the CO (he was thirty-five), explained that they had removed the ball turrets from the planes to lighten each ship. This would allow us to carry more Frenchmen.

There would be no flak jackets either, the CO declared. This news hit me hard. I had been used to sitting on mine as I flew, trying everything I could to protect my private parts. A man has to know what's really important.

The CO's last announcement, however, was greeted with pleasant surprise. He said we were to fly individually. There would be no formation, and we could choose our own altitude. After having flown exclusively from 19,000 to 23,000 feet on all missions, to me this was an open invitation to get a close look at some of the damage the war had done to German cities. And, to have some fun.

We pilots jumped at the chance to cross the English Channel at about one hundred feet above the waves, and then to hedgehop our way across Europe. It's been fifty-five years, but I can still see the fear and anxiety that flushed the face of a cyclist in France who turned to see our four props bearing down on him.

We were like kids in a candy store. Come to think of it, we were kids. I had just crossed over my twentieth birthday and, with few exceptions, the rest of our crew was about the same age.

For some magical reason, we all felt indestructible that day, like we were going to live forever. We were on our way to make somewhat of a heroic rescue. We let loose and stole the moment.

Along the way, I remember flying under a suspension bridge on the Rhine River. I also remember spotting what must have been about 100,000

German prisoners lounging in an open field. We veered toward them and, as we passed over their heads, almost every member of the crew took the opportunity to use the relief tube. I guess you could call it our last commentary on the war.

Shortly after landing at the German air base at Linz, the newly released French troops began arriving. They were a ragged bunch, filthy dirty, their uniforms tattered. After five years in captivity, it was understandable. The poor guys seemed utterly exhausted. Still, they held their heads high with dignity, even when our doctors were spraying them with DDT to kill the lice. They just kept smiling.

The bad part for us was the doctors insisted that every airman be sprayed as well, since we were to be in very close proximity on-board the plane. I didn't relish the idea, but it did make sense.

I don't know how many men we packed into the cockpit with us, but they were literally all over us. You could feel their relief at being free, but it was somehow restrained until the moment we crossed over the border into France. In broken French, we announced the news over the intercom. It was pandemonium. The Frenchies were cheering with joy, hugging each other, reaching over to hug and kiss us and then crying with happiness. It was a moment not easy to forget.

We landed at Chateau-dun and bid our liberated passengers *au revoir*. I can close my eyes today and still see hundreds of French men kissing the ground as we roared down the runway heading for home.

Back in the air, I couldn't help thinking of those men and all the opportunities that lay ahead of them. Sitting at the controls, I took stock of my own future as well. I knew that upon my return from the war, my parents expected me to finish college and become a professional – which, to them, meant being a doctor, lawyer, or accountant. Those were my choices.

Prior to enlisting as an aviation cadet, I was just another student at the University of Illinois. Before going overseas, I had already concluded I wasn't cut out to be a doctor, and I wasn't smart enough to be a lawyer. In my mind, I had settled on becoming an accountant. The two years at the University of Illinois, however, suggested I wasn't exactly accountant material, either. My lowest grades were in algebra and cost accounting.

As I flew over Aachen, Germany, I peered down at what must have once been a charming village and was now sheer destruction. Not a single rooftop was in place. I wondered if perhaps I had been too focused, too scared, too intense, and too well-trained to notice while the war was in full swing that life can be incredibly cruel and is invariably precious. The site below also made me more fully realize how fortunate I was to be an American. Thinking of all the liberties that awaited me back home in Chicago, I became convinced I could not pursue a career that didn't suit me. As admirable a profession as accounting is, I needed to find something that inspired me, something I could feel passionate about and was fulfilled by. I needed a career that required my strengths and appealed to my interests. I wanted a job that was both exciting and fun.

I left the Army Air Corps (it didn't become the U.S. Air Force until years later) in November 1945, and headed back to Champaign, Illinois, home of the University of Illinois, determined to discover my true calling. The campus seemed to have changed in the three years I'd been gone, yet there remained a comfortable similarity as well. As returning veterans, we were considered real hotshots. I had the crushed pilot's hat and the wings, and I felt ten feet tall. The underclassmen treated us veterans with great respect, but that attitude soon disappeared and we all became just students again.

The University of Illinois was enjoying its greatest days – and so was I. The "Whiz Kids" won the Big Ten and the NCAA Basketball Championships. The Illinois football team went to the Rose Bowl and my fraternity won the all-university softball and football intramural titles.

Perhaps because I was more attuned to the value of my education, the subjects I had struggled so hard with in the past now seemed incredibly easy. I still had no idea which career path to take, but I enjoyed classes that challenged my creative instincts. I had a feeling it might involve some sort of communication work.

WE WERE REALLY POOR

Money was always something I had to be creative about. For as long as I can remember, it was the obstacle that couldn't be ignored. My family had been really poor. If not for family pride, we would have been a charity case. In college, I was lucky. The G.I. Bill helped, and I earned extra funds when I was hired by the University to teach flying to returning veterans. On top of that, the Sigma Alpha Mu fraternity gave me a job washing dishes, which paid for half my room and board.

The fraternity's kitchen detail was made up of an amazing group of guys. Like myself, each of them needed help meeting financial obligations.

In looking back, it's fascinating to realize that every one of the men in that kitchen – hired to clear garbage off plates and wash and wipe dishes every night – became tremendously successful in business and life.

In my senior year at Illinois, I took every English, writing, journalism, salesmanship, and advertising course they offered. Writing just seemed to come naturally to me, and I enjoyed it. Because there was no such thing as "public relations" yet, that wasn't an option. I finally decided that advertising might be my forte, and that's essentially what put me on the corner of Randolph Street and Michigan Avenue on that brisk winter day in 1947.

The fact that I was not able to speak with a person of prominence in any one of those Michigan Avenue agencies made quite an impact on me. I admit that I laughed about it in later years because they certainly passed on a good bet. I also learned a lesson that throughout my career I tried never to forget. That lesson centers on opportunity and responsibility.

The competitive nature of today's corporate culture tends to demand certain etiquette in how one pursues employment, but I think every company ought to consider its responsibility to provide ample opportunity to those actively interested in a particular type of work.

Having experienced the disillusionment of not being given a chance myself, I would not feel comfortable turning the tables on someone else. Regardless of time demands, any person seeking a position at our agency who has written, called, or paid a visit to another staff member, or me, has been granted an interview.

It's true that not all of those meetings resulted in a new hire, but every once in a while I would come across an unusually bright, intelligent, and creative person who I thought would be a good fit for our organization. In many cases in which we were not in the position to hire anyone else, I would refer him or her to colleagues who I knew were interested in expanding their staff.

But, back in '47, my inability to find an agency job with a downtown firm eventually led me to shift my focus toward corporate positions in the advertising field and, finally, I got what I perceived was my big break.

I came across a job listing for an assistant ad manager with an industrial firm called Triangle Industries. I interviewed for the job, and, when it was offered to me at forty-five dollars per week, I immediately snatched it up and signed on. The glamour and excitement of it all soon faded when I found myself relegated to writing catalogue copy for an electrical supply house. In a period of three weeks, I went from ecstatic to miserable.

I'm a bit embarrassed to say that the highlight of my experience at Triangle Industries had little to do with the lofty craft of copywriting. It had a lot to do with a prostitute who lived in an apartment across the street from our offices. Because both her business and her shades were open during the day, quite a crowd gathered to watch her work. We, on the other hand, got very little work done during her busy times.

Luckily, my father called one day and essentially breathed new life into my dreams of more fulfilling work. Skipping any small talk, he asked if I knew anything about the publicity business. Frankly, I had never heard the word "publicity" and "business" used together before, so the irony that my co-workers and I had unknowingly publicized the exotic vocation of our female neighbor was completely lost on me.

I'd like to say my father's work was his life, but it was really the other way around. He had worked one job after another since he was twelve. That's the year his father died, when his horse and wagon fell into the Chicago River in the middle of winter.

As far back as I can remember, Essaness Theatre Corporation of Chicago employed my dad. He went to work when most people went to bed. Every night after the box offices closed, he would drive to each of the company's theaters to pick up accounting receipts, not money. With Essaness owning more than thirty theaters, he drove from ten at night to eight in the morning, seven days a week, 365 days a year. With only one car in the family and dad's unusual working hours, I was flying four-engine planes before I learned how to drive.

During the days and early evenings when dad wasn't working for Essaness, he landed some unusual side jobs – the most unusual being a stand-in for Groucho Marx. Because he was a dead ringer for Groucho, Paramount Pictures often hired dad as a promotional double. With a touch of make-up to widen his eyebrows and square off his existing mustache, the rest was easy. Dad always chewed a big cigar and he had Groucho's long stride and bent limp down to an art form. He was known as "Groucho" to everyone on film row.

I'M IN SHOW BUSINESS

When he called me that day, he knew I wasn't thrilled with my job at Triangle. Always listening for an opportunity for me, he heard that Essaness was looking for a publicist for their Oriental Theatre on Randolph Street. At that time, the Oriental and the Chicago Theatre were the two Grande

13

Palaces in the city, both showing first-run motion pictures, and both featuring big name stage shows.

Dad's tip led me to an interview with Edwin Silverman, the head of Essaness. I'd met Mr. Silverman several times in the past, when dad took me into the office and introduced me to everyone. Still, I couldn't help but be a bit intimidated. Here's the boss of one of the biggest theater chains in the city looking for a top-notch publicity man, and I wasn't even sure what publicity was.

The interview didn't last long. Mr. Silverman immediately asked if I could write. I told him that's what I was trained to do. He instructed me to go to the Oriental Theatre that evening and catch the 10:30 stage show starring Dorothy Shay, *The Park Avenue Hillbilly*.

"Write a review of the show," he said, "and have it back on my desk by eight the next morning."

It was freezing that night when I walked into the theater. I watched the show, headed back to the office, and immediately sat down and began writing. At 2 a.m., I placed my review on Mr. Silverman's desk. His secretary called the next morning to tell me I had the job and it paid fifty dollars per week. I took it.

I was so excited that I called my girlfriend, who was at home in St. Louis, and proposed to her over the phone. Ironically, her name was Doris Silverman, though she was not related to Edwin Silverman.

Doris had been in my life since college. I was dating a sorority sister of hers and, when I went to the sorority house to pick this girl up, I saw a very attractive girl standing in the stairwell. Someone told me her name was Doris and that she was from St. Louis. It began with a phone call and a dance date, and we've been together ever since. With three children and ten grandchildren, we recently celebrated our fifty-fifth wedding anniversary. And they said it wouldn't last.

With the job in hand, I felt marriage was the next logical step for us. Nothing else stood in the way. It didn't seem important that I hadn't the faintest idea what I was supposed to do as publicity man for the Oriental. Monday morning, beaming with both eagerness and pride, I dutifully reported for work. Showing the proper respect, I waited in the reception room to be invited in. I'd sat in that same spot so many times as a guest. Now I was an employee.

I was instructed to report to a man I had met many times before at social functions with my father. As I approached his office, I had quiet confidence and enthusiasm. I was ready to set the world on fire. But, that changed in a hurry.

When I walked into the room, my new "boss" looked at me but never got up from his chair. He was a short man, but his opening words to me were filled with the swagger of a corporate tyrant.

"I don't know how you got this job," he said with venom, "but I don't want you, and I'm going to get you out of here in a hurry."

I remember mumbling to myself, "Welcome to the publicity business." What a put-down. I was shocked. I literally stood there speechless. It couldn't have been something I said, because I hadn't spoken a word.

This guy was just downright nasty, I thought to myself, as I glanced past his shoulder at a wall full of service awards. The front of his office was made of clear glass, so he could easily look out over his staff of two artists, one production man, and the publicist for the Woods Theatre. It was obvious he'd been around a long time, and was used to being in control.

Before I could say a word, the boss called everyone into his office. No names, no introductions, not even a half-hearted welcome. "This is Cushman," he announced to the staff. "He has just been hired for the Oriental job. He is here on a thirty-day trial, and I want to know exactly what he knows. Therefore, there is to be no conversation between you and him at any time. You are not to make suggestions to him or offer him assistance. Anyone seen disobeying my orders will be summarily discharged. Do you all understand?"

The nervous staffers stood there in stunned silence, and, one by one, they turned and marched back to their desks. I never felt more alone in my life. At that moment, I longed for a nice mission over flak-filled German skies . . . almost. I later discovered the boss had promised this job to a girlfriend.

Several days went by, with me still completely in the dark as to the duties of my new position. I really wanted to be a success, if only to spite my boss, but I didn't have the slightest idea of how to go about it.

SUDDENLY THE LIGHT WENT ON!

Everyone on staff knew I was green, and, slowly, over the next few weeks, guys like Dick Felix, Harry Bryan, and Joel Mink began slipping me notes. One might say, "Check page 4, column 3 of the *Tribune*." I'd stare at that spot in the newspaper for what seemed like hours, desperately trying to understand what they were telling me. Then, I began to get the idea. It was like someone opened the door and a bright light went on.

As a publicist, I was supposed to make news. I was supposed to use the notoriety of the theater and its personalities to gain media attention. I was supposed to plan activities and pitch stories that would interest the city's reporters.

Fantastic! I was no longer in the dark. It was an epiphany of sorts, and I grabbed it and ran. I guess I've been running ever since. I fell in love with the job, and the great sense of accomplishment that came with each successful media placement for which I was responsible.

More importantly, I began to realize how critically important my role was in drawing audiences and contributing to the bottom line. For that, I owe a great deal to Dick, Harry, and Joel.

This really was a dream job, for the simple fact that I was able to learn the publicity craft while working with so many great stars of motion pictures, recording, and stage. How could you miss with that kind of product to merchandise?

I began to build extensive personal media contacts. Within a few weeks of taking the job, columnists from each of the city's papers and anchor people from the radio shows were calling me to gather activity highlights and to set up personal interviews. Suddenly, the theater was receiving media coverage to a degree it hadn't enjoyed in years, and my boss had backed off his promise of getting rid of me as soon as he could.

Unlike today's circumstances, media doors were wide open and everyone – well, almost everyone – was receptive to a creative, newsworthy idea. This was the era of popular Chicago columnists like Jimmy Savage, Herb Lyons, Irv Kupcinet, Tony Weitzel, Bill Leonard, Maggie Daley, Nate Gross, Noreen Foley, Roy Topper, Aaron Gold, and entertainment editors like Charlie Dawn, George Dougherty, Sam Lesner, and Mae Tinee. It was an era that required ingenuity and imagination, and I felt like I was loaded with it.

Though I was confident of my own potential, I was smart enough to realize how much I had to learn. Will Harris produced each stage show for the Oriental Theatre and, at age seventy, he experienced everything that was possible to do on stage and off, and some things that may not have been possible. He taught me a great deal about stage backdrops, lighting, and sound. Arthur Steagle was the theater manager and a very practical showman. He knew what voluminous publicity meant to marketing each show and was more than willing to offer me everything he knew about each attraction.

HELLO, UNCLE MILTY

Our shows changed every few weeks, and part of my responsibility was the preparation of a giant lobby display that provided our customers with a preview of the upcoming act. That display was easily twenty-five feet wide and fifteen feet tall.

My baptism by fire with that display involved the arrival of Milton Berle. I had arranged a schedule of interviews for Uncle Milty and sought his approval before making firm commitments. That same morning, we stopped at the theater and I noticed Mr. Berle staring at the lobby display that featured his name. He finally looked down and asked if we would get him a ladder and a ruler. Knowing what a great comedian he was, I assumed he was joking. He wasn't. I couldn't imagine what he was thinking, but my job was to satisfy his request.

The stagehand brought the ladder and I handed Berle the ruler. I nearly fell on the floor when he began to climb the ladder right there in the lobby. He stopped at the top and, using the ruler, began to measure the size of his name compared to the second attraction. I knew his contract called for one hundred percent top billing and that no other act could be more than seventy-five percent. After a few mental calculations, Berle climbed down and appeared satisfied.

Will Harris took me aside later and explained how important billing is to entertainers. "Sometimes," he said, "it's more important than money."

SEX SYMBOL JANE RUSSELL: HOT COPY

Meeting Berle was quite a treat, but it wasn't until I met Jane Russell that I realized the true perks of my job. Russell was booked into the theater shortly after completing her first motion picture, *The Outlaw*. Howard Hughes had recently discovered her and, although she was already considered the next sex goddess, she had never made a personal appearance of this kind.

Jane Russell was hot copy, so it was a real coup for Essaness to land her. As soon as word got out that she was coming to Chicago, my phone jumped off the hook. It seemed as if everyone wanted her for pictures, interviews, and charity appearances.

Capitalizing on her popularity was a piece of cake for me, but I had absolutely no idea what to expect when she arrived. Let's face it, people have fantasies about working with a sex goddess. Eager anticipation probably best described my mental state when she showed up at the theater one morning just in time for rehearsals.

She truly was beautiful, but seemed to me to be the antithesis of someone who had been tabbed as the short skirt, plenty of cleavage variety star. Jane wore a modest turtleneck sweater and was tall enough to stand head and shoulders above Will Harris.

As this was her first real personal appearance, it was not surprising that she was unfamiliar with even the simplest techniques of walking on and off stage. Will made clever use of me by having me act as her stand-in, just to demonstrate to her the way in which he wanted her to enter and leave the stage. My father doubles for Groucho; I double for Jane Russell.

Jane was not only intelligent, warm and friendly, but to Will's great pleasure, she was quick to pick up all the nuances. Working with her day to day, I found her to be highly religious, sensitive, and an utter delight.

THE THREE STOOGES: MADNESS ON THE HOOF

Another act that I found a pleasure to work with happened to come in threes. I can still see them running through their act.

Moe and Larry standing stage center, as Shemp enters stage left.

Moe, gesturing toward a security man backstage, shouts, "Close the alley door, everything is coming in here!"

To me, The Three Stooges were incorrigible and hysterically funny. Of all those who came through the Oriental, they were certainly among my favorites – as talent and as individuals. I wasn't sure how their brand of humor would play in Chicago, but to my amazement the Stooges quickly became one of our biggest box office grosses.

People loved them and, in fact, their shows drew new patrons to the theater. When they hit town, our audience changed from sophisticated to family. Parents and kids lined up along Randolph and Dearborn streets, sometimes waiting for hours to get tickets. After witnessing the way the Stooges were received, I wasn't surprised when they made their lasting mark in television.

On stage, each of them was riotous. Off stage, you'd think you were mingling with . . . well, accountants. All three of them were actually very serious men. It was almost as if they not only left their wild facial expressions on stage, but their whole comical demeanor, as well.

At times I'd walk around the city with one, two, or all three of them. No matter where we went, not a soul recognized them. I guess people just couldn't notice them out of costume – even though their costuming consisted of nothing more than a set of highly coveted combs, baggy business suits, and three brains full of zany antics. The combs were key, because in thirty seconds, adroitly used, they transformed three normal human beings into wild, untamable rogues, i.e., The Stooges.

But when they were on, they were nonstop. Tell them it was a publicity appearance, and, bang, three seemingly normal, middle-aged men would transform themselves into real-life stooges. They'd mug for any camera in sight, improvise on the spot and honor all requests for autographs. They were true "*menches*," good people.

In fact, one of their first requests of me was to tell them which children's hospital they could visit. It was the only personal appearance they made in which they insisted I not do my job of seeking publicity. Thank God we didn't need the coverage. There were so many demands for their time that the only way we could honor all the events was to split the Stooges up and have each one attend specific engagements. While I loved to see these guys move on to great success, I hated to see them leave Chicago.

The parade of stars through Chicago and the Oriental continued for the next three years. The names included Nat "King" Cole, Ella Fitzgerald, Sarah Vaughn, Louis Prima, Keely Smith, The Ink Spots, The Four Lads, The Pied Pipers, Louis Armstrong, and the Mills Brothers, among others. Gene Autry and his famous horse, Champion, took the stage at the Oriental, as well as Tony Martin and the gorgeous Lena Horne.

Each act brought its own challenges, and it was then that I was able to see these stars as individuals. Some, of course, were better than others. Many times, there seemed to be as much drama playing out backstage at the Oriental as there was on-stage. Any time, day or night, you could find twenty, thirty – sometimes up to fifty – stage door Johnnies and Jennies lingering about in search of a fantasy fulfilled. Most of them were just kids, and the girls seemed to be far more aggressive than the boys. The girls' hue and cry went from, "Please, just an autograph" to "C'mon, just give me five minutes in his dressing room alone." They were persistent, too. There was a security man at the door, but I couldn't count the number of young girls who sneaked past him. Occasionally, I'd enter a star's dressing room and find one or two young girls fulfilling their fondest desires.

For the most part, however, I found these celebrities to be upstanding people as well as extraordinary talents. Some just wanted to be left alone between shows, while others craved publicity and wanted to take advantage of every free moment to go and do, see and be seen.

THE TOASTMASTER GENERAL OF THE UNITED STATES

George Jessel was a special case. George came out of the Eddie Cantor and Al Jolson era of performers. Without a doubt, he was an outstanding *raconteur*. He was endowed with an amazing gift of gab and knew when and how to use his talent. George was also president of Twentieth Century Fox and had been responsible for producing several of the studio's most successful motion pictures.

Billed as the "Toastmaster General of the United States," George was wise to the value of publicity, and eager to do every interview and radio talk show I could arrange for him. It was "open sesame" as far as generating media coverage for him. We kept each other motivated, and the results were incredible.

George was also very "Hollywood." By that, I mean he was a top-flight namedropper. He seemed to know everyone in the world and, while there's no question he wielded substantial influence and power, he was quite impressed with his own importance. I admit I was a bit impressed with his importance as well. George continually offered me a job in Hollywood. I realized there was a bit of song and dance to it, but I was always flattered by the idea.

For various reasons, I'll never forget the last words George ever spoke to me. I dropped him at the airport one afternoon and, in typical Jessel style, he turned to me and declared, "You be sure and call me whenever you get to the West Coast. There's a job waiting for you at Fox."

While notions of working at Fox gave me a real morale boost, my job just continued to get better. There was a minor shake-up, however, when Essaness sold the Oriental to Jim Booth in 1949. But it was good news all around. My boss and his crew disappeared, and Mr. Booth brought in new and capable people to handle the advertising chores. Seeming more than satisfied with the work we were doing, he kept the rest of the theater personnel intact.

At about the same time, a close fraternity was developing among all the theatrical press agents in the area. Talk about wonderful guys. Eddie Sequin was my counterpart at the Chicago Theatre, which was owned and run by Balaban & Katz. He, along with Jack Garber, had been there for years. Ben Katz was Midwest publicity manager for Eagle Lion Films and the most experienced man doing world premieres. Eddie Solomon was in charge of Twentieth Century Fox Pictures. They were wonderful mentors. As the new kid on the block, I spent hours just listening and learning from the best.

One particular character of our fraternal clique stood above all others: Frank Casey of Warner Bros. Pictures. Frank was close with all the political bigwigs of the Midwest. That included Chicago Mayor Richard J. Daley and the city's second most powerful Democrat, Dan Ryan.

Frank was without peer in the "proper" utilization of expense accounts. He was recognized as the past master of expense account exaggeration. Everyone who knew Frank was aware of his specialty, including the hierarchy at Warner Bros. Yet his minor misdeeds were overlooked because everyone loved the guy. He could get more done, had more important contacts, and carried more quiet influence than any other publicist of his time. He was truly one of a kind.

While I was learning quite a bit from these men, I was still too much of a neophyte to recognize that there were widespread differences between the duties of theatrical press agents, publicists, and public relations consultants. It didn't seem to matter. The Oriental was packing them in. Across the street at the Chicago Theatre, Jack Webb's personal appearance brought lines of patrons that snaked around the block, and their booking of Frank Sinatra tied up State Street for weeks. In 1948 and '49, the world had a rosy hue, and I was sure I had found my niche.

NOTHING STAYS THE SAME IN SHOW BUSINESS

There was something I hadn't yet learned about this business. There's no such thing as a typical day in the entertainment industry. I learned that the hard way, when I strolled into the office bright and early one morning. As I passed the receptionist, she practically shouted after me, "Aaron, there is someone who wants to see you."

I immediately stopped and turned back to her. After a pause I said, "Who?"

"The new owner!"

This was news to me.

Without a second thought, I headed to Mr. Booth's office and knocked on the door. "Come in."

The voice was deep, and before I opened the door I knew someone was sitting at Booth's desk. Leaning way back in his chair, the gentleman's feet were propped up on the desk like a man intent on proving he was in charge. The stranger chomped on a big, brown cigar, looked up at me and barked, "Who the hell are you?"

I introduced myself and said, "I understand you were looking for me."

The man looked me straight in the eye and said, "If you're Cushman . . . you're fired."

It didn't sink in for a few seconds. I stood there motionless before finally gathering the courage to ask why. "You're the last employee left over from the Essaness regime, and I want you out."

I had never been fired before. I was shocked. Rather meekly, I asked him how soon he would like me to leave. "I'll give you five minutes to clean out your desk and be gone." Within five minutes, my whole world seemed to fall apart. I was devastated.

It took me more than a week to gather the courage to tell Doris. Each morning I'd get up, get dressed, and head out the door as if nothing happened. Instead of going to the office, I'd walk the Loop, stopping in to see friends to let them know I was in the job market.

I gave myself four weeks to find another position. In the meantime, Eddie Sequin and the guys at Balaban & Katz invited me to use their offices as a home base. They offered me the use of their phones and typewriters, and even said they'd be glad to take messages for me. Not bad for fellas I'd been competing with for news space and broadcast time. Like I said, it was a small fraternity.

A NEW BEGINNING

I finally had to come clean with Doris and, as I should have known, she was incredibly supportive. The good news, I told her, was that in walking the streets and keeping up with colleagues – you'd call it networking today – something unusual was happening. Small business people had begun asking me to represent them.

I guess I just kept running into the right people. First, a woman who headed a talent agency approached me about taking over her account, and then a restaurant owner requested my services. Soon after, I had interest from a nightclub, a hair styling salon, and even a place that provided grooming for poodles.

Over Sunday breakfast I must have had a faraway look because Doris asked me what I was thinking. I told her I had earned $600 per month at the Oriental and suddenly, three weeks after being fired, five small businesses were each offering me $200 per month to handle their publicity. "That's a thousand bucks," I said. "That's more than the job was paying me. Maybe this is what I should be doing instead of searching for another position somewhere."

Not long after that conversation, we came to a decision. With Doris' help, I started the Aaron D. Cushman Publicity Company in the middle of 1950. Initially, I operated from our apartment, telling myself that as soon as we added another two or three clients, I'd pick a Loop location.

With a start-up business, I was on a fast track going from 8 a.m. to 8 p.m., six days a week, and reveling in it. I was capitalizing on the media contacts I'd made and the know-how I picked up in my three-year stint at the theater. When my peers preached, I had been a good listener.

I tried to learn more, but publicity was such a new field, there weren't any textbooks on the subject. There were no seminars and no courses offered in local colleges. So, it was fly by the seat of your pants – trial and error – a method that is not likely to work today.

A PERSONAL LETTER FROM HARRY TRUMAN

Fortunately for me, more ideas worked than didn't. Our company was up and running, our clients were happy, and we were flying high. This was an adventure, and the future seemed bright, until the President's telegram arrived in September of that year.

It was more like a form letter. Harry Truman had written that it was impossible for the United States to successfully participate in the Korean police action without my help. In short, I was being recalled to active duty.

I couldn't believe it. I was an old married man of twenty-six who hadn't flown anything in five years. What could I possibly contribute to the war effort? How could I be called back, having already served my country with such pride and conviction?

I knew exactly how it was possible. In a weak moment, as I was being mustered out of the Air Force in 1945, I signed on to become a member of the inactive reserve. They had a perfect right to call me back.

In fact, I should have seen it coming, because I had read somewhere the Air Force was in need of experienced public information people. Considering my most recent experience, that reason for recalling me would make sense. But the Western Union wire clearly made note of my pilot's credentials and specifically stated I was being assigned to the Strategic Air Command. It said I was to report to the 97th Bomb Group at Biggs Air Force Base in El Paso, Texas, for transition training in B-50s and B-29s.

Believe me, I tried to erase any chance of getting in the pilot's seat of another bomber. I even went to Washington, D.C., to plead my case to General Sory Smith, the commander of all Air Force public information.

After getting lost in the Pentagon for half an hour, I was able to gain a brief session with the General. I hoped to convince him I'd be of far greater value to the Air Force as a public information officer. "Son," he said, "everyone assigned to SAC (Strategic Air Command) whose primary duty is to pilot, must fly. As much as we would like to have you in PIO, my hands are tied. As soon as you're off combat crew, we may be able to do something for you. Until then, it's just tough."

I was disappointed. I wasn't prepared to leave my business, and I certainly wasn't prepared to fly again. But I had no choice. Doris and I gave up our apartment on the city's North Side, sold most of our furniture, packed up the rest, and headed south.

I really felt bad for my clients. We'd had such a short run and things were going so well. But, in an effort to save what I could, I made a deal with a couple of friends in the business. We agreed they would service my accounts and keep any and all revenue until I got back . . . if I got back. You see, I always felt each of us carries a little bag of luck on our back, and it seemed as though my bag was pretty empty at the end of World War II.

It's strange how fate seems to keep pulling me back to Chanute Air Force Base in Rantoul, Illinois. I enlisted through Chanute in 1943 and passed my first military physical exam there. Now, headed back for another physical before moving on to El Paso, I couldn't help but remember how close I had come to flunking that first exam and avoiding military service altogether.

Only eighteen at the time and an active athlete, everything checked out okay. Even the eye tests went well, 20/20, until we reached a little matter of eye convergence.

In this test, the caring Captain placed a twelve-inch ruler at the bridge of my nose and proceeded to put a small pearl stuck to the end of a tiny pin atop the ruler. He asked me to follow the pearl as he moved it closer and closer to my face. After a couple of tries, he stopped.

"Sorry, Aaron," he said. "It's just not working." He told me it was a simple muscle exercise. If I practiced bringing my finger to the bridge of my nose, I should be able to pass. He suggested I go back to Champaign (I was in my sophomore year at the University of Illinois) and work at it for a week. So I did.

I used almost every waking moment to practice. On top of that, I began eating carrots like they were going out of style, since I heard they were good for the eyes. The week came and went, and I went back to the same

Captain, getting the same result. He told me it was really too bad because all my other tests had been so good. If I couldn't pass this baby, however, it was time to forget about learning to fly. I talked the Captain into giving me one more week to practice. It was back to the fraternity house, and back to the carrots.

God, how I practiced. Everyone at the frat house thought I had lost my marbles, sitting in the chapter room night after night with a ruler in front of my face and a mouth full of carrots. I drove back to Chanute the following Saturday, and again I flunked the exam. This time, the Captain said there was nothing more he could do or say. Dazed and on the verge of tears, I put my tail between my legs and followed him to the flight surgeon's office, where I was sure to be washed out of the aviation cadet program.

The flight surgeon was a bird Colonel, and, after looking at all my records, he stood up and half-shouted, "What kind of shit is this? Damn it, son, there is no good reason on earth for you to fail this test!" With that, he commanded me to sit down. He grabbed a ruler and then a pearl. With a dark marker pen, he drew a semi-circle on the face of the pearl. With the Captain looking on, the Colonel asked me, "Do you see that?"

"Yes, sir."

"Well, for your information," he barked, "that represents a girl's breast." Then he drew a single dot and asked, "Can you see that?"

"Yes, sir," I quivered.

"That's the nipple on her breast," he bellowed, "and you damn well better follow it."

Like the Captain before him, he slowly moved the pearl up the ruler until it poked me between my eyes. Unlike the Captain, he slapped me on the back and said, "You passed, son." I guess it just hadn't been properly explained to me before.

This time, however, we passed through Chanute without any trouble, and before long were unloading our bags at Biggs Air Force Base in El Paso. I reported to Colonel Donovan, the CO, and after a brief welcome, he asked me if I'd like to get in some flying time that day. He was going up in a Gooney Bird (C-47) and suggested I come along. Everything was very surreal. There I was back in the air, desperately trying to act like I knew what I was doing.

We flew the area for about two hours, and I was at the controls for a good part of the time. It was not exactly like riding a bike, but I was surprised at how comfortable I felt. Finally, Col. Donovan suggested we head for home and asked me to fly a GCA. He must have seen the lost look on my face because he asked what was wrong.

"Colonel," I stuttered, "what's a GCA?" He laughed and then asked me how long it had been. When I told him my last military flight was about five years ago, he smiled and explained that every landing in SAC had to make a GCA, or a Ground Control Approach. In short, we were to be vectored in by a radar operator as though we could not see the ground. I handled the maneuver okay, but this trip gave the Colonel a clear picture of my flying proficiency, and the next day I was deep into ground school with some B-29 transitional flying mixed in.

Fortunately, Korean combat crew was short-lived, and in a few months it was back to El Paso and a new job. Just as I had hoped, I was assigned as base public information officer. I was now a staff officer and invited to attend each of the commander's staff meetings, which were called whenever he had a subject of importance to discuss. They were held in a large room where tables were set in a giant square. Each department head (i.e., operations, adjutant, judge advocate, meteorology, maintenance, etc.) attended these meetings.

THE AIR FORCE AID SOCIETY NEEDS MONEY

We learned at one such meeting that General Curtis LeMay, commanding general of Strategic Air Command headquarters, had assigned the 97th Group the monumental task of raising $50,000 for the Air Force Aid Society. Apparently, each base in SAC had been given a quota based upon per capita personnel. Col. Donovan continued the meeting by wondering aloud how we were going to comply with orders and raise the money. As he often did when examining an issue, Donovan went around the room inviting thoughts and ideas.

Keep in mind I was low man on the totem pole and practically the last to speak. One by one, each officer, all field grade (Major or above), basically shook his head and shrugged his shoulders. As a last resort, Donovan turned to me. Very softly, almost whispering, I said, "I can raise the money, sir."

Almost as one, every head in the room turned in my direction. The doubt on their faces was obvious. Donovan stared at me a moment before asking, "And just how would you plan to do that?"

I told him I had been in the entertainment business before being recalled and had many friends in Hollywood. Then, I outlined my plan. If the Colonel were to give me a B-25 to fly to Los Angeles, a staff car and accommodations at the Hollywood Roosevelt Hotel, within four to six weeks I felt that I could bring back to El Paso a planeload of movie stars, with whom we could hold a benefit show that would attract enough people to make the $50,000.

To this day, I'm not sure that Donovan believed me, he just had no other option. He did not want to have the only SAC base unable to meet its quota. Within twenty-four hours, he approved the idea and agreed to provide me with what I needed. "California, here I come."

The Hollywood Roosevelt was a top-of-the-line hotel back then. With a luxurious room and the staff car at my beck and call, I must admit I was soaring so high, my ego could have used a parachute. Still, I was focused on the mission and the idea of failing never entered my mind. After all, so many stars had given me their numbers and invited me to call.

Actually, I was expecting success with the first call. George Jessel, Mister "you've-got-a-job-waiting-for-you" himself, was still head of Fox Studios. And I was his boy. I knew George had the power and prestige to make things happen. Just a few calls from him to the stars under contract to Fox, I figured, and our problem would be solved.

I dug Jessel's private number out of my black book and dialed him up. "Mr. Jessel's office," snapped the voice of an obviously sharp-tongued woman. I told her who was calling, that I knew Mr. Jessel, and asked if I could speak with him briefly. "May I tell him why you're calling?" she demanded.

"Please tell Mr. Jessel that it's Aaron Cushman from the Oriental Theatre in Chicago and that I am not looking for a job. Tell him I'm in the Air Force, and on behalf of the Air Force Aid Society, I am seeking his help."

So confident that he would be the next voice I heard, I agreed to hold while she transferred the call. It didn't happen. In fact, I placed five calls to George, and he was always in a meeting, reviewing a script, or previewing yesterday's shoot.

I panicked. George was the key to this whole thing. If I couldn't reach him, how would I pull this off? What if I had the same experience with my other contacts? Clearly, I'd be screwed. The old man would eat me alive and, worst of all, I'd look like a fool to all of my superiors. I'd be the laughing stock of the whole base.

I reviewed my options. Out came my trusty little black book of numbers. Determination, I reminded myself in pure Hollywood style, is my middle name. I would not, I could not, take "no" for an answer. After making several calls, hope began to emerge. Eventually, I was led to Sybil Cohn, the wife of Harry Cohn, who was head of Columbia Pictures.

Mrs. Cohn invited me to her home and, during a short meeting, she not only agreed to help, but also recruited Hal Wallis' sister to join us. Hal Wallis was a major Hollywood producer at the time. Without the help of these two dynamic women, my mission would have been impossible.

The three of us sifted through the names of stars, looking for those who were not on location shooting films. Many were unavailable. Of the stars I had known personally, some, like The Three Stooges, signed on immediately. This is another interesting lesson I'd take with me into agency work: to learn to identify who is for real and who is simply mouthing the words.

Five weeks after that fateful staff meeting, I called Colonel Donovan and told him I had thirty-six Hollywood stars who had agreed to come to Biggs and help make his quota. I requested that he call MATS (Military Air Transport Service) and arrange for a Stratacruiser to pick them up. I flew home to El Paso, satisfied that we had gathered the tools and talent to make this event a huge success.

The next step was to build local excitement through the consumer media in advance of the stars' arrival. As productive as the Hollywood part of the job turned out to be, this was what got me excited. I was handling the event's publicity and, for a change, completely confident in what I was doing.

Our strategy was to feed the media one or two big names at a time. This sustained the coverage over several weeks. In the meantime, with the Colonel's help, I was able to secure thirty-six convertibles for our giant parade of stars through downtown El Paso and into neighboring Juarez. Each convertible would carry one of the thirty-six stars, with the star's name emblazoned on the door to be readily identifiable to persons on the street.

With the cars ready and waiting on the tarmac, Ann Sheridan led the group of celebrities out on the runway. Hundreds of airmen in the gathering crowd went berserk. She was gorgeous, and as she stepped down, she waved and blew kisses to everyone. Margaret O'Brien followed with her pert smile. Then came Marta Toren, Eddie Bracken, the Stooges, Wanda Hendrix, Gussie Moran, Leo Carillo, Martha Tilton, Coleen Gray, Nancy Guild, Florence Marly, Bill Connors, and all the rest of those wonderful people who had given up their free time to help us out. The fact that none of them were being paid rekindled my faith in humankind.

Slowly winding through these two small towns, the parade drew overflow crowds to the base that weekend. With so much talent, it was easy to package an irresistible show. The great Henry Mancini, leading a pick-up band, anchored the three-hour program. Prices were low and the payoff was high. Not only did the show receive widespread press coverage, our box office and concessions sales easily put us over the $50,000 mark.

Ten days later, I was transferred to 8th Air Force headquarters at Carswell Air Force Base in Fort Worth, Texas. While I was encouraged to maintain my flying proficiency, I was now a full-time PIO. I didn't need too much encouragement because I wanted that extra flight pay.

It was at Carswell that I met Colonel Kalberer. He was the head of PIO for all SAC bases, and perhaps the finest officer I ever met. Kalberer knew he didn't have a chance of getting a General's star as long as he stayed in PIO. He was close to General LeMay, and everyone knew that one day Kalberer would get a bomber command and be elevated to General. It eventually happened.

Col. "Kal" was a stickler for proficiency. "If you are a pilot," he'd say, "be damn good at it. If you're a PIO, you better know your stuff." I was lucky because the true experience level of most SAC PIO's wasn't very strong. Early on, the Colonel seemed to gain respect for me and came to rely on me for assignments that otherwise would have gone elsewhere.

LIFE MAGAZINE, ED MURROW, AND ARTHUR GODFREY COME TO SAC

When *Life* magazine's Margaret Bourke-White came to SAC to do a photo spread on the B-36, I was assigned to escort her through Carswell and other bases where we flew the B-36. That aircraft, with its six pusher propellers and four jet pods, was our country's major deterrent during the Cold War days and the Russian threat.

Ms. Bourke-White knew her business. You don't become one of *Life*'s top photographers because you have political pull. I watched her work everyday for about three weeks and, while she never lost her sense of humor, she demanded respect and cooperation, and she got it. I don't think she missed a single angle in photographing the big ships and their crews. I still treasure copies of the eight-page story, though I never saw her again.

The other plum assignment Col. Kalberer steered my way was to work with newsman Edward R. Murrow. Murrow was filing a story on SAC and it was my assignment to be of help to him in any way that I could. Murrow had been through the London Blitz and had seen enough war to make his feelings about peace eminently clear.

With a razor sharp mind, cool demeanor, and penchant for chain smoking, Murrow defined the era's image of the gutsy but distinguished anchorman. It was through him that I realized the vital importance of meeting deadlines in the broadcast news business. This would come in handy down the road.

It was also under Col. "Kal" that I was introduced to crisis management, the hard way. When one of our ships crashed, I was one of the first military personnel on the scene. The plane had exploded on impact and we lost several airmen. I wasn't at the location more than twenty minutes when the media arrived en masse.

The crash occurred off the base, and the press was interviewing anyone and everyone who thought they had seen what happened. In the tension, with the atmosphere fraught with apprehension and fear, some of the quotes were wild, inaccurate and inappropriate. My job was to get the names and hometowns of every man in that crew to the press as fast as possible, but only after notification of next of kin.

It was my first experience facing a frenzied media so intent on gathering information that the actual facts seemed secondary. Photographers tried to crawl over every inch of the wreck . . . shooting, shooting, and shooting. It seemed as if everyone had lost any semblance of dignity or humaneness. The feeling I had was the media smelled blood, and, no matter what, they were going to get their story.

Under more sane circumstances, Col. "Kal" gave me another great assignment. Arthur Godfrey, perhaps America's most prominent television personality, had been a strong proponent of Strategic Air Command and a personal friend of General LeMay. On his weekly network television show, Godfrey had been an outspoken advocate of SAC and its deterrent program. Now he wanted to see the bases and the planes firsthand. Godfrey was a pilot himself, so he was well-informed of the latest aircraft and equipment.

In touring the command with him, I realized he had a serious problem walking. Although his limp was quite obvious, we never discussed it. Without having actually witnessed it, I'm reasonably certain that Arthur Godfrey was one of the few civilians ever to fly in a SAC combat ready aircraft – and I would not be surprised if he didn't actually spend some time at the controls.

In February 1952, Colonel Kalberer sent for me. He told me he was aware that my tour of duty was over in about thirty days. He asked me if I had a job waiting for me at home. I told him no. By that time I knew, despite the help of my colleagues, that most of my clients had moved on without me.

Kalberer told me there was a war brewing in the Far East that he felt the U.S. would be involved in very soon. If I were to stay in the service, he said, he might be able to arrange a promotion fairly quickly.

He must have read the look on my face, because with a hint of frustration he asked, "Why are you getting out?"

I paused before answering. The truth was, I was through flying military aircraft. The last time I sat out on the end of the runway, I knew I had already spent too much time checking magnetos, prop pitch, and feathering props. At the controls, the old devil-may-care attitude was gone. I was being too careful – if being too careful was possible. In my gut, I knew it was time to hang it up. It was definitely time to start building a future, planting some roots, and to begin thinking about raising a family.

"Colonel," I said, "This is just not a job for a nice Jewish boy." He laughed, and we left it at that.

CHAPTER 2

The Republican Convention
and the Chez Paree _____

Many reporters bring their own agenda to the assignments
they cover. Because they know what they want going in,
they direct their questions and don't let up until an answer
eventually shifts the subject's focus in their desired direction.
Then, their story is made, while the original – perhaps more
important – information is virtually ignored.

In March 1952, upon our return to Chicago, Doris and I started all over again. We opened an office at 307 N. Michigan Avenue. We had one desk, two chairs and one typewriter. The plan was for me to bang out the stories and Doris to cleanly type the material. Then, I'd rush the copy to the papers. We were back in business. Our only problem was we didn't have a single client.

Although we were essentially starting from scratch, I never viewed it that way. At twenty-eight, with the adventures I'd encountered, I felt like I'd already spent half a lifetime handling publicity. Intertwined with two tours of duty, I not only enjoyed three incredible years at the Oriental, but I had launched my own agency. Ironically, it was my Air Force experience that provided me with the best opportunity to hone my publicity skills, to make some excellent national contacts, and to gain the discipline and confidence to get my career back on track.

Within a week of opening up shop, I got a lead on a possible account, a potentially high-profile account, that had nothing to do with an actress, actor, or theater company. It involved the campaign to help make Dwight D. Eisenhower a candidate for the U.S. Presidency.

Citizens for Eisenhower funded the campaign, and the political leadership came from Senator Henry Cabot Lodge of Massachusetts. Ike, the hero of World War II, was hesitant to become a candidate, and Senator Lodge was touring the country to build a grassroots outcry for Ike to throw his hat into the ring.

Obviously, it worked, but Ike did need some convincing. Lodge was quite a political force himself in those days, and without his impassioned stumping, who knows if Ike would ever have held the highest office in the land.

I vividly remember one trip Lodge made to Chicago in support of Ike. It turned out to be a bizarre lesson in the antics of the media. George Fry, who was the Illinois chairman of the campaign, asked me to set up a press conference for Lodge at the Blackstone Hotel. The room was packed with political writers and broadcast media. One of the last reporters to enter the room was John Madigan of the *Chicago American*, which, at that time, was a Hearst newspaper. Almost immediately after Senator Lodge took the podium and started to speak, Madigan started in on him.

With seemingly every comment by the Senator, Madigan would interrupt him with some outrageous question or comment. Lodge maintained his cool and patience, while Madigan continued to harangue and interrupt. Finally, Lodge had enough. He turned to his security staff and demanded that Madigan be removed from the press conference.

Of course, the *American*'s first edition front-page banner the next morning read, "Reporter forcibly removed from press conference."

It was clear to me that Madigan, a solid reporter, had been specifically assigned by his city editor to disrupt the conference and make himself such a pest that Lodge would have no choice but to throw him out. In my opinion, that was the pre-arranged story line. It was the first time I saw it happen, but certainly not the last.

Many reporters bring their own agenda to the assignments they cover. Because they know what they want going in, they direct their questions and don't let up until an answer eventually shifts the subject's focus in their desired direction. Then, their story is made, while the original – perhaps more important – information, is virtually ignored.

Ironically, it was a few caring media folks who recommended me to the local leadership of Citizens for Ike. I was given the opportunity to compete for the account against several much larger agencies and won. I'm sure that my being a returning veteran pilot helped.

When Ike did become a Republican candidate, I had no qualms about working to help make him our next President. Ike knew war, perhaps better than anyone. He had seen all its horrors and I felt confident if there was one human being who would try his level best to keep our country out of another conflict, it would be Dwight Eisenhower.

With our client-agency relationship almost as an afterthought, I jumped head-on into the election effort. The enthusiasm was contagious. Everywhere you looked, it was "I Like Ike." It was on buttons, signs, buses, hats, ties, and blouses. The slogan appeared almost daily in the media. My personal preference for Ike was obviously shared by millions across the country. He was the candidate, and the Republican National Convention was headed to Chicago.

Jim Haggerty was anointed Ike's press secretary, and, early on, he recognized that the national media would pour into Chicago for the Convention. He also realized the delegates who streamed into the city would undoubtedly get their morning news from Chicago papers, radio, and television. He was in need of someone not only familiar with the local media, but a person who was on a first-name basis with many of its personalities. I just happened to be in the right place at the right time. When Jim added me to the convention team, I knew it would be a learning experience at a whole new level.

BUILDING MEDIA CONTACTS

My job involved press relations, and while I was already used to dealing with different personalities, I do remember an incident that called for a peculiar brand of ego massaging. Ike was in town, staying at the Blackstone Hotel, ensconced in around-the-clock meetings. The wheeling and dealing never seemed to stop. Being way out on the periphery, it was mind-boggling to watch the ebb and flow of key national leaders going in and out of his suite. On one such afternoon, I was headed down in the hotel's elevator. Someone in the rear of the elevator was ranting and raving, "I don't give a damn about Eisenhower! If Haggerty won't even give me five minutes with Ike for a photograph, he can go straight to hell as far as all of my papers are concerned." This guy was really peeved, and he didn't care who knew it.

As the elevator opened and those getting off peered over their shoulder at Mr. Loudmouth, I swung around behind him, tapped him on the shoulder and said, "Excuse me, I couldn't help overhearing what you said and I'm wondering if I might be of help." I introduced myself and explained that I was a member of Eisenhower's public relations staff.

This man told me he was Hubert Messe, the owner and publisher of twenty-seven community newspapers in Chicago's northwest suburbs. He told me he was accustomed to running a picture of himself and the candidate that he backed on the front page of each of his papers.

Messe clearly had an ego that wouldn't quit and apparently Haggerty had refused to allow him to take a picture with Ike. I told Messe as long as he had come all the way downtown from the suburbs, wouldn't it make sense to wait just another few minutes to see if I could change Haggerty's mind? He agreed it was worth a try.

I told Haggerty getting this guy a quick photograph with Ike was not only worth keeping him from going home angry, but it also might be worth the suburban coverage. Hubert Messe got his photo with Ike, and, oddly enough, we ended up being lifelong friends.

It's obviously the little things in life that count because, from that day on, Hubert was open to running or writing stories involving any of my clients that made sense for his readers. He helped me recruit *all* the publishers of suburban papers into one contest after another. These were businessmen who guarded their papers' territory like Fort Knox, and yet, with Hubert's help, we ran mutual promotional campaigns that covered over 150 community newspapers.

Despite the fact that he occasionally lost his cool and wanted everyone within earshot to know how important he was, Hubert Messe could be generous and kind to a fault. I grew to have genuine respect and admiration for him and his wife, Dina.

During the actual convention, I spent most of my time as a runner, carrying messages and releases to the media. I did have the chance to bang out a few secondary stories for Haggerty's approval, but the excitement for me came with simply watching the national politicos frantically rush from meeting to meeting with state delegations. To stand at a distance and observe the precision of network television newsmen like Walter Cronkite and Huntley and Brinkley was an education unto itself.

Eisenhower won the election, and everyone involved celebrated wildly. Ike came to Chicago briefly after the election, and I had the chance to both meet and talk with him. He was very gracious and surprisingly friendly.

I always had the impression Ike really didn't want the job, but that the country insisted he have it. For me, the victory brought with it a sense of pride. I felt as though I played a small role in making history. I also felt as if the experience gave me an advantage in marketing my new agency. I was back in town and back in business, and I wasn't shy about spreading the word.

THE BUSIEST NEWSMAN HAD THE MOST OPEN DOOR

One of the first to learn of my latest venture was *Chicago Sun-Times* columnist Irv Kupcinet, the busiest newsman I've ever known, and the man with the most open door for everyone. His daily column may still be the first page readers turn to in the morning to find out what's really going on in the city. He was and continues to be "Mr. Chicago."

In his heyday, not a single major political or entertainment personality would come through Chicago without calling on "Kup." From President Harry Truman to Bob Hope, he was a wanted man for lunch, dinner, drinks, or private conversation.

His column was dynamite, but his schedule was downright incredible. There were days when I'd see Irv in his office at eight in the morning and then meet him for a drink at two the next morning. His secret, although it wasn't all that secret, was his ability to catnap. It wasn't unusual to see Kup fall asleep in a taxi in the midst of a five-minute ride.

His other secret is, and this isn't all that secret either, he was blessed with excellent secretaries over the years. All of them were amazing, able to juggle their work, his schedule, and all of the requests to reach him, while still providing people with access to Kup and his column. One secretary in particular, Stella Foster, has been a fixture in his office for close to twenty years. I'd bet she knows how to reach any newsworthy individual in the world.

In the fifty years I've known him and read him, I've never seen Kup take pot shots at anyone or be unkind in his column. In fact, I know from personal experience that he's made a habit of helping people. In my early years at the Oriental, he was always quick with a smile, a compliment, or even a word of advice.

I remember visiting with Kup shortly before leaving for El Paso on my second tour of duty. I told him how I would have to put my career on hold, but I planned to get back in one piece. I let him know that if I came across a story or two in my military travels, I'd try my darndest to get it to him exclusively.

In my eighteen months of duty, I had plenty of opportunities to offer him solid news tips without breaking security. He had been so helpful to me, I wanted to reciprocate in some small way. By giving him a twenty-four-hour lead on a breaking story, Kup had the jump on every newsman in the country.

In telling Kup that I had once again launched my own publicity agency, he couldn't have been more encouraging. He offered me a firm vote of confidence and a promise to take a look at anything I sent his way. His words were a big boost at the right time, and he later proved to be more helpful than I ever imagined.

WE START BUILDING THE AGENCY

In the meantime, I signed my first commercial clients, Mary and Mart Dooling. Mary was CEO of Talent, Inc., which as its name would suggest, was an agency representing radio and television talent. Her clients ranged from commercial advertising voices to dramatic actors to news specialists.

Mary had come to Chicago from St. Louis, where she'd been employed by the Catholic Archdiocese. How this prepared her for a career dealing with an array of temperamental personalities, I could never understand. She was so soft-spoken, so gentle, and almost nun-like in her demeanor – except when negotiating contracts for her people. She was unflappable in the heat of monetary discussions, and yet never raised her voice or, God forbid, uttered a four-letter word.

Mary's people were demanding, at times unbelievably difficult, and in a business where it was customary to switch agents whenever it seemed advantageous, I seldom if ever heard that she lost a specific talent. Everyone loved Mary, and I admit to being a party to that sentiment. It was her own unique personality – she was genuine to the core – that made it possible for us to sell several major feature stories on the company.

We picked up another client working in the thick of the entertainment industry when Harry and Elmer Balaban signed on with us. Harry and Elmer were related to, but did not work for, the Balabans of Balaban & Katz, which for many years ran the largest chain of theaters in the country. Harry and Elmer owned the Esquire and the Surf Theatres.

With each new account, we slowly turned from a mom and pop operation into a small business. Uhlemann Optical Company, Sheridan Art Galleries, Michael Kirby's Ice-Skating School and Norman Granz "Jazz at the Philharmonic" also joined the firm in our first year. Doris and I were digging in and enjoying our embryonic success. Little did we know things were about to get even better.

The French have a word for it, "*cabaret*," meaning a restaurant where guests dine while being entertained by a variety of performers. Although the Chez Paree in Chicago was referred to as a nightclub, what it offered more neatly fit the meaning of a *cabaret*.

Dave Halper, an owner of the Chez Paree, contacted me following a recommendation from Irv Kupcinet. I was obviously flattered by the good word. I knew the club was top of the line, and for me, it represented the prospect of acquiring a major piece of business that was loaded with prestige.

Having been established in 1932, the Chez Paree was one of the oldest nightclubs in the country. This wasn't just a Chicago hot spot, either. It enjoyed a national, and even international, reputation. Sophisticated travelers considered an evening at the Chez a must when in the Windy City.

It was difficult to miss the club's bright marquee at the corner of Fairbanks Court and Ontario Street. Standing tall under that marquee each night was a sturdy doorman, cloaked in the costume of a Russian Cossack. He even spoke in a clear Russian accent, and getting into the club took more than flashing him a picture I.D.

Visitors to the Chez were squeezed into a tiny elevator and carried up to the action on the third floor. At peak performance, the elevator carried eight to ten people at a time. With literally hundreds waiting in line to see acts like Dean Martin and Jerry Lewis, I marveled at how they were ever able to get them all inside.

From what I knew about the Chez, I approached my initial meeting with Dave Halper with great interest, but some trepidation. Mr. Halper spent only two minutes with me before turning me over to Jay G. Schatz. It was then that I learned four partners owned the Chez, each with a different area of expertise. Dave Halper, "Dingy" to his friends, was in charge of hiring talent. Don Medlevine, "Donjo" to his friends, was responsible for buying the booze. Al Kaiser, who also owned a food company on West Randolph Street, was the club's food specialist. Finally, Jay Schatz, "Jack" to his friends, ran marketing and operations.

Jay, or "Jack," started by telling me he didn't know much about public relations, but he was smart enough to know that in previous years, he hadn't had any. I learned later that Jack was a board-approved practicing attorney and a qualified auditor, so he was indeed one smart man. He even knew I had recently returned from military service. He asked how long I'd been in and where I had served. We really connected when I told him I was with the 351st Bomb Group at Polebrook.

Turned out Jack had been with the 351st as a bombardier. He was shot down in late 1943 and spent almost two years as a POW. He fractured his hip when bailing out of the plane and was left with a slight limp. We traded a few war stories that day and then made an agreement that stood for ten years. He would teach me the nightclub business, and I would teach him the public relations business.

Initially, Jack could not understand how I could represent the Chez and not be in the club every night until at least midnight. Their previous publicist had spent most every evening bent over the bar, and didn't do much in the way of gaining them any media exposure. I explained to Jack that with the exception of gossip columnists, most media people worked a normal nine-to-five shift. There was no way I could accomplish anything on behalf of the Chez by trying to reach media in the middle of the night. I told him I planned to be in the club during every opening event, whenever the club hosted a media person or whenever there was a between-shows publicity activity involving our stars.

Jack bought into my thinking. We also agreed to meet at the club every Tuesday evening, at which time I would give him a complete report on the results of past activities and the planning of future special events. Jack quickly became adept at the publicity aspect and even began contacting certain columnists himself. Although I felt this was not his role, I didn't make a big deal of it because I knew he really enjoyed the personal contact.

PR FOR THE CHEZ PAREE: A WIN-WIN SITUATION

The enduring success of the Chez Paree centered on two long-established policies. One was the club's strict dedication to the quality of its food and beverages, and the other was the consistent promise of superb entertainment. For $5.50 and tax, the Chez offered an exquisite seven-course meal, the enjoyment of dancing or simply listening to the music of two fine orchestras, and a first-rate performance by headliners that included Jimmy Durante, Danny Thomas, Joe E. Lewis, Sophie Tucker, Ann Sothern, Joey Bishop, Metropolitan Opera diva Helen Traubel, and Tony Martin, among others.

What a field day I had placing feature articles, fashion layouts, and even promotional tie-ups with commercial establishments in return for advertising!

The Chez's financial records showed the club had approximately twenty to twenty-five weeks of bookings with major attractions that guaranteed maximum attendance every year. Well aware of those numbers, Jack and I developed a marketing program that strove to find ways to improve flagrant reversals in the business chart in the remaining twenty-seven weeks. We set about emphasizing the fact that an evening at the Chez Paree was relatively economical. As a way of proving the Chez was the best entertainment buy in Chicago, we used a factual but hypothetical situation to point out the club was actually less expensive than having dinner at a fashionable restaurant and attending a legitimate show.

In 1953, after analyzing attendance charts and operating expense statements, we projected our marketing program two years ahead and adopted a combination of publicity and advertising designed to educate the public to what their dollar amount could buy at the Chez.

DANNY THOMAS: PERENNIAL FAVORITE

For one thing, they could buy an evening with Danny Thomas. He was one of the first entertainment giants I promoted for the Chez. Danny was a long time Chicago hit from his early days at the 5100 Club, and he claimed Chicago as a favorite among his many ports of call. I picked him up at Midway Airport (O'Hare had not yet been built), and, after introducing myself, Danny instantly said, "Please take me to Little Jack's for cheesecake." The man loved the cheesecake at Little Jack's. It was as if he could smell it from the air, because it was always the first stop when he rolled into town.

In his shows, Danny performed all the classic routines that made him such a big draw. There was "The Wailing Assyrian," "The Jack Story," and "You're Over the Hill." His performance changed dramatically in later years, after he starred in several motion pictures in which his singing talent was featured. On stage, he was able to transform himself from comedian to singer. Though some of his loyal fans were disappointed, Chicago audiences loved him no matter what he did. Every show was a guaranteed sellout.

BEDLAM WITH DEAN MARTIN AND JERRY LEWIS

Our biggest attraction, however, had to be Dean Martin and Jerry Lewis. This was before they went their separate ways. Working with those two was a real kick. Jerry was always on-stage, totally uninhibited no matter where he was. He played Dean's foil perfectly, and, as far as I could tell, he loved doing it.

Jerry made his nightly entry onto the stage from the rear of the room rather than from the stage wings. He would actually walk on top of tables as people were dining. Despite an occasional spilt soup or martini, his first impression never failed to break the audience up. They roared with laughter and applauded until their hands were raw.

While Jerry did more than his share of personal appearances, Dean spent most of his time between shows in the Key Club, a private club within the Chez. Jerry was tough. He demanded a thorough explanation of every item on the publicity agenda. The slightest delay or change sent him flying into a temper tantrum or a fit in which he'd threaten to pull out. But that was the surface Jerry Lewis. Within five minutes of his blowup, he'd usually apologize, saying he knew the delay was not my fault. As I said, working with those two was a real kick.

Sherman Wolf, a former fraternity brother of mine and a key member of our staff, reminded me that we once convinced Jerry Lewis to push a wheelbarrow loaded with pieces of luggage for a publicity stunt in support of his picture, *The Bell Boy*. Sherm had the plum assignment of providing the luggage and supervising the photo session.

There were a number of unusual stunts Jerry was willing to take on. He rode atop a giant pumpkin in a State Street parade, sold tickets in the box office of the Chicago Theatre, and played first base in a charity baseball game at Comiskey Park. As always, Sherm helped pull these events off without a hitch. Well, almost always.

There was one occasion when Jerry was in town, not only for an appearance at the Chez, but to help promote his latest motion picture, *Cinderfella*, which was making its Chicago premiere. The premiere was to be followed by a black-tie ball in the Sarah Siddons Room of the Ambassador West Hotel.

On the night of the event, Jerry was scheduled to grant five radio interviews in the hotel lobby. As expected, the lobby was jammed with people. Jerry's first interview was with Jack Eigen, and when it ended, Jerry turned livid, screaming and yelling about what a dumb idea this was. Sherm was the one taking the heat until, finally, the manager took Jerry into his private office.

The ball, meanwhile, was to begin officially with Jerry brought out on a sedan chair, carried by two of the Pump Room's plumed and costumed servers. Sherm had been embarrassed by Jerry's previous outburst, but was happy to see the opening ceremonies unfold as planned. Relieved, he headed for the door. Jerry must have noticed Sherm leaving because he headed directly across the ballroom, where he stopped Sherm and offered him an apology.

When Jerry was in town for another event, we received a call from Chicago's Cardinal Stritch, who asked if Jerry Lewis would be willing to spend a few minutes with a nun and three children who had survived the tragic fire at Our Lady of Angels Church. The fire had killed nearly one hundred children and nuns, and injured many others.

We got the news to Jerry and he quickly agreed to the Cardinal's request. Again, Sherm handled the assignment. Jerry met the nun and the children at the Chez and took them backstage to his dressing room. Sherm waited in the lobby.

After several minutes, the nun and the children emerged from the dressing room smiling, their arms loaded with gifts. The nun told Sherm that Jerry wanted to see him. When Sherm knocked on the door he heard sobbing. Upon entering, he found Jerry, his face in his hands. "Those poor kids," Jerry was saying through his tears, "how I wish I could speak to and touch the ones who didn't make it."

In our view, when the *Damn Yankees* cast sang "You Gotta Have Heart," they were telling what the real Jerry Lewis is all about.

JIMMY DURANTE: NOSE TO NOSE WITH TURTLE WAX

Jimmy Durante was another incredible draw for the Chez. His "Ink a Dink" routine drove me nuts. I couldn't stop laughing. Jimmy was also one of the nicest, most genuine people I ever worked with in show business. He came to town annually with at least six beautiful chorus girls, and he knew exactly when and how to work them into his act.

Always looking for ways to tie the Chez's attractions in with our commercial clients, Sherm Wolf and I concocted an idea we felt was a natural dual promotion between Jimmy Durante and Turtle Wax. Turtle Wax is a wax enamel used primarily for automobiles. It's been well-advertised for years, but, at the time, the company had branched out into household items. In 1953, the auto enamel finish was their anchor product, and Sherm managed the account for our firm.

At the three-way intersection of Madison, Ogden and Ashland streets, atop a twelve-story edifice, Turtle Wax built a giant glass turtle designed to help Chicagoans to better anticipate the weather by changing its color with each revision in the climate. The electrified turtle was scheduled to be turned on for the first time on a day that dovetailed with Jimmy Durante's engagement at the Chez. Since the turtle and Durante represented the two biggest noses in town, we wanted Jimmy to actually throw the switch that would light the turtle, and, to throw that switch with his nose.

Jimmy seemed to get a kick out of the idea and agreed to go along with it. Sherman and I discussed the plan with the city desk at each major newspaper in town, and got nothing but enthusiastic responses and promises to send photographers and reporters to cover the story and interview Durante. The stunt was scheduled for noon.

On the morning of the event, I sent Sherm to the Drake Hotel, where Jimmy always stayed. Sherm was to pick him up and have him at the site by 11:45 a.m. At about that time, Sherm was back at the site, but no Jimmy. He told me he could not reach Jimmy, that Jimmy had placed a hold on his phone, and the hotel clerk refused to ring his room.

With the media beginning to rumble, we both went back to the hotel. I demanded to see the manager, and when I explained the situation, he relented and rang Jimmy's room. There was no answer. Now he was genuinely concerned and decided to take a passkey and check the room out himself.

As he put the key into the lock and headed into the room, Sherm and I were hot on his trail. We couldn't believe our eyes. Jimmy was stretched out on a couch in the suite's living room, sound asleep in his underwear. In every corner of the room lay one of the chorus girls in bra and panties. They too were sound asleep. It looked like the second Battle of the Bulge. It was clear Durante was not going to rub noses with anything but the Sandman.

Sherm and I got back in a cab, returned to the site and apologized to the media. We told them we goofed, that there had been some confusion in Mr. Durante's schedule. Another lesson: we must always protect our clients.

SOPHIE TUCKER: MARKETER PAR EXCELLENCE

As for the hardest working headliner to play the Chez, in my view, it was Sophie Tucker. No question about it. Deep into her seventies and well past her prime, Sophie was still belting out "Some of these days you're gonna miss me, honey . . ." She is now long gone, but she was right. I do miss her and think of her fondly and often.

Sophie was a special breed, clearly from the old school. She was also her own best marketer. She liked staying at the Ambassador West Hotel, which was just minutes north of the Chez. Every afternoon, you could find her in her suite writing personal cards to a host of people whose names she kept in files on three-by-five-inch cards. She was writing to fans, nightclub personnel, and members of the media in the towns she was scheduled to appear in next. She'd just drop a personal note, saying something like, "I'll be in Minneapolis September 9 through 21 at the 'xyz' club and would love to have you stop by and say hello. Love, Sophie." Every card was hand-written and she averaged about 300 a day. At night, after each performance, she'd sit at a table in the club's lobby and hustle her book, with all revenues going to one charity or another. People leaving the club would stop and chat with her or request an autograph. Invariably, she'd always manage to sell them a book as well.

After two weeks of decent, if not great business, Sophie was all packed and ready to leave the hotel when I ran into her. She gave me a big hug, a sincere thank you and then she slipped some money into my hand. "Sophie," I protested, "you really are great, but I cannot accept this. I'm well-paid by the Chez, and I don't think it's right to accept this kind of gift." She looked at me and in Yiddish said, *"Zie nicht a knar,"* which means "Don't be a fool." Then she said, "I want you to have it. It's my way of saying thank you."

JUST A SQUEEZE ON THE ARM: "EVERYTHING'S OKAY"

Every opening night, the club hosted entertainment editors and columnists. I usually sat them at a large table together and arranged for the show's star to come by either before or after the performance. On most of these evenings, while I was waiting for our media guests to arrive, I'd stand near the *maitre d'*, where I could best greet the press representatives and their wives. At every opening for ten years, Mr. Jimmy Allegretti would stop by and squeeze my arm. He never said a word to me in ten years; just squeezed my arm.

Now, Allegretti was no editor or columnist. In fact, I don't know for sure what he was, but knowledgeable folks referred to him as "the man who controlled Rush Street." As long as I worked at the Chez, I was aware of the rumor the club was, in some way, backed by gangster money. To this day, I'm not certain there was any truth to that.

Allegretti always arrived and left with an entourage. After he and his pals walked out the door one evening, I decided to mention this arm-squeezing thing to "Donjo" Medlevine. Donjo told me it was Jimmy's way of saying, "Kid, everything's okay. Just keep doing what you're doing."

Donjo was just one of those intuitive guys who knew how to interpret a good arm-squeezing. A similar episode involving Donjo occurred one night during Tony Martin's engagement. We had scheduled a personal appearance for Tony between shows, and I remember getting him back to the club around 12:30 in the morning. As always, I parked my car directly across the street from the club's marquee and took Tony to his dressing room. He was just in time to freshen up for the second show and I was ready to get back in my car and head home for a few solid hours of sack time.

When I got back into my car, the typewriter I had left in the back seat was gone. Angry and frustrated, I ran back upstairs to the private office, picked up the phone and called the police. As I was describing the incident to the desk sergeant on the other end of the line, Donjo put his giant hand on my shoulder and said, "Hang up the phone."

"But, Don, you don't understand, someone copped a typewriter out of my car right in front of the club," I tried to explain. He insisted I hang up the phone, and then asked me when this happened. I told him just a few minutes ago. He told me to sit tight, stay in the office and stay away from the cops. Donjo Medlevine was not the kind of guy you want to argue with, so like a dummy I sat in the office contemplating my navel.

Within a half-hour, the Russian doorman came into the office and in his heavy accent said, "Your typewriter is back in your car." I never asked who, what, when, or why. All I knew was I had my typewriter back.

QUICK-DRAW MAN: SAMMY DAVIS, JR.

The Will Mastin Trio starring Sammy Davis, Jr., was another outstanding act that "Dingy" Halper tried to book at the Chez at least once each year. Halper would have taken the group every day for a year if it were possible. That's how big an attraction they were.

Will Mastin was Sammy's uncle, and the third member of the group was Sammy's father. In a quiet moment, Sammy would say Will and his dad taught him everything, and as long as they lived he intended to keep the act together. Though a bit past their prime, neither gentleman was a slouch when it came to dancing.

Sammy was not only quite a song-and-dance man, but also an avowed quick-draw man. He loved to demonstrate his prowess with a gun, twirling it in his hand and sliding it in and out of its holster. It seemed his free time was spent either listening to the recordings of friends like Frank Sinatra and Dean Martin or flipping a gun around. He was equally adept with his

46

left hand and his right. We eventually figured out a way to take advantage of this off-stage skill.

Already fairly sure of his answer, I asked Sammy if he would be willing to take on challengers in a quick-draw contest we would hold some afternoon at the Chez Paree. He liked the idea, so we pushed a few magic buttons and sold it as a promotion to one of the morning papers. Then we tied in a radio station and, with all the advance publicity, we had quick-draw candidates coming out of the woodwork. Actually, some seemed to come straight out of the woods.

Of course, no ammunition was permitted and all guns were carefully inspected at the door. Sammy arrived in casual tight pants and an open sport shirt. The challengers were tough, but so was Sammy. In the end, the event itself was a draw. The judges ruled Sammy and another gentleman as dead even. Sammy invited the co-champion and his wife to be his guests that evening for dinner and the show.

In mid-week of that same engagement, I set up an appearance for Sammy at a retail establishment that sold records, stereo equipment, and television sets. Sammy had recently announced his new religious choice, Judaism, so he was in the headlines even more than usual. Besides that, the store had done a good job of promoting his appearance on their radio and television spots, which included credits for the Chez Paree, so we were correct in expecting quite a crowd.

Sammy always traveled by limousine and his driver, Big John, was a very big man indeed. He was a black man, standing at least six feet five inches, weighing about 300 pounds. Ironically, Sammy's actual bodyguard was no bigger than Sammy. Also black, he was short, thin, and wiry, but there was no mistaking the large bulge that always protruded from his coat.

The four of us attended the event and Sammy did not disappoint the many who had gathered to see him. He signed loads of autographs and, as usual, entertained everyone with his charm and wit. Afterward, the four of us climbed back into the limo with Big John up front and the three of us in back for the ten-minute trip back to the club. I just happened to wind up in the middle seat, Sammy on one side and his bodyguard on the other. The limo pulled away from the curb, as Sammy leaned forward and very quietly asked Big John to close the window that separated the front of the limo from the back. As the window slowly rose, both Sammy and his bodyguard pulled out their snub-nosed revolvers and before I knew it, I had a gun pressed up against me on each side.

Sammy looked at me and in almost a whisper he said, "Do you realize that you are the only motherfuckin' white person in this car?" For what seemed like a full minute, I said nothing. I just kept looking down at the two guns. Finally, I glanced up at Sammy and said, "Yeah, Sammy, but I'm Jewish." The three of them laughed, the guns disappeared, and some color slowly began returning to my very white face.

FUNNYMAN SAM LEVENSON

There was another performer named Sam who, while he could never be compared with the talent of a Sammy Davis, Jr., certainly had an impact on me. I met him in a hotel lobby. I thought I recognized him as the comedian who was scheduled to play the Chez the following week. He had a pinkish face and was slightly rotund, like the comedian I was looking for, but he had with him three large, metallic file cabinets. When he noticed me staring at them, he said, "That's my act for the Chez. I carry all my jokes in this file. Before I go on stage each night, I select those that are most apropos, depending on the city, the time of year, and the crowd."

He introduced himself as Sam Levenson. Suffice it to say he was a teacher turned comic. Although he was professorial about his act, there was something down-home about Levenson that I liked immediately. He talked about his family often and he was an entertainer who really enjoyed telling and listening to his own jokes. He was almost impish, with a peculiar giggle that tickled the audience and seemed to bring them closer to him.

That first time I met him, we worked together only three days when my father died. After the funeral, our friends and family sat Shiva at our home in Lincolnwood, a northern suburb of Chicago. At about six in the evening, a taxi pulled up and in walked Sam Levenson. He entered my home like a regular member of the family, gave me a big hug and whispered his sympathies.

He had taken a forty-five-minute cab ride to sit with someone he had only known three days. I was deeply touched. I soon learned that was typical Sam. Never one to stand on ceremony, and even with the acclaim and applause of the audience in his ears, he was a very humble, gentle man.

I never forgot his thoughtfulness. In subsequent years, when Sam came through Chicago (by then we knew he loved Jewish home cooking) my mother gave him the full treatment with dinner at her apartment.

No, he never drew crowds like Sammy or Durante, but Sam Levenson consistently gave the owners two weeks' worth of solid, profitable business.

He was always welcome at the Chez Paree, and he was always welcome at our home.

THE CHEZ PAREE ADORABLES

For some people, the Chez Paree was home. There was never a dull moment with its rotating cast of characters, including guests, staff, and entertainers. The most permanent residents of the club had to be the Chez Paree Adorables. The Adorables opened each show with a new routine choreographed by Donn Arden. Clad in skimpy but colorful costumes, the eight glamorous women who made up the Adorables were talented dancers. Well, at least six of them were. In dance lingo, they are called "ponies," meaning legitimate dancers, while those tall beauties who seem to do little more than decorate the backdrop are referred to as "horses."

The turnover of these chorus girls was surprisingly small. Each year, we'd lose one or two to marriage or an invitation to work in Las Vegas, but many stayed with the group for years. I would periodically request their cooperation to model for a promotional picture, and sometimes I'd dig up a particularly interesting background on one of them and turn it into a feature story.

One night between shows, I was milling around backstage when four of the girls grabbed me and literally threw me into the shower. Thankfully, it was not running at the time, but I was startled nonetheless. The other four joined these, and I quickly found myself backed up against the wall. Eight gorgeous girls wearing no more than pants and bras and, as ridiculous as it may sound, I tried to get away. But these girls were strong, and determined. I couldn't imagine what they were up to.

"We finally figured you out," the leader of the group said to me. "You've been here for years and have never made a pass at one of us. You have to be gay." That broke me up. I laughed so hard that they all backed off. The word fidelity had never entered their minds. Married a short time, I had always been told by Doris, "Look, but don't touch." I could never lie. The temptation was there, but it was controllable.

Long before becoming synonymous with "60 Minutes," Mike Wallace was another personality of the Chez. He and his wife, Buffy, held court in the Key Club, where they hosted a nightly radio show. It was an entertainment talk show that was well-known in Chicago, and when Wallace went on to bigger and better things, the Chez Paree and radio station WMAQ hired Jack Eigen to take over as host.

The contrast between Mike and Jack was wider than the Grand Canyon. From day one, Jack's show was anchored in controversy. At five feet, three inches, Jack had all the earmarks of the "little big-man" disposition. Opinionated, argumentative and unappreciative of anyone else's viewpoint, Jack had a penchant for creating problems. But the radio audience liked the guy, and the ratings put him in a position of power. He was on the air from 10 p.m. to 1 a.m. each night. Every press agent in town would bring their star attraction down to the Chez to try to get a placement on his show. Night after night, there was some new controversy, and more often than not it made the papers. This was a case of our own media causing us problems.

EARLY LESSONS IN MEDIA ETHICS

While handling the Chez, I got more than a few lessons in media thinking. Some of what I was seeing and hearing I hated. Like most Americans, I was brought up to believe that whatever was published in the newspapers had to be the unvarnished truth. Ostensibly, they were the guardians of our cherished freedom of speech, and their ethics were never to be questioned. Chalk it up to inexperience and *naïveté*.

I would never question the media's right to pick and choose what is news. However, when a newspaper begins comparing your client's advertising expenditures to published news coverage, I do begin to wonder. Frank Ward, once in charge of the entertainment pages of the *Chicago American*, had the habit of weighing ad space against editorial. I once told Frank, "If you don't think it's news, don't publish it. But don't ask me the size of our weekly ad budget for your paper."

On another occasion, I approached that same newspaper with a news picture that tied entertainer Lena Horne to the Chicago Heart Association campaign. This was not a typical publicity still one would hope to place on the amusement pages, but a news item. The photo editor studied the picture and noted that it wasn't bad. Then he asked if I realized, "This paper doesn't publish pictures of blacks in our news pages." Even though this was the mid-fifties, I simply couldn't believe what I had just heard.

In the PR business at that time, there was no court of appeal, meaning if you went over the editor's head to the city editor or managing editor, you were writing your own obituary as far as any future placements were concerned. So, I shook my head, returned the photo to my attaché case, and slowly walked out.

CREATIVITY VERSUS GOOD WRITERS

Interestingly, when I recognized the need to add staff to my own growing agency, I found myself searching for people with a particular background. You couldn't ask for an educational background in publicity because I knew no one was teaching it. With journalism giving me an increasingly sour taste in my mouth, and by now having spent several years working closely with professional entertainers, I was drawn to people who radiated creativity. Writers, I felt, weren't hard to find, but you had to delve deeper to discover the idea people. It was those people, I was convinced, who would ultimately make the hallmark of Aaron Cushman & Associates known throughout the country.

For too many years, I found too many supposedly experienced public relations people fall into a safe routine that let them plod along and take the "Don't rock the boat" attitude by trying not to be too innovative. This was an attitude I abhorred. I wanted thinking people who were risk-takers. Slowly, one by one, I found a coterie of folks who ultimately built our national reputation. Many of them came to me with a show business background.

In the early days, there wasn't another agency in our market area that had anything but disdain for anyone who had a show business background. In their minds, there was no way a theatrical press agent could have the native intelligence to ever work with corporate executives. Though we had not as yet crossed the line into industrial and corporate clients, I was confident we would eventually take that step without losing a beat.

BUSTING SOME PR MYTHS

Amazingly, there were also many clients, at that time, that felt all you needed to do to place a story was entertain the reporter. And "Jack" Schatz at the Chez was no different. Take the newspaperman or woman out for cocktails, and you've got it made. Nothing could be further from the truth.

In most cases, media people have so many invitations that they couldn't care less about them. How about the antiquated idea of payola? Just drop a few bucks; that'll work. To think that top corporate executives could ever believe that turns my stomach. However, I am familiar with at least one Chicago editor who used a similar approach for years before his "retirement."

He was a photo editor who, in previous years, had been very helpful, particularly to young publicists. However, I watched him grow bolder as the years passed. If a publicist were to bring him a photo, in many cases he'd study it, perhaps point out how it could have been made more appealing, while assuring the person it was definitely usable — that is, until he turned the picture over and examined the photo studio's stamp. "On second thought," he'd say, "you're using the wrong photographer. Now, if Photo Ideas had shot this picture, they would have done such and such to make it much better." Every publicist in Chicago knew this guy owned Photo Ideas. Is that payola? Maybe not, but it's not exactly my idea of ethics for a professional journalist, either.

Sometimes, you're forced to work with difficult people in order to get the job done. Typically, planning an advance publicity campaign for each new act at the Chez meant following a specific routine, which included providing photo shots of our stars to the entertainment editors two weeks in advance. Every newspaper (there were four in Chicago at that time) had varied deadlines for their amusement, or entertainment, pages. By Tuesday at 3 p.m., the *Sunday Tribune* had to have, in-hand, whatever material we wanted to place. Monday at 4 p.m. was closing for placement in Sunday's *Sun-Times*. *The Daily News* did not publish a Sunday edition. Their big entertainment section broke on Saturday, and they required pictures and stories in their hands by Wednesday at noon. *The American* broke most of their amusement page stories on Friday and had a forty-eight-hour advance deadline. Both the *Sunday Tribune* magazine and Saturday's *Daily News* magazine required good color photos at least four weeks in advance so they could do proper color separation.

DUPLICATING IS A CARDINAL SIN

I always tried to be fair with the columnists at each paper, rotating exclusive notes from one to the other in sequence and never duplicating, which could be a cardinal sin. I'd offer an item, and if the columnist told me he or she planned to use it, I'd wait three days. If it didn't break by day three, I always felt free to try to get it placed somewhere else.

In most cases, each item had a news time limit. If it was not published within a certain time period, it was no longer news and was considered dead. My staff and I continually tried to educate our clients to the fact that publicity must precede advertising. Once you have advertised the product, you have removed the possibility of it being carried as a news item. At the Chez, management always thought advertising was the only way to sell. With Jack's help, and a lot of repetitive pressure from me, that attitude gradually changed.

PROGRAMMING, THE ART OF THINKING AHEAD

The real challenge of programming for each attraction began after routine placements were made. We studied the media and recognized that they always let you know what they want. Daylight Savings Time, Halloween, Thanksgiving, and, of course, Christmas were occasions and holidays the media was committed to inform their readers about. Weather, changing seasons, major variations in the stock market, and Chicago sports teams were all subjects of interest to their viewers and readers. As a result, by utilizing our name talent with any and all of those scenarios, we were able to combine exposure for the Chez in a news item. The media outlet could rationalize its use of our material because they were providing a public service and reminding readers and viewers of important occasions.

This was a strategy I wanted those in our agency to always keep in mind. I was a bear about making sure our account personnel read each of the four newspapers every day from cover to cover. True creativity emerged when you were able to find a way to cleverly wrap a promotion in a news item. If Chicago was sweltering in ninety-degree heat over a period of a week, or stuck in a deep freeze, it was headline news. When either of those situations occurred, photo editors were desperately anxious for interesting pictures that would help them tell that story.

Similarly, when baseball begins its spring training, the papers are looking for baseball tie-ins. Don't try selling football stories in March and April, but come late July or early August, suddenly everyone is receptive to pictures of glamorous personalities alongside husky football players. Once you understand some basics, this business is not so complex.

UNPREDICTABLE FORCES

Of course, there are always unpredictable forces that threaten to drive you right out of this business. This almost happened to Buddy Arvey.

Buddy was the son of Jake Arvey, who in the mid-1950s was a Democratic dynamo and political kingmaker. Illinois gubernatorial and mayoral candidates alike sought his support. He grew so powerful within the Democratic political machine that he was able to cast a giant shadow into national politics as well.

But, in 1954, Buddy set his sights on one of the biggest musical concerts ever. Many still consider "Star Night" a brilliant concept. It was to be a three-night extravaganza that opened on a Friday night in August at Chicago's Soldier Field before moving on to Briggs Stadium in Detroit on

Saturday, and then to Cleveland's baseball stadium on Sunday.

Buddy booked three major orchestras for the event, with the plan that Ralph Marterie, Ray Anthony and the Sauter Finnegan Band would rotate on the same giant stage. Then, the big players would perform, and Buddy had them all lined up as well. There was Louis Armstrong and his quintet, Nat "King" Cole, Eddie Fisher, Sarah Vaughn, Ella Fitzgerald, Patti Page, Julius La Rosa, and Dick "Tiny" Marx. My company was hired to handle the promotion for "Star Night" and in all my life I've never seen an amalgamation of top stars on one billing that's ever equaled it. Only Soldier Field, with its seating capacity of 75,000, could handle the draw this array of name talent promised. Detroit's seating was limited to about 45,000, but Cleveland's stadium could accommodate at least 80,000 people.

Opening night was definitely one to remember. The advance publicity heralding the event was remarkable, if I do say so myself. Advance ticket sales exceeded 60,000 before the big Friday night in August; but, the forecast called for rain.

The show was scheduled to begin at 7 p.m. and a light drizzle fell at about 5:30. Once the stands were filled with people, it began to pour. People covered their heads with newspapers, umbrellas, wide-brimmed hats, and whatever else they could, but not a soul left Soldier Field.

By 7:30 p.m. the show had not gotten underway, and the crowd was getting restless in the downpour. We all felt that at any moment the mass exodus would begin, with people demanding their money back. Buddy Arvey and his backers were on the edge of a panic. Our performers were disappointed, but dry, as they waited in a dugout area located just off the field, but in view of most of the crowd.

With the crowd going nowhere, Buddy and I went up and down the line of stars pleading for someone, anyone, to go out there. No one budged. They looked at us as if we were insane. They had guaranteed contracts, so if it was a catastrophe, there was no way they could get hurt.

Suddenly, "Tiny" Marx and his small group of musicians gathered their courage and raced through the rain out to the stage. Covering themselves with oversized golf umbrellas, they began to play.

For a few minutes, they were able to pacify the crowd, but the rain was now falling in a torrent. With no one else moving in the dugout of stars, it looked like doomsday. Then Julius La Rosa jumped up, took off his suit coat, opened his tie and said, "What the hell!" With that, he went running across the field. By the time he reached the stage, he was soaked to the bone. Without even wiping the rain from his eyes, he reached for the microphone and announced to the crowd, "I guess if you folks have enough guts to sit in the rain, I'm going to get wet with you while I sing my heart out." He cued Tiny Marx and began to sing.

Previously on the verge of becoming unruly, the crowd went deathly silent. As Julius finished his first number, they stood up and screamed their approval. Without blinking an eye, Julius just kept singing one song after another. He must have been out there thirty minutes, and by the time he took his last bow, the rain had subsided and the show went on as planned. He absolutely saved the day. The guy had brass balls.

The entire show had chartered a train for Detroit, where we not only enjoyed good weather, but a full house. However, Sunday in Cleveland was another story. The 35,000 to 40,000 folks who came to the stadium looked lost in that cavernous establishment. Whatever money Buddy Arvey made the previous two nights went down the sewer in Cleveland.

THE "ITALIAN NIGHT OF STARS"

Early one evening, Dave Halper and I were in the office at the Chez when he asked me if I was familiar with the "Italian Night of Stars." It was a one-night benefit event held each year at the Chicago Stadium. He told me he had been asked to produce this year's show and wondered if I would be willing to handle the promotion pro bono. Without hesitation, I agreed. I knew Dave would gather the annual stalwarts like Frank Sinatra, Dean Martin, Jimmy Durante, and others, and I knew there was no way you could miss selling out the 20,000-seat Stadium with those kinds of names.

I worked on the show for six weeks and, although the media reception was terrific and the public grabbed up the tickets quickly, it had been a lot of work. It was a Saturday afternoon and the big names were in rehearsal. I found myself sitting in the front row of a nearly empty Chicago Stadium, watching Frank Sinatra walk through his routine.

At that moment, two men who I'd never met before stopped in front of me and asked if I was Aaron Cushman. I nodded my head and they sat down beside me. They were neatly dressed in shirt and tie and the leader of the two introduced himself; I'll refer to him as Mr. Anthony. He told me he was a spokesman for the Italian community and on their behalf he just wanted to thank me for all my efforts in making this benefit such a huge success. I thanked him in return and the two men left shortly thereafter.

The following year, Dave again asked me if I would handle the show's promotion and again I agreed. With much the same talent, the show was a great success as well. *Déjà vu*; I was sitting in the front row of the stadium, watching the stars run through their acts, when, out of the corner of my eye, I saw the same two men approaching. "Hi," said Mr. Anthony. "Another wonderful show and another financial success for the Italian community. And we owe a lot of it to you."

I tried to make light of it by pointing out that with these kinds of attractions, anyone could have done the job. Mr. Anthony was persistent. He told me they had many friends and points of influence in Chicago's corporate world and would like to help my agency and me by leading us into some major new clients. He rattled off at least ten corporate names that I would have given anything to call our clients. He kept telling me all they wanted to do was show their appreciation and reciprocate for all I had done for them. They asked if they could come to my office on Monday to talk in more detail.

I knew who they were, and who their constituency was, and still I agreed to the meeting. If they were sincere and all they really wanted to do was help, I thought, why not? There was never a doubt in my mind they had those corporate connections and knew which buttons to push.

They arrived at my office at 10 a.m. sharp. I offered them coffee, and, after a few sips, Mr. Anthony again reiterated their desire to help. He told me I shouldn't expect immediate action from the companies mentioned because most of them had existing contracts. However, he made it clear that as soon as those annual contracts were fulfilled, he was certain some, if not all, could become clients. I was excited. I listened hard. Did I really want to get involved in this? How fast did I want my agency to grow and in what direction?

Mr. Anthony recognized my apparent interest and continued. "Once what we have helped you get in new clients equals the volume you presently have," he said, "I would like to ask you a favor. I would like my friend here," he pointed toward his associate, "to be given a position in your firm without salary, and be given the opportunity to learn the business." My hand began to shake as I imagined a situation a couple years down the line when this young man was more qualified. I could foresee someone providing me with a ticket to Afghanistan (a one-way ticket), and at that moment I became downright angry.

We were facing each other across the desk and I asked Mr. Anthony, "Do you really want to help me? If you do, please just leave me alone. I appreciate your coming here," I continued firmly, "but I would rather fight the battle without your assistance." He never blinked. He simply said they were grateful and sincerely wanted to help. "No pressure, no problems. We wish you the best . . . and if you should ever need our help, make a phone call and you've got it." With that, the two of them stood up, we shook hands and, to my great relief, I've never seen either of them since.

I never thought I'd run into anyone who made me more uncomfortable than Mr. Anthony and his aspiring sidekick did that day, and I guess I still haven't. But I did come close.

THE BANKING BUSINESS BECKONS

It was a warm summer day, and I was headed to an appointment I had looked forward to for some time. I was to talk PR with the leaders of one of Chicago's major banking institutions. LaSalle Street was crowded with the usual mix of attorneys and stock market analysts. Because of traffic problems, I jumped out of a cab about two blocks short of the bank and walked sprightly toward what I was certain would be a great presentation.

I was ready. We had done our homework and the staff had loaded me with many solid creative ideas. We had a complete understanding as to why this particular financial institution needed a fresh approach to their public relations. Their target market was clear, and I was sure we could make serious inroads toward achieving their goals.

I purposely wore my most conservative navy blue suit. Thinking of the mentality and age of those about to scrutinize my capability, I was also careful in the selection of a shirt, tie, and cuff links. With every pocket bulging with confidence, I approached the receptionist and asked for the Chairman. Yes, he was expecting me.

Five minutes later, I was face to face with eleven men, similarly attired and with a prominent amount of gray hair. The presentation lasted about one hour, after which I invited questions. Priding myself on being a top salesman, I felt as though they were sold and about to buy.

After cleanly fielding several good questions, one gentleman looked at me a little crooked and asked, "Are you the same Aaron Cushman that represents the Chez Paree?" He had come across my name periodically in Kup's Column. Kup, who was always there to help, would occasionally write, "Aaron 'Chez Paree' Cushman reported that . . ." It was Kup's way of trying to bring me recognition, which I always appreciated; but, this time, it backfired on me.

The moment I responded affirmatively to the question, I felt the atmosphere in that room change dramatically. Suddenly, those eleven men looked at me as though I were wearing a dirty shirt, had half a cigarette hanging from the corner of my mouth, and spoke in dee's, dem's and do's, their picture image of the theatrical publicist.

It was immediately clear the meeting was over. It was inconceivable to them that the same person handling public relations for a nightclub could understand the ramifications of representing a large, conservative banking establishment. Every point I'd made in the presentation now seemed forgotten. I was history as far as they were concerned.

I rose from the table, picked up my papers and blindly stumbled for the exit. I remember standing on the corner of LaSalle and Adams Streets without moving for a very long time. As a matter of fact, one of Chicago's finest inquired if I was okay.

My emotions were running deep at the overt rejection. I could have understood it if that judgment had been made because my presentation was lacking, but to turn me away because some of my clients were in the entertainment business left me shaking my head. Was this the way it would always be if I tried to gain industrial and corporate clients? Was it going to be showbiz or nothing?

As I began the long walk back to Wacker and Michigan, I thought about the only two ways to get into the PR business. Either your family was wealthy and well-connected and had close social ties to key corporate leaders, in which case you had a running start, or, your family was not wealthy or well-connected and didn't have close social ties to key corporate leaders. In that case, you scratched and clawed to get your start in an agency and then you took any legitimate account that came your way. You then began learning and polishing your craft in a fashion that allowed you to slowly build national recognition and respect.

I knew the latter situation fit my story and, as I continued my walk back to the office, I knew exactly what I was going to do. If they weren't going to let me live on both sides of the tracks, I was going to pick the corporate world. It was a bold and even frightening move, but I was positive my agency's future lay in that direction.

That evening, I stopped by the Chez and told Jay Schatz I would no longer be representing the club. It was a difficult conversation. We had had such a great run at the Chez, and I had enjoyed every minute of it. Jay tried to convince me to stay, but my mind was made up. It was time for me, and our agency, to move on.

The very next morning, I called my staff together and announced my decision to resign each and every one of our entertainment accounts. Their faces told me they thought I'd gone mad. As companies go, we were small potatoes, grossing less than $500,000 annually. But we had all shed blood, sweat, and tears to get and successfully service that business, and now I was closing the book on it.

Sadly, the Chez itself would close only a year and a half later. Its demise had nothing to do with my leaving, but was a result of the rise of Las Vegas. Through loyalty and gratitude to Dave Halper, the club was able to hang on to its top-notch performers for several months while similar clubs in other cities were simply priced out of existence by the new venues of Vegas. When it caught up to the Chez, it was the end of a twenty-five-year era. It had been the longest operating nightclub in the country when it closed in 1961.

When I severed ties with the Chez and other entertainment clients, I knew people on my staff feared for their jobs. I assured them no one would be fired. We would find a way to replace the entertainment business. It was an end, but a beginning as well. Later years showed the error of the management of that initial bank, since we went on to represent The Exchange National Bank, The American National Bank, Marina City Bank, Cole-Taylor Banks, and Labe Bank in Chicago, along with others in St. Louis and Los Angeles.

CHAPTER 3

The Public Relations Equation _____

I never found a way to provide a quarter-pound of
public relations.

Ground zero is not a fun place to be. Despite my bravado in canceling all of our entertainment accounts, it's safe to say I had not fully considered the challenges that now faced our organization.

We still had to meet payroll as well as cover rent, insurance, suppliers, telephones, and so on. Fortunately, we had set aside a few bucks against the proverbial rainy day. At this point, it was pouring, but I was confident we could make it. We were determined to pick up new clients and begin to roll again. But first, it was important that we knew who we were and where we were going. This fresh start allowed us the chance to reconsider the definition of public relations, and the role we play as public relations professionals.

Back in the early days, the mid-to-late 1940s, as public relations struggled for recognition, it was true that the only measurement of results was newspaper coverage. You were judged by the number of clips that you could show a client. Despite what many may still believe, the job of public relations encompasses much more than getting your client's name in newspapers, magazines, or on broadcast media.

So, what is public relations? Although public relations has come of age and earned its professional position as a respected and essential management function, that's a question that I'm still frequently asked today.

Consider for a moment that in the case of a corporation, there are at least eight completely diversified "publics," without whose goodwill and acceptance this business is sure to encounter a stormy future. Corporations operate in a community that includes stockholders, employees, distributors, suppliers, bankers, government, competitors, and consumers. Business needs income and capital. It also requires labor, supplies, service, and a favorable climate of law, policy, and public opinion.

Therefore, business must maintain constructive relationships with the people who accommodate its needs. With customers who provide income, with employees who make up their labor force, with stockholders and bankers who assist with capital, and with suppliers who make available the services and raw material necessary to deliver a finished product to market.

It is vital that any PR agency understands both the structure and concept of such interdependence before moving ahead as a nurturing force in these business relationships. It is also important that we continue to resist the ideas that others might hold of our true function.

TERMINOLOGY

One issue that has long stood in the way of clearly defining the role and impact of proper public relations is the confusion over terminology. Three titles that have often been used interchangeably are press agent, publicist, and public relations counsel. Are they the same? Only if you think a bookkeeper performs the same role as an auditor, or a cook has skills equal to those of a chef. Yet, the media often continues to use the terms press agent, publicist, and public relations counsel indiscriminately.

These terms actually describe different levels of proficiency and, in my mind, each of these jobs serves a distinct purpose. The press agent is the clip seeker, consumed only with landing the client's name in the press. Despite what many of my colleagues may think, I believe the age of the press agent, or huckster, is not gone. The problem comes when firms or clients mistake this singular effort as public relations, rather than just one aspect of an ongoing campaign.

Instead of relying on writing skills, the secret weapon of the press agent tends to be the telephone. Remove a press agent from the phone and he's incapacitated. Press agents are not afraid to stray into gray areas of the truth, or to manufacture a stunt or tale. The good ones are crafty, tenacious, creative, and talented. I have always respected these characteristics, and have periodically sought out these specialists for staff positions.

A publicist is a trained mechanic, one who can quickly recognize a good story and, with adept writing skill, can expertly put it to paper. Effective publicists have a thorough understanding of the news distribution system, and they understand what role they play within the marketing team. Programming and budgeting are seldom part of a publicist's responsibility.

Those who can rightfully claim the title of public relations counselor are part of the management team. They are expected to contribute to the corporate "big picture." They have the responsibility and capability to plan year-round programs and to budget their anticipated expenditures. They make a significant impact on shaping the corporate culture and generating sales. A counselor knows that a key part of his or her job is to be heavily involved in corporate decision-making prior to the implementation phase. Counselors remain cognizant of the reaction of all publics to management decisions. They are relied upon to anticipate media reaction to any corporate announcements. A strong counselor will direct all marketing elements to support a sales effort into existing markets and to build a pre-sell into new markets. He or she knows that publicity must precede advertising – that's so obvious I hesitate to even mention it. At this level, public relations counselors perform a respected, essential management function and report directly to top management.

Publicity by its very nature is a form of news, and if you have advertised the product, the news is gone. Today, public relations programs are more targeted, more focused and more results-oriented than ever in the past, with heavy emphasis on research and planning.

Sadly, the business of public relations has not reached a position of controlled professionalism, which means almost anyone can hang out a shingle. The Public Relations Society of America has instituted an accreditation program replete with a written and oral examination in an attempt to upgrade the practice at all levels, but in some markets, advertising people and journalists are trying to pass themselves off as experienced public relations professionals. The result, poor performance and unsatisfactory work, is one reason why so many companies have been soured by what they thought they were buying.

EDWARD BERNAYS: "MAKE NEWS, NOT NEWS RELEASES."

I have often been asked why a competent newsperson would not succeed in his or her moonlighting effort in the PR arena. The answer seems simple enough to me.

Visualize a city editor, on any major daily publication, on the receiving end of a phone call advising him that a fire of substantial proportion has been spotted emanating from a downtown hotel. The editor turns to a staff reporter and instructs him or her to grab a cab, get to the scene, and cover the story.

The reporter gets to within two blocks of the fire and is stopped by curious crowds and traffic. The reporter leaves the cab, takes one look at the fifteen-story burning building and sees ten people standing on the roof ready to jump. Six floors are engulfed in flames; four people have already jumped to their deaths.

The reporter counts twenty-four pieces of firefighting equipment and ten squad cars, and estimates the crowd at 5,000. The reporter picks up the phone and calls in the story. That's the reporter's job. But, it's the job of the PR professional to light the fuse, to motivate the editor to send the reporter to cover the story.

It's true that there's creativity in writing, and, once they get beyond writing obituaries, reporters are challenged every day to find enticing leads for their assigned stories. But it's entirely different when striving to create the news.

Edward Bernays, who some say gave birth to the business of public relations, was by everyone's account a true icon. It was he who said, "Make news, not news releases." He was a master at using the media for his client's purposes, and he did it in a way that also gave the media what it most needs: real news.

In PR, there's nothing more effective than wrapping a client or product around real news. Sure, corporate marketing directors understand there is a growing awareness on the part of today's consumers that advertising messages are not only paid for, but are also carefully prepared to be appealing. Those consumers are also attuned to the fact that the appeal of such advertising depends upon the media selected to carry the message, the age group it is intended to reach, the affluence of the viewer or reader, and, particularly in the case of broadcast media, the time selected for transmission of the message. With sufficient repetition, this marketing tactic is indeed powerful. But in complete juxtaposition, and despite media errors, even the savviest consumers still believe in the integrity of information presented editorially. To paraphrase an old saying, they believe: "If I read it in the paper, saw it on the TV news, or heard it on the radio, it must be true."

PR BEGINS WITH THE INDIVIDUAL

From the beginning, there were several basic concepts I tried to establish and follow religiously. I concluded long ago that public relations is everyone's business. We all market our own public relations. It's not the exclusive terrain of any individual who bears title to that responsibility.

Unless you are the officially designated PR man or woman within your corporate structure, you probably have no formal training in this area. You've never written a news release in your life and the closest you've come to the inside of a newspaper is when you open it over coffee in the morning. You couldn't be expected to know a deadline from a double truck. Yet, you play a vital role in public relations.

However lofty or low your position on the corporate ladder, you create an image of your company, and yourself, every minute of every day. That image is every bit as vital to your business success as the composite publicity the company's designated professional will accrue. The way you dress, the way you speak, the organized manner of your presentation are always being tabulated by the listener or viewer, who then decides how they wish to respond – if at all.

Long ago, I told my staff we need to look at ourselves as others see us. This is our PR quotient. I asked that they consider whether they thought of themselves as a positive or negative force in the marketing mix. When sitting in a prospect's office, I wondered, is your mouth saying you are definitely interested in having his or her business, while your body is telling him or her you really don't care? How organized is the material in your portfolio? If you have to scurry through papers to find the correct element, your personal disorganization may be symbolic of your company.

Are you following up your personal calls promptly? Are thank you letters in the offing? Do you prepare an analysis of your prospect's problems with critiques and comments on your discussion after each meeting? What you do or don't do creates an image of you as a person who cares, one who is truly interested in a prospect's problem. Most importantly, you are symbolic of the entire staff that is waiting to service this account.

When it comes to letters, many people insist upon a style that fits the business mode of Victorian England. Correspondence which begins with, "Regarding your inquiry . . ." or "Pursuant to our conversation . . ." has all the excitement, warmth, and enthusiasm of warm beer. This approach immediately conveys a stodgy, tired image. It creates distance rather than rapport. If your advertising and publicity is meant to create an image of sizzling steaks and beautiful people, don't send letters which place you in the Stone Age.

YOUR PR QUOTIENT

Our individual PR quotient is also concerned with tone. Everyone's phone technique is different and is a reflection of their own personality. Our receptionist knows that next to bookkeeping, she may be the most important person on staff. She is the first source of contact with the office and she knows the sound of her voice, the welcome she transmits when she says hello, the courtesy expressed and the speed with which she transfers the call creates a mental picture of the company in the mind of the caller. By the tone of your voice, your listener decides whether you are young or old, friendly or antagonistic, capable or stupid. The best marketing program can go right down the sewer if the operator handles the incoming call improperly. Even worse, in this day of direct dial and e-mail, the caller may never hear a human voice but is offered a "menu" of topics; is asked to punch in the first three letters of the last name of the party he or she is calling; and when the caller finally gets through, he or she almost always gets an answering machine. Modern-day phone systems may be expeditious but won't help your public relations image. I'll take that warm, living, breathing human voice every day.

It's a good idea for each executive to explain to phone operators the way that he or she would like their calls to be handled. I've asked mine to say, "May I tell Mr. Cushman who is calling?" They are never to ask, "May I tell him why you are calling?" And, no matter what your corporate title or whether you are buying or selling, never keep a person waiting if you have had your office initiate the call. When the recipient picks up the phone, he or she is ready to talk, so you'd better be on the line and ready as well.

Another element in our PR quotient relates to the speed with which we return calls. Should you be out or in a meeting, the caller will expect a return call promptly. If you return the call the following day or, worse, a couple days later, you've already told him or her plenty. You've told that caller he or she is not all that important to you, and you've probably lost their business.

With those working for me, I've tried to stress that this PR image is not restricted to the outside world. Fellow employees should see you in the same shining light in which you hope clients view you. These are the people who will make or break your marketing effort, particularly if they are involved in customer contact.

I believe executives should show genuine interest in personnel and their problems. "Please" and "thanks" are still the ABC's of the PR alphabet. Ask staffers for their input, treat them as though your job depends upon their opinion of you, because oftentimes it does.

Today, with help wanted ads and training program costs becoming exorbitant, acquisition and retention of personnel is as important as getting and keeping clients. The overhead expenditures that come with major staff turnover can result in profit exiting out the back door while new business is coming in the front.

As public relations professionals, we recognize that poor employee relations programs are as disastrous to a profit and loss statement as improper sales techniques. Impressions of any company are developed by the interpretation and communication of policies, and by personal relationships with management. It's just one more reason why I believe, after fifty years in this business, that public relations is everyone's business.

Once you're armed with a plan and are clear in your purpose, I believe as did Woodrow Wilson, "Nothing in the world can take the place of persistence. Talent will not. Nothing is more common than unsuccessful men with talent. Genius will not. Unrewarded genius is almost a proverb. Education will not; The world is full of educated derelicts."

Although our entertainment accounts were behind us, we had vision and ambition on our side. As we set out to build the future of Cushman & Associates, I was convinced persistence and determination alone were of prime importance.

I believe it was that attitude that led us to Marvin Frank. Marvin operated a mid-sized advertising agency housed in the Pure Oil Building in Chicago's Loop. His firm specialized in radio broadcast commercials, and Marvin specialized in people.

Meeting Marvin is truly an experience. Every conversation began with, "Have you heard the joke about . . ." It was a never-ending laugh session with him. What a marvelous personality. The first time we met, it took about ten seconds to set me at ease. This wonderful man was telling me he'd heard good things about our organization, that he had several clients he would like to talk to me about. Was I interested? Talk about manna from heaven. There was no innuendo about not trying to steal his clients. No concern about funds being diverted from advertising for public relations.

No questions about systems and methods. Just plain open trust between two men who had never met before.

Marvin knew his clients needed more exposure than their small budgets could afford to purchase through advertising. His primary interest – no, his only interest – was his clients' welfare. It was a position that very few, if any, of the major advertising agencies I worked with later ever expressed.

Marvin was smart. Smart enough to be aware that many advertising agencies in the early '60s looked at public relations as a way to earn an additional easy buck. Many Michigan Avenue and Madison Avenue agencies began building small PR departments and selling its services to their advertising clients.

The concept was doomed from the start. There was no way a one- or two-person agency could compete against established public relations companies with large, competent staffs. In addition, at that time, most advertising agencies looked down their respective noses at the business of public relations. They were treating their new PR staff as second-class citizens and telling them how to conduct a PR campaign. It was a scenario headed for disaster.

Within two years, most ad agencies not only lost their PR business, but also in many cases, their clients were so angry at unfulfilled promises and lack of performance in PR that they cancelled the advertising contracts as well.

Marvin saw this coming. He admitted he knew nothing of public relations and had no intention of building his own department. He was staying with his strength – radio advertising.

He introduced me to Gingiss Tuxedo Co., Z. Frank Chevrolet Dealership, and William A. Lewis (a women's fashion retailer). All three companies quickly became clients. We were off and running. True, it wasn't AT&T or Xerox, but it was a departure from the entertainment world.

Marvin Frank was certainly instrumental in our agency's early strides in a new direction. It's rare that any person achieves success in business alone and without help. I'm indebted to Marvin for the confidence he showed in us, and the push-start he provided. I still count him among my best friends. Just past his eighty-seventh birthday, Marvin passed away. I miss our phone conversations that began with, "Have you heard the one about . . ."

With a head of steam behind us, we continued to seek out new business. One client in particular, the Evans Fur Company, was a real dichotomy. A.L. Meltzer was the company's owner, CEO, and marketing guru. He built his firm's volume on what the trade called "schlock advertising." Full-length Black Diamond mink coats, mink stoles, Persian lamb coats, and white rabbit furs were splashed across large newspaper ads, all offered at "unbelievably low prices." Meltzer was clearly appealing to the masses.

There was another side to Evans' merchandise. The company did carry a complete line of impeccably designed couture garments, purchased in Paris at the fashion houses of Ballenciaga, Balmain, and Givenchy. However, based upon the image of the company portrayed in its newspaper ads, affluent women with taste would not consider shopping at Evans. A.L. Meltzer recognized this problem and decided to explore a new area of marketing for his store: public relations.

I may not have had the entertainment contracts any longer, but I still maintained my contacts and understood exactly what was needed to ease Meltzer's marketing predicament. Our plan was to expose Evans' finer garments in Chicago's most fashionable and prestigious locations, and to drape them over the shoulders of the country's most recognizable female personalities.

The star: A $5,000 mink stole. The setting: Booth #1 of Chicago's legendary Pump Room in the Ambassador East Hotel. The shoulders: None other than stars like Hollywood's Susan Hayward.

Employing this technique as often as possible over the next few years, and making sure of consistent media coverage, this campaign transformed the image of Evans Fur Company. But don't for a single moment think they gave up their routine of schlock ads. The PR was simply another dimension, and it worked.

Today, Evans is a multi-store, multi-city publicly traded corporation. A.L. Meltzer is gone, but his son David continues to build this impressive company.

Our own company's initial growth started with retail clients, then moved to small manufacturing companies, and, in later years, to national and international corporations, eventually even including foreign governments. In the beginning there was Lyon & Healy, Field Paper Box Company, Jim Moran "Courtesy Man" Auto Dealer, *Downbeat* magazine, Little City, Multiple Sclerosis Foundation, Villa Venice restaurant, and a piece of business from Evinrude Outboard Motors.

Over the years, our client list blossomed into national and international business clients that included Marriott Hotels worldwide, Ramada Inns International, Keebler Co., Motorola, Warner Lambert, Century 21, Chrysler

Corp., American Motors, Pickett Suite Hotels, Maremont Corp., Chicago Tribune Entertainment Corp., Eveready Batteries, AT&T Consumer Products, Seiko Consumer Electronics, Maytag Company, Revere Camera Co., Armour Food Co., Con Agra Frozen Food Co., Hires Root Beer & Orange Crush, McDonald's (Illinois & Northern Indiana), Ralston Purina Co., The Seven-Up Co., Tribuno Wines, Tuborg and Meisterbrau Beer, Philip Morris USA, Ideal Toy Co., Hasbro Toy Co., and many more. Our foreign government client list included Mexico, Singapore, Cayman Islands, Canada, Sweden, and South Korea.

THE MARKETING MIX

I have always been, and remain to this day, an advocate of a marketing mix that includes both advertising and public relations. These days, product marketing directors point to the ever-increasing cost of television time and to the fact that attractive time slots are difficult to secure. Tremendous advertising clutter clouds the issue further, and more and more television broadcast and cable channels have meant a steady decrease in consistent ratings, all of which adds impetus to the strategy of marketing public relations.

Although public relations consists of many sub-specialties such as financial, community, government, hospital/medical, internal, corporate, and employee relations, our forte has always been marketing. Keeping this in mind, another basic concept for our organization was the creation of what I termed the "public relations equation."

THE PR EQUATION

Exposure = Awareness = Sales is the success formula for any marketing-related public relations program. Today, any corporate campaign has access to many forms of communication, including media, point of purchase, internet, direct mail, word-of-mouth, and public relations. For the formula to be effective, there must be a continuity of exposure. No single or small series of exposures will provide awareness. A full-page advertisement or PR story in the *Wall Street Journal* or *New York Times*, while effective, will not be sufficient to provide awareness. However, once that continuity of exposure has guaranteed awareness, sales will result, with the proviso that the product or service is of quality and fulfills a need.

The target for every manufacturing and service-oriented corporation is one hundred percent market penetration. Once you extend beyond detergent makers, some beer and soft drink companies, automotive builders like General Motors, Chrysler, Ford, and Toyota, some computer industry leaders, pharmaceuticals, major insurance companies, and gasoline purveyors, you soon run out of those financially powerful companies that do have the ability to purchase one hundred percent market penetration.

What then happens to the great percentage of business entities in the United States that fall into a category that limits their financial ability to purchase complete market penetration via paid advertising? Progressive management, seeking new and better ways to expand their acquisition of exposure within their limited budgets, in many cases has turned to professional public relations.

Visualize a pie chart with the entire perimeter representing full market penetration. Then draw in that chart exactly what percentage of the whole pie your company can afford to buy through paid advertising. One quickly comes to the conclusion that a large element of that penetration pie remains uncovered. Because of its credibility and cost efficiency, public relations remains the only possible answer to help close the "ad gap."

THE MEDIA

Let's look again at the media. Until recently, the average consumer tended to believe as gospel those elements of information they have read in newspapers and magazines and have seen and heard on radio and television. The basic reason for this is the implied, disinterested "third person endorsement" provided by the editorial staff of whatever media is involved. Ostensibly, this type of exposure carries believability.

Unfortunately, in the past few years, over-enthusiasm on the part of some members of the media has resulted in reporters publishing error-laden articles. These errors have also been spurred by an increased reliance on "sources," a lack of fact checking, and the continued effort by managing editors to be first with the news, regardless of accuracy. Although editorial corrections tend to be printed in some tiny spot hidden deep within the publication, the media's gradual slip into recklessness has led to a loss of public confidence.

Some recent examples of overemphasis and multiple inaccuracies on the part of the media include reports of the October 1999 aircraft accident that tragically took the life of John F. Kennedy, Jr., and the November 1999 crash of Egypt Air Flight 990. Television reports of Kennedy's accident went virtually uninterrupted for days, despite the lack of new information.

In the case of Egypt Air Flight 990, numerous reports were later retracted after they were determined to be either false or unfounded rumors.

Perhaps the most current flagrant example of media inaccuracies can be attributed to the *New York Times*, a publication that many regard as the world's finest. With the discovery that their byline reporter Jayson Blair was guilty of fabricating many portions of his material, the *New York Times* summarily discharged Blair and subsequently has gone through a major revise of their editorial management group.

CREDIBILITY

Aside from these incidents, however, the key word remains: credibility. Consumers, regardless of their level of sophistication, have been "had" so often by misleading advertising claims that they tend to become disbelieving. Even when making a purchase, the anticipation is usually somewhat less than what was promised. Conversely, there remains a reliance on news media to provide truthful and factual information.

Whether fact or fiction, corporations are still prone to slaying the messenger. The negative image article on the business page is the responsibility of management, not the public relations designate. First, it must be made clear that there is no way to kill a bad story. The best that companies can hope for is to locate the heart of the problem, correct it, and perhaps induce the writer to return within a reasonable time span.

Don't bury the real problem, which may have been a poorly planned program or ill-conceived product, by claiming the PR person should have had enough ability and contacts to keep bad stories from being published. I'm reminded of the Broadway producer eagerly awaiting reviews of opening night. The reviews are poor and he immediately fires the PR person. That is totally ridiculous. The director, choreographer, stage manager, and perhaps the talent should be fired. A poor production is not the fault of the publicist any more than bad food served in an elegant restaurant is the fault of the wait staff. Fire the chef, not the *maitre d'*.

CLOSING THE "AD GAP"

Earlier, I referred to the "ad gap." Certainly not a derogatory comment. The "ad gap" is simply the difference between the portion of the market you can afford to reach by advertising and the market's total potential. A strong public relations program can help close that gap, and at a fraction of the cost of advertising.

Without question, corporations with either products or services to sell have found that the most successful programs are those with a sound balance of both advertising and public relations. They not only complement each other, but also have different roles to play.

Using hotels as an example, you can meet short-term goals such as building attendance for dining rooms or one-night or one-week entertainment attractions through advertising, with PR playing a secondary role. On the other hand, long-term goals such as higher occupancy, increased utilization by corporate meeting planners, consistent traffic in restaurants and lounges, and, perhaps most important, the ability to recruit and retain key personnel are public relations assignments achieved with advertising support. These are year-round jobs that cannot be resolved with piecemeal, stop-and-go programming. I've never found a way to provide a quarter-pound of public relations. It takes an experienced professional to get the desired results, not a part-time secretary with a flair for writing who "just loves to work with people."

INFLUENCING BEHAVIOR

In its simplest form, public relations is the act of influencing behavior. We all possess that ability whether we know it or not. To make it a positive force requires the molding and control of all individual and corporate relationships. In business, through skillfully planned, carefully researched strategic transmission of information, we dynamically move to influence behavior toward specific individuals, countries, corporations (and their products and services), financial institutions, and environmental issues.

CHAPTER 4

16 Ways to Achieve
Positive Media Relations

*The role of public relations as a marketing support tool can
be tangible and measurable.*

A malignancy that is more certain to bring fiscal destruction to individuals, politicians, or companies is "bad press relations." The careers of innumerable personalities either ceased abruptly or suffered slow, lingering termination. Earl Butz, the former Secretary of Agriculture, is one who comes to mind, as well as daredevil Evil Knievel, and even lovable Charlie Chaplin. The end result was an outgrowth of unpopular positions they held. Among these were indifference, lack of professionalism in their communication techniques, or outright disdain for the power of the press.

But the opposite is equally true. The media's support of people, services, or products can potentially skyrocket an unknown commodity into overnight prominence. Recognizing both the positive and negative results of relationships with the news media reminds management of the importance of this aspect of public relations.

It is only logical that before the media's assistance is sought to tell the corporate story, it is necessary to first convince the media of the worthiness of your corporate position, product, or service and all of its unique elements. Once an understanding of media's key role has been established, how can companies develop the most positive image to ensure the strongest possible support?

There are at least 16 ways to help achieve strong, positive media relations:

1. Understand the media's interests. Media outlets, whether electronic, print, or broadcast, are not in the public relations business. Your interests are not theirs. What your company feels is exciting may be too self-serving or too commercial in the eyes of the media's editorial staff. Their interest is in the acquisition of viewers, listeners, and readers, i.e., ratings, circulation, and advertisers. Providing news is coincidental to acquiring one of the aforementioned goals. The media is first and foremost a commercial institution and we should never forget that. To get their attention, your material must appeal to their readers, viewers, or listeners.

2. Know how to transmit your information. Editors are constantly besieged with material from all corners of the globe and have heavy demands upon their time. They themselves aren't certain as to what method of transmission is most appropriate. I've heard some say, "Please use e-mail." Others have said their computer is overloaded, so mail in your releases. Still others have said that a timely news tip should be transmitted by phone. Personal contact with editors and reporters in your community will provide the answer to which method they prefer.

3. Prepare your written material properly. The receptiveness on the part of editors depends on their realizing that they do not have sufficient staff to adequately cover their market thoroughly. They need professional PR people to supplement their own reporters and photographers. The key word is "professional." Your material should be well-thought-out and written in a news style. Get the salient points in your lead paragraph because if the news desk isn't "grabbed" by the uniqueness of your lead, your story will immediately be headed for file 13 – the wastebasket.

4. Deadlines. Young people on our staff get the hand-holding treatment until we are certain they know every columnist's style and deadline. Mass distribution of releases is one giant waste and only serves to alienate reporters who receive material they could care less about. It tells the media person you either didn't do your homework or perhaps you just didn't care.

5. Don't duplicate. There isn't a PR person alive who wouldn't like to hit all stations and all papers at once. If it's legitimate news, your corporate PR person is entitled to transmit it simultaneously to all media. If it's a feature story, place it exclusively with one media outlet and, in the future, rotate your selection so all media are treated equally. If the same column note or story appears on the same day in two different sources, you have committed editorial suicide.

6. Respond quickly to queries. When a newsperson calls with a question, break your back to get the answer fast. The editor will appreciate prompt reaction and will be encouraged to contact your company again, which could mean increased positive exposure.

7. Be honest. Build credibility by providing straightforward and inherently honest material. Be as thorough as possible while still protecting private and privileged information.

8. Your response should never be, "No comment." Advise management to avoid this phrase, even when demanded by legal counsel. Find an alternative response that says the same thing. As is usually the case, what is said depends upon whose ox is being gored. Media members dislike "no comment" and are often free to express themselves accordingly – that is, except when the phrase is applicable to themselves. Not too long ago, the *Chicago Sun-Times* editorial staff was on strike against management. When opposition media queried the *Sun-Times* management, they were repeatedly told "no comment."

9. Be brief and accurate. News space and editorial time are at a premium. Avoid superfluous information not relevant to the story. Leave the adjectives and spectaculars to the advertising copywriters. For those of you who remember television's Sgt. Friday, make it "Just the facts."

10. Be creative. A good newsperson will enjoy a clever new concept. They will even admire a well-thought-out publicity stunt. But, by all means, search for a fresh approach.

11. Level with your editorial contacts. Even with a potentially negative story, you'll stand a better chance of gaining media understanding if the press doesn't think you tried to fool them.

12. Be considerate and provide for the media's needs. If you're hosting a major event and anticipate prolonged time periods of media being on your premises, try to meet their basic requirements. Do they need a pressroom stocked with multiple computer outlets and numerous phones? Is a 220-volt line readily available for television camera people? What about modest refreshments?

13. Have dignity that reflects your business or corporate client, even if the press does not reciprocate in kind. Don't ask for favors. You may get your positive placement at the cost of your self-respect. Let the quality of your material speak for itself. Earn the media's admiration, however grudgingly, and you have taken a giant step towards gaining positive press relations for yourself and your company.

14. Be scrupulously fair. Avoid taking the line of least resistance and spread your material without playing favorites. Even in this day of twenty-four-hour cable television news, it pays to rotate release dates, giving AM's the lead story one day and PM's the next.

15. Keep management visible. Counsel them against hiding in the face of negative press.

16. Guide your business or company toward achieving recognition as a good community corporate citizen. Through your daily activities, build a storehouse of goodwill against the day your client or company may need that extra consideration. It could be any one of a hundred potentially damaging stories, and some deft care in which the media handle such material can be extremely important. Negative problems such as strikes, product recalls, industrial accidents, suicides, fires, zoning disputes, storm damage, or simply a downturn in sales volume and profits are platforms for media expression. You're seeking their understanding that, although the event did occur, your company and management are either blameless or taking aggressive steps to correct the problem. That's the time the friendships you have worked so hard to build may stand up and be counted. When this happens, your management will realize that their investment in public relations and their confidence in your ability and judgment were indeed warranted, for you will have tangibly demonstrated that you have helped your company achieve positive press relations.

POWER MARKETING

A major change in consumer products and services is creating a new emphasis on marketing-oriented public relations. This trend is due in part to the fluctuating economy and demands new approaches to marketing expenditures while it places emphasis on new, cost-efficient ways to reach sales goals.

Labor costs have recently been at an all-time high. So too are raw materials, freight, and warehousing. And the cost of money has been kept under control by the Fed. Print media continually raises advertising rates while broadcast media, growing fat from the stepped-up demand for prime time slots, is enjoying a true sellers' market.

Faced with these facts, and a slowdown in consumer expenditures, product managers must struggle with the problem of bringing their products to market at a price that will include profit. Innovative, even radical, changes in marketing thinking must take place or manufacturing could start to stare at red ink. Fortunately, there is a vehicle that can provide the cost-efficient marketing alternative to skyrocketing media advertising costs.

Until now, in most consumer product and service programs, advertising has carried the bulk of the responsibility for product exposure and movement off the shelf. In recent years, some progressive manufacturers have employed joint public relations/advertising marketing efforts to varying degrees, but funding for the PR element has been hesitant and minuscule compared with the escalating advertising appropriation. There is a growing awareness among sophisticated companies that public relations can be a strong player in the motivation of sales.

Today, the role of public relations as a marketing support tool can be tangible and measurable. With investors and stockholders demanding the continuation of high profit margins, I see the next few years providing an opportunity for management to reduce the size of total marketing expenditures without reducing effectiveness.

Unfortunately, many companies with relatively sizable advertising budgets take only a side-glance at public relations and allocate small fractions of total budget for a national campaign. Certainly, some support for product exposure can be anticipated at that expenditure level, but it is clearly insufficient to achieve major inroads. Management, insecure in its allocation of PR budgets, leaves the sales goal only partially achievable because of the lack of financial commitment.

I'm suggesting that this is the time to reduce advertising expenditures and to use selective public relations to fill any gap in the drive to gain one hundred percent market penetration. The result should be to sustain product impact at all distribution levels with increased credibility and cost effectiveness. An additional benefit from this concept, which I call Power Marketing, will be a definite increase in advertising productivity. Keebler Cookie Company successfully competed against Procter & Gamble and Nabisco when it introduced its soft-center cookies into the $2 billion market with the power marketing concept, and achieved over a thirty percent market share in the first year. The believability that an expanded public relations program brings will increase consumer acceptance of the advertising's action message.

It is possible, through analysis of the selling proposition, for public relations techniques to be aimed at pinpointed targets: distribution, quality control, productivity, printing, shipping, warehousing, or finance. It is possible to accurately direct the program to the precise target group. This control will eliminate most waste circulation and, with it, cut expenditures. It's time to review the respective roles of advertising and public relations and to provide sufficient funding to enable competent marketing-oriented public relations practitioners to implement a program based upon research that is large enough to bring the desired sales results. In short, cut your budget by reducing advertising and placing greater emphasis on PR. Increase your PR budget to enable it to fulfill your expectations, but increase PR far less than the reduction in advertising appropriations. By doing this and using competent professionals, you should be able to reach forecasted sales goals and still return a portion of former advertising expenditures to bottom-line profits.

CHAPTER 5

Evolving – and Devolving – Ethics _____

If truth and trust are inherent in media business success,
I fear for their future.

Speaking of the bottom line, "spinning" is a word that has crept into our lexicon by way of those who refuse to let the truth get in the way of the bottom line. The truth, it seems, is no longer fashionable. My learned colleagues swear up and down they will never be party to spinning. For those not familiar with this shifty new art form, spinning refers to the twisting of facts to make them read or sound more positive. If most accomplished public relations leaders refuse to ever report anything but the unvarnished truth, then who is doing the spinning?

Let's start with government. It's become quite acceptable to tell the American people half or partial truths. The public's cynicism about the government's ability to tell the unvarnished truth has probably reached new heights as a result of (at the least) exaggerations by President Bush about reasons for the second U.S. invasion of Iraq. Then there was President Clinton's explanation that he did not have sex with Monica Lewinsky. Consider President Reagan's stance on the Iran/Contra issue. The Iraqi, Iranian, and Soviet governments constantly spin in their reports relating to current events. India, Pakistan, and innumerable South American countries stretch the truth when reporting disasters. In this country, many true facts are kept "classified" or out of the public's reach for years.

Regrettably, spinning has also become a common technique used by American and foreign corporations when reporting unfavorable information to United States citizens. Everyone is seeking to sound a positive tone in their negative information and, if it means resorting to an occasional spin, so be it. It is indeed a sorry situation and further depletes the average American's confidence in editorially published information.

The media also practices spinning when, on a daily basis, newspersons quote sources who have provided information on the guarantee of anonymity. Too much inaccurate information has been reported and later retracted, often too late to undo the damage done to innocent people when it is a *fait accompli*.

It is refreshing then to come across the occasional embarrassed or outraged newsperson who finds the strength to chastise his or her colleagues for this increasing habit of writing questionably reliable material. In the November 28, 1999, issue of the *Sarasota Herald Tribune*, columnist Janet Weaver wrote, "Every time I read another story about the Egypt Air crash, I get angry at my profession all over again. If ever there was a textbook example of the problems in building a story around anonymous sources, this one is it. First, the anonymous sources are quoted as saying there is nothing unusual on the cockpit voice recorders of the plane before it began an erratic ride into the Atlantic Ocean, killing all aboard.

"The next day, almost before the ink was dry on the paper, with television anchors' words still ringing in our ears, the anonymous sources are being quoted quite differently. Now, they say, the tape reveals the suicidal mutterings of the co-pilot as he intentionally put the plane into a dive.

"Go one more news cycle, and the sources' whispered words shift again. It wasn't the co-pilot, whose life by now has been examined in stories searching for a clue to why he would do this. No, it was the relief co-pilot, a man who was intended to work as part of the second crew on the long overseas flight.

"What's most frustrating to me," Ms. Weaver continues, "both as a journalist and as a reader, is that there was never any way for me to evaluate the sources of all this shifting information and decide for myself whether they were credible. The irony for me is that the Egypt Air story was unfolding as I was attending a meeting for journalists on the issue of credibility. The journalists who gathered in Chicago are all dedicated to the idea that we have to do something to rescue our declining credibility as a source of information. Attending were editors of other papers, like the *Herald Tribune*, participating in the Journalism Credibility Project sponsored by the American Society of Newspaper Editors."

TRUTH IS NO LONGER FASHIONABLE

In December 1996, *Esquire* magazine published an eight-page article accusing PR pros, ad people, pollsters, the media, and just about everyone else of spinning the truth. At the time, it caused a tidal wave of concern in the PR community. Using a broad cross section of top PR industry leaders, Jack O'Dwyer, in his monthly *O'Dwyer Report*, sought reaction to the *Esquire* article. Particularly, he sought reaction to a key quote used in the article by former *New York Times* ad columnist, Randall Rothenberg. It was a statement attributed to Richard Edelman, president and CEO of Edelman PR Worldwide, in which he was quoted as saying, "In this era of exploding media technologies, there is no truth except the truth you create for yourself."

Heated denials poured in from every corner of the PR world. In that same article, I was quoted backing Edelman's position. I said, "Sadly, Rich Edelman is right. The truth is no longer fashionable. In today's society, perception is the fact. Everyone spins, from local retailers to entire countries. Even the media spins its own aura to the public. I spent fifty years in PR being scrupulously honest and I feel old-fashioned."

Spinning, of course, is tied to the issue of ethics. In the case of the media as a whole, I believe that in recent years ethics have been all but ignored in the name of competition, ratings and financial reward. For any active practitioner of PR to take a swipe at the media is to expose himself to media reprisals. Having been retired for a number of years, I'm unconcerned with any reaction my finger-pointing might spur.

THE MEDIA MUST ALSO ASSUME RESPONSIBILITY

Ethics is a two-way street. There's no denying that PR wrestles with its own problems, but for years I have watched "well-meaning" writers attack the public relations industry with most of the criticism being unfounded. The Public Relations Society of America has formed one committee after another to respond to allegations against the industry, with little or no meaningful action ever taken. Within their hallowed halls, PR executives know that a strong response is needed, and yet none is ever forthcoming. It's time someone bit the bullet and tried to set the record straight.

Let me just offer a few personal experiences that shed a bit of light on some of the media's ethical misconduct and plain lack of common courtesy.

1. Some media persons refuse to honor release dates. Information transmitted, whether by mail or electronically, is usually marked, "For

release after X o'clock on such-and-such a date." Some publications and/ or broadcast outlets choose to disregard the date and time and jump the gun.

2. Let's say your company announces it will hold a press conference tomorrow at noon. The subject matter contains solid news. Sure enough, at least one media representative will call requesting an advance copy of the material to be announced, knowing perfectly well that by complying with their request, you do an injustice to other media representatives who plan to attend.

3. You have a CEO of a major public company coming to your city. Four weeks in advance of his or her arrival, you contact the marketing columnist of a major paper in the city to query his interest in interviewing your client. The columnist says he will take the interview providing no other interviews are set, including broadcast outlets. He is absolutely adamant about this being an exclusive. You comply, and set the date, time, and location of the interview. Of course, your client is advised and preparations begin to brief him on the interview subject matter. On the morning of the interview, with the client en route on the plane, the columnist calls and informs you that he is canceling the interview because he has found what he considers a better one. It's too late to re-book your client because the columnist insisted on exclusivity.

Yes, it actually happened. Whose ethics are these? The famed marketing columnist of the *Chicago Tribune*, George Lazarus. Mr. Lazarus also had a penchant for screaming over the phone and using four-letter words. On one occasion, a female staff member came into my office with tears streaming down her face. She had just gotten off the phone with Mr. Lazarus, who was unhappy because another writer had gotten a story he thought he should have had. Five minutes later, I was marching into his office. I moved past his secretary and stood in front of his desk until he looked up. Mr. Lazarus is a short man with a somewhat roly-poly body. Every PR person in the country is familiar with his nasty personality. He stared up at me, saying nothing. I quietly said, "George, the next time you call my office and scream at anyone on my staff, I will come back here and kick you right in the ass." Some years later, Mr. Lazarus had a heart attack and his demeanor improved markedly thereafter.

4. A broadcast producer calls requesting your client for an interview on his network talk show. You review the intended subject matter and are told that the interview will center on new products, with specific interest in

a unique robotic manufacturing technique. Your client is briefed and accepts the invitation. One minute into the interview, with the product forgotten, the broadcast personality turns hostile and attacks the company's hiring practices. The producer later beats his chest and proclaims innocence. If the subject matter was to be hiring practices, why not say so when inviting the guest? One is forced to believe the PR person and his client were intentionally deceived. Is this ethical?

5. There is no such thing as "off the record." I've been in interviews where the media person says, "Talk to me off the record," and the next day everything that was said in confidence is published with quotes. Ethical?

6. Freeloaders still exist. Many are the media persons who call requesting hospitality in either hotels or resorts claiming to be on assignment. A quick check of the assigning publication uncovers no such commitment. Let us also be clear in the understanding that media representatives accepting hospitality have no obligation to write positive material simply because they were guests. Every PR professional I know, in extending the invitation, only expects the writer to write with complete freedom and with no cloud of obligation.

7. Earlier I made mention of the ongoing practice by one major Chicago newspaper photo editor of carefully examining both the content of the picture and the back side to check the photo studio that actually shot the picture. If the studio was not the one in which the editor had a financial interest, the probability of seeing that photo in print was practically zero.

8. Was cash ever exchanged for real or imagined favors? Dan Ryan, the second most powerful Democrat in Chicago during the Richard Daley, Sr., administration, was my client for twelve years. He ran for Chairman of the County Board three times against William Erickson and won each time. The super highway that stretches through Chicago's South Side carries Ryan's name. Dan was a premier gentleman and the picture image of the smiling Irishman. His home was close to the Ambassador East Hotel, and he and Mrs. Ryan made the famed Pump Room their headquarters on most evenings. Doris and I were rare attendees for dinner, but each time we were there, Mr. Ryan would come to our table, put his arm around my shoulders, and guide me through the room, from table to table, saying, "I want you to meet the man that got me elected."

I can assure you this statement was a gross exaggeration, but that was the kind of man Dan Ryan was, and I was always proud to represent him.

Dan was a great tease and full of fun. Early one morning, I was in his office when he called to his secretary through the open door to her office. "Please call Bill Stritch," he instructed her. I was dumbfounded that he, an ardent Catholic, was talking about the Cardinal and quickly asked, "Dan, do you always call Cardinal Stritch by his first name?" He nodded and assured me that he did. At that moment, the phone on his desk rang and, as Dan lifted the receiver, he said, "Good morning, Your Eminence."

On the previous day, I had taken a photo depicting three generations of Dan Ryan's family. Both his son and grandson were in the photo, which I had hand-carried to the editor of Chicago's *American*. The editor assured me the picture and caption would run in the morning's first edition. I filled Dan in on this information, and shortly thereafter Dan's secretary told him a reporter for the *American* was waiting to see him. Dan asked me to stand behind the door, out of sight, before ushering the reporter in. He walked up to Dan's desk and placed the opened first edition in front of him, with the picture placement on top. "Had to pull some strings to get them to use this shot," the reporter said, "but I pulled it off." Mr. Ryan smiled, pulled out twenty-five dollars, and handed it to him with a warm thank you.

When he left, Dan simply shrugged his shoulders and laughed. We both knew it was a media sham.

9. A social function has been planned for any number of reasons. It might be the grand opening of a major edifice, or something as simple as a Christmas party. In either case, the location is a Four Seasons-type hotel. Invitations are issued to media, and two scenarios occur. First, the media invitee responds positively, and does not attend. Second, the invitee does not respond at all, but shows up with two or three guests that he has casually invited. Discerning media people would never handle their personal affairs in this manner, and yet, because they are members of the fourth estate, a certain number choose to disregard common courtesy and take advantage of a given situation.

10. PR people are constantly criticized for not preparing their material more thoroughly. It works both ways. A specific case in point relates to Mrs. Frank Lloyd Wright, who was head of her deceased husband's famed architecture firm, Taliesen. She had just signed a contract to design modestly priced homes for National Homes Corp., of Lafayette, Indiana. It represented a major change for her firm, which made the nation's press very interested. Among other outlets, we queried the producers of the NBC's "Today Show" and they expressed strong interest in interviewing Mrs. Wright. While admitting recognition of her fame, the show's producers were concerned

about her ability to speak on television. They requested a pre-show interview.

Though somewhat surprised at the request in light of the fact that Mrs. Wright had authored eight books and been written up by most major national magazines (including three times by *Life* magazine), we honored the show's request. On the appointed morning Mrs. Wright, a small contingent of associates, and I were huddled in the Plaza Hotel in New York, awaiting the arrival of the "Today Show" representative.

Promptly at nine o'clock, the representative called from the lobby and was immediately invited to Mrs. Wright's suite. In waltzed a young woman who could not have been more than twenty-one years old. After being introduced, her first question to Mrs. Wright was, "Mrs. Wright, how old are you?"

Mrs. Wright, a very strong personality, immediately rose to her feet and said, "Young lady, I want you to leave immediately. I have been written up in every *Who's Who* imaginable, by *Life* magazine and innumerable others, and, if you had even the slightest interest in preparing for this interview, you would know how old I am."

With that, the young woman was ushered out of the suite and we said good-bye to the "Today Show."

11. A business page writer, who covers many subjects in his daily column, reports that after initially scrutinizing a dozen agencies, Century 21 real estate has selected three finalists for their regional PR account. The writer further reports that the review committee is meeting the next day to select their winner.

Up to this point, the information is interesting, factual, and timely. However, his next sentence is, in my opinion, a breach of ethics. He decides to editorialize and advise the review committee which agency they ought to select. Without having access to any of the presentation material or knowing the specific account personnel involved, he contributes his well-thought-out opinion.

Did it actually happen? Of course it did. Was the writer correct in his suggested selection? Happily, the review committee didn't think so.

12. Sam Smith, one of the most erudite, honest, and well-informed sports columnists anywhere, does his writing for the *Chicago Tribune*. His beat is the National Basketball Association. Sam did a fascinating column on August 20, 2000, in which he devoted most of his story to Mark Bartelstein, who represents dozens of professional athletes from his Chicago-based management firm. Before quoting Bartelstein, Sam said, "Ninety-

five percent of what you read in newspapers is true, except the five percent about which you have personal knowledge."

After quoting Bartelstein, he goes on to say, "The media have a problem and, as a result, so do I. Value often is determined by perception, so I have to keep an eye on everything that is said and written to make sure it's accurate. You can't imagine how much time NBA executives spend on the Internet reading newspaper (and other) reports to try to figure out what's going on around the league. And general managers and coaches, like everyone else, believe what they read. Yet, there has been more misinformation out there now than anytime I can remember. It seems like there is this incredible race to beat someone to a story, and the more negative, the better.

"So, I have to call teams and say, 'How much of what is written about your team is accurate?' and they say, 'Basically nothing.' "

Sam, in that same column, goes on to say, "All the media really have is their credibility. It's the basic tenet of the business: If readers cannot trust what they read, the outlet is out of business." If truth and trust are inherent to media business success, I fear for their future.

A former newspaper reporter, now turned public relations professional, explains one additional difference between her previous and current position. Journalists aren't exactly known for their diplomacy skills (a gross understatement). The reporter goes on to state that media representatives don't need to be diplomatic, so they don't practice that technique. Asking a direct question as a reporter is considered an attribute; in corporate public relations, it's more likely to be perceived as rude and tactless. I could never understand why most media people care so little about common courtesy.

These ethical points are not meant to be all encompassing. Some may not be ethical questions, but those related to common courtesy. In any case, the point to be made here is that media persons are not "holier than thou." They do make errors and, before directing additional attacks on the public relations industry, they would be wise to put their own house in order.

THE UNCONTROLLABLE ELEMENT

Unlike most industries or professions, PR possesses an inherently uncontrollable element. To be a participant in this field is to be constantly aware that you are not completely in control. No matter the hard news aspect. No matter the lofty level of writing. No matter the complete understanding of media deadlines and the various electronic distribution systems, there is always that which is uncontrollable, whether it be breaking news or simply that your editorial contact is having a bad day.

If your story is only good on this particular day, and for whatever reason the media isn't buying, you must face the fact that you will not have success this day. There is no Court of Appeals. To go over your contact's head is tantamount to ending any relationship that may exist. So, you put your material back in your attaché case and quietly walk away. It may hurt, but you know you will live to fight another day.

CHAPTER 6

"Hi, I'm Bill Veeck."

He was driven to prove that he was better with one leg than most men were with two. I don't think he ever knew how much I cared. I would have worked that account for nothing.

What I loved most about my job was not knowing whose business I was going to get into next. On any given day, I could get a call from almost anyone inquiring about our services. That's what made it exciting.

I had been in the PR business about ten years when the day of all days came in November of 1958. I was sitting at my desk that morning and the phone rang. I lifted the receiver and heard an unfamiliar voice say, "Hi, I'm Bill Veeck."

Everyone in the Chicago area knew Mrs. Dorothy Comiskey had just sold the White Sox to a group partnership headed by Veeck. The team had been in the Comiskey family since the days of Charles A. Comiskey, alias "The Old Roman." It seemed inconceivable at that time that anyone outside the Comiskey family could own the team.

I didn't know Mr. Veeck and couldn't imagine his calling me, so I responded rather briskly to the call. "Yeah, and I'm President Eisenhower." Bill laughed before confirming that it really was baseball's bad boy. He told me he was searching for a PR/marketing man to join the White Sox organization and asked if I was interested. He had no way of knowing that the day I was born in Mt. Sinai Hospital, on Chicago's southwest side, the nurse handed me over to my mother wrapped in a blanket covered with White Sox logos. Talk about an authentic, wild and crazy White Sox fan –

that's me. Was I interested? He didn't have to ask me twice. Bill invited me to join him for breakfast the following day. That two-hour session led to lunch and dinner the next day, and the day after that.

Just by being an avid baseball fan and dedicated reader of the sports page, I knew Bill had owned the St. Louis Browns and the Cleveland Indians. I knew he'd won a pennant with the Indians, and I remembered the Eddie Gaedel midget stunt he pulled in St. Louis. I knew he was thought of as a creative maverick, and sort of a mad genius. I was also aware of his dichotomy with baseball. Owners who considered themselves baseball purists were not banging any drums for Bill and his brand of sports marketing. In contrast, the media, and many fans, saw Bill as a breath of fresh air.

What I didn't know was how Bill had gotten my name. He told me his PR man and good friend in Cleveland, Mar Samuels, had sent him to the W.B. Doner Advertising Agency in Detroit. They referred him to the head of their Chicago office, who just happened to be Marvin Frank, the advertising man who had already been so helpful to me.

After hiring Marvin's firm to handle advertising for the team, Bill asked him if he could recommend a good public relations agency. Bill told me he took Marvin's recommendation to several media people who agreed that I might be his kind of guy. Suddenly, it was all real. I was officially representing the Chicago White Sox.

In those two days of togetherness, Bill told me the story of how the Sox became available and explained some of the machinations he had to go through to finally close the deal. Evidently, when Charles "Chuck" Comiskey's father, Lou, died in 1939, his mother, Mrs. Grace Comiskey, battled the team's trustees, who were determined to sell the club. She put up a successful fight and assumed the title of president.

In addition to her son, Chuck, Mrs. Comiskey had a daughter, Dorothy. When Mrs. Comiskey died in 1956, her will stated that the White Sox shares be split equally between her two children, except for an additional 500 shares which she left to Dorothy. She named Dorothy executor of the estate and gave her control of the team. That meant Dorothy owned fifty-four percent of the stock and Chuck forty-six percent.

Dorothy made Chuck a vice president, along with her husband, John Duncan Rigney, a former White Sox pitcher. Chuck was furious and initiated multiple lawsuits. He lost them all. Well, almost all of them. The legal action he did win cost him any chance of regaining control of the team.

With Dorothy's majority interest giving her three members on the board of directors, and Chuck only two, he successfully navigated a series of legal maneuvers that helped him gain equal representation on the board. This created a complete deadlock. Dorothy was left with no choice. Since she could not operate the club her way, her only alternative was to sell.

Bill had been out of baseball about six years, and when he heard about the Chicago situation, he hurried to town to follow-up the lead and, hopefully, find a way back into the game he loved so much. After negotiating for some time, he made an offer of $2.7 million. Dorothy Comiskey made it clear that her brother would have the right to match Bill's offer, and if he did, then the team was Chuck's.

Under those circumstances, Bill was certain Chuck would take the White Sox, and that all this activity was an exercise in frustration. For the next six months, Bill continued doing color commentary on "Baseball's Game of the Week." When his attorneys contacted Mrs. Comiskey again, they were amazed to learn Chuck Comiskey had offered his sister about one million dollars less than Bill. Bill was back in the game – or so it seemed.

Charley Finley became his next obstacle. With that impish smile, Bill told me how sweet ol' Charley, who at that time was a well-known insurance magnate, threw him a curve ball that almost cost him the team. Charley had called Bill to ask if he could get in on the action. Bill welcomed Charley into his group, until he found out Charley was bad-mouthing him to some Chicago sportswriters, claiming that Bill would never exercise his option on the deal because he would lose his backers. Then Bill discovered that dear Charley had gone to Mrs. Comiskey and signed a purchasing agreement that would go into effect if Bill allowed his option to lapse. In a quick phone conversation, Bill invited Mr. Finley out of the deal. Up to this point, Bill had only put up one hundred dollars. Charley immediately offered Bill $250,000 for his option, and was firmly turned aside.

It took until late April 1959 before Veeck accomplished what Mrs. Comiskey could not. After winning a court case, he was permitted to enlarge the board and he became the new director. Within a week, Bill was named team president. The final sale price for the team was $2,525,000, because Bill and his financial backers were only able to obtain eighty percent of the White Sox stock. His inability to convince Chuck Comiskey to sell him his twenty percent cost Bill over $1 million in extra taxes. The ridiculous part of the deal was that forty-six percent of that million was Chuck's money. As stubborn as he was, Chuck finally resigned in the early part of 1960.

Bill's backers included prominent stockbroker A.C. Allyn, Sidney Frye of the legal firm of Schiff, Hardin & Waite, and Baseball Hall of Famer, Hank Greenberg. Some other funding came from Cleveland. These people were not only behind Bill financially, they were loyal supporters throughout the grueling negotiation process.

Bill and I seemed to hit it off at that first meeting, but neither of us had any idea our business relationship – and our friendship – would last another twenty-five years. I spent most of the winter and spring of '59 getting to know Bill, discovering what a driven, energetic, and complex person he was.

He grew up in the Chicago suburb of Hinsdale. His Daddy – that's what Bill always called his father – was one of the leaders of the Chicago Cubs organization. As a youngster, Bill worked part-time on the team's maintenance crew. After each game, he'd spend hours sweeping the outfield bleachers. Bill always spoke with such reverence about the ivy-covered outfield walls of Wrigley Field, as if he were referring to the Holy Grail. I got the impression Bill's father was responsible for the initial installation of the ivy. Although he played basketball in high school, the time he spent around Wrigley is certainly when he developed his love of baseball and his interest in every aspect of its operation.

Like a lot of young men at the beginning of World War II, Bill enlisted in the Marines. I knew he'd been injured in Bougainville in 1943 and, because he didn't like to talk about himself, the best I could gather was that the recoil of a piece of heavy artillery hit him in the leg. Before he could be removed from the combat field, an infection that he called "jungle rot" had set in. He spent the next eighteen months going from one hospital to another, trying to fight off the popular prognosis that his leg be removed.

He went on with his life, even became an owner of the Cleveland Indians, but his leg problems persisted. Bill made them put the inevitable off until after the 1946 World Series, which featured his pennant-winning Indians. By then, he had been convinced by doctors that any further delay placed his life in danger. They cut off his leg below the knee in November of that year.

HE DISLIKED THE WORD "HANDICAPPED"

Ten weeks after the amputation, his new prosthesis leg arrived. In typical Veeck fashion, he wore the leg that evening to an affair with 1,000 guests. The stump was still raw but, of course, no one heard him complain. That's part of the Veeck philosophy. "Don't coddle yourself." From that day to the moment he died, Bill felt he had to be better with one leg than most men were with two. He disliked the word "handicapped." In complete contrast to the socially accepted way of describing someone who had lost a limb, Bill felt he was not handicapped, but crippled.

Over the years, he never let on to the daily pain he was going through. I knew this because we would often hold meetings at his South Side apartment early in the morning, and I would find him soaking his stump in a hot bath. Bill seldom slept more than four or five hours each night. Between five and six in the morning, he read. He was a voracious reader. It wasn't unusual for him to go through a book every twenty-four hours. Those early morning meetings with Bill were amazing. He'd lie there in the tub, soaking his stump, and spout idea after idea. His mind was ticking every second, and not just on baseball.

But as smart as he was, Bill was also driven to prove his strength, his athleticism, and his virility. He put in the time and effort to become an excellent dancer. He and his wife, Mary Frances, took pride in their prowess on the dance floor. Bill was a good racquetball and tennis player as well. He had great anticipation. He'd read his opponent's move so he could position himself properly. I always considered myself a pretty good racquetball player, and he easily cleaned my clock. On the tennis court, I would stand in disbelief at his agility. The fact that he had fathered ten children, four by an earlier marriage and six with Mary Frances, just added to the Veeck mystique.

MARY FRANCES VEECK

Everyone who knew Mary Frances seemed to admire her. I was no exception. I marveled at the way she was able to stay close to Bill, to be a part of his baseball life, to be an important confidante, and still be an exceptional mother to her growing family. You had to know Bill to understand how challenging it was for Mary Frances. They had a wonderful, loving relationship, but Bill was not easy. He kept long hours, frequently coming home well after midnight after making three or four speeches, and having a few beers. She seemed to always be there at the right time, either hosting an informal event in the Bards Room where the White Sox served meals to their VIP's, or just sitting in the owner's box.

Mary Frances had been in public relations, serving as director of one of the major professional Ice Shows that toured the country. She was an excellent writer, very smooth on her feet in interview situations, and bright as hell. I never felt Mary Frances was along for the ride. She was an active participant.

As for me, being part of the Chicago White Sox organization was the living end. Bill's gone now, and though I never told him, I would have worked that account for nothing. I don't think he ever knew how much I cared.

You see, long before play-by-play men Ken Harrelson and Tom Paciorek, before Bob Elson, Jack Brickhouse, and Harry Caray, there was Hal Totten. As a kid, I couldn't wait to dash home from elementary school to tune in to Totten and the White Sox game. In those days, without lights, each day's broadcast began at 3 p.m. A kid's imagination is a miraculous thing. At about eight or nine years of age, I played make-believe baseball against the brick wall across from our Lawndale Street apartment. I was completely oblivious to any traffic. I would follow my own game plan and, from moment to moment, I would change characters. I'd become the strong-armed great White Sox pitcher, Ted Lyons, offering my own radio play-by-play. "Lyons winds up, stretches, looks toward first, and fires a strike right over the heart of the plate."

As I spoke, I reenacted the scene. After winding up, I would fire the sponge ball against the wall. Somehow, I always imagined playing against the New York Yankees. "Bill Dickey smashes the ball towards short," and suddenly I was transformed into Luke Appling. "Luke scoops up the ball and fires it to Zeke Bonura at first for the out." And so it went, hour after hour, and day after day. My White Sox never won anything, but I loved them anyway. I lived through the era of Bullfrog Dietrich and John Duncan Rigney, as well as Ted Lyons and Bill Lee, and was mesmerized by the triple K's, the double play combination of Kennedy to Kolloway to Kuhel. Even though the Sox were perennial losers, each spring there was a new ray of hope.

There is a not-so imaginary line that runs through the heart of Chicago separating north from south, Cubs from Sox. Madison Street runs east to west through downtown. Everything north of this barrier is considered Chicago Cubs territory. Everything south of Madison is Chicago White Sox country, and never the twain shall meet.

From the very inception of major-league baseball in Chicago, there have always been two major-league teams in town, with no neutral territory. Fans have favored either one or the other, and emotions run deep – deep enough in some cases to describe it as downright hatred. Although I've lived north of the city most of my life, my first thirteen years were spent on White Sox turf. That was enough. Despite my northern migration, I remained a fiercely loyal Sox fan.

When Bill Veeck took over, it was like nothing I'd ever seen before. The fans went absolutely ape over the team. There had been so much hype in the press, from Chuck Comiskey's seemingly never-ending legal antics to Bill's reputation as a true winner and relative genius, that people couldn't wait for the start of spring training.

Al Lopez was the team manager when Bill took over. Al was an easygoing guy himself, so sitting down with him and Bill was a laugh a minute. Al kept telling Bill he thought they had enough to win the pennant. Bill, always a strong proponent of the combination of pitching and power, felt the Sox of '59 were in dire need of some power. He kept trying to get Roy Sievers from Washington. Sievers was a well-known home run hitter for the Senators. Despite Washington's need for money, they wouldn't part with their big bopper.

EXCITEMENT IS CONTAGIOUS

Bill's first order of business was to create an atmosphere in which things were not only going to change, but change for the better. With ever an eye on ticket sales, he wanted to build excitement. Bill repeatedly said, "Excitement is contagious." He knew from experience that excitement and anticipation stirred up the fans, and that spirit spilled onto the playing field and infected the players as well. He felt that after years of going nowhere, the Sox weren't about to become pennant contenders unless he made the most of the positive buzz surrounding his takeover. He knew he had to instill that feeling of reinvigoration from the top down, and to sustain it over the course of a long season. Although rarely spoken, I think Bill felt Chicago was his last chance to grab the ring. He had been through Milwaukee, St. Louis, and Cleveland. I think he knew Chicago was his last stop.

Having had ten years in the publicity business, I was used to the ongoing struggle of trying to land media attention for one account or another. It was a real eye-opener to walk into the White Sox offices every day and find reporters actually waiting there. More often than not came the question, "Any good story ideas for tomorrow's paper?" Talk about accessibility. I wasn't prepared for this kind of largesse. My, how things had changed.

In his first book, *Veeck as in Wreck*, Bill did me the great honor of writing, "And, again my luck held: I went into a new operation and found exactly the man I most needed. He was Aaron Cushman, about the brightest young PR man I have ever come in contact with, and my luck in bumping into him was the first sign that the dice were going to fall for me in Chicago."

When the team got off to a good start, the momentum ran into the streets. A confidence seemed to be taking over the city. Even Cubs fans were jumping on the bandwagon.

It was as if people had the feeling we were headed down the road to victory. The media declared the White Sox were on a roll. Bill and I agreed that the beat sportswriters seemed to be coming to the park earlier and earlier, and leaving later and later. By mid-season, many of the community papers began sending their sports reporters to some games.

VEECK: A MASTER AT MEDIA RELATIONS

He was a master at hospitality, particularly when it came to the press. Bill greeted media members individually and would often escort them to the Bards Room. He would hold court around a big circular table in the middle of the room where reporters would shoot questions at him in an informal atmosphere. He loved it.

One of the true barometers of the team's success was the arrival of the sports columnists. We knew the beat reporters were assigned to cover the Sox every day, but the columnists had the freedom to pick and choose their subjects. When they started making the Bards Room a part of their daily routine, I knew it wasn't because of the food. That's not to say guys like Dave Condon and John Carmichael were shy about their nutritional intake, but the team was making noise and it was good to have them around.

Al Lopez liked the look of this team. "Pitching and defense with a little speed thrown in," he said, "could win it for the White Sox." More power would be welcome, but he felt he could win with the team we had.

Bill wanted to bring Satchel Paige to Chicago. Only God knew how old Satchel was at that point, but Bill was convinced Satch could throw as well as anybody for a few innings of relief. Never one to impose his will upon a manager, Bill made the suggestion to Señor Lopez, in his own quiet and inimitable fashion. He knew full well Al wanted no part of dealing with a troublesome or non-conformist player, and Al was certainly aware of Satch's history of doing his own thing and occasionally missing a team bus or plane.

It never happened, but it was indicative of Bill's thought process. To him, image was everything. Almost every move he made was designed to endear himself and his team to the average man and woman on the street. He loved the so-called little people. In the office, he was probably the most accessible business executive in the nation. He always took his own calls; when you phoned the Chicago White Sox and asked to speak to Bill Veeck, his was the next voice you heard. He handled the good calls, and the bad.

When Bill took over the team, he chose not to move Chuck Comiskey out of the big office he had always occupied. Instead, he set himself up in a tiny cubicle formerly used by a secretary. This was his private office.

A BASE HIT AT THE RIGHT TIME

"How you doing, Bill?" People who'd run into him on the street repeatedly offered him this greeting. His typical response became one of his favorite expressions: "Just give me a base hit at the right time."

Another Veeckian comment came in response to requests for an autograph: "Anyone who doesn't enjoy doing this is a liar." This was in direct contrast to several of today's highly compensated athletes who like to be paid for providing their John Henry to adoring fans. Things certainly have changed.

Bill's daily routine included a complete walking tour of the ball yard every morning. He'd make his rounds in search of ways to improve the park and make it more pleasant for the fans. The first day I walked into the park, Bill had a crew of hundreds washing down the stands and seats with soap and water. By the following year, he had a steam-cleaning unit that kept the stands spotless. Next came the renovation of the men's and women's restrooms. He also had additional restrooms put in. Not long after that came an increase in the number of concession stands, and some diversification in the type of food served in those stands. Instead of building fancy private dining rooms for box seat holders, Bill had a picnic area built beneath the stands in left and right fields and added a beer garden as well. In retrospect, some of these moves may not have been altogether altruistic. Bill did have a keen eye for increased revenues.

The image of Comiskey Park compared to Wrigley Field was night and day. No pun intended. Beautiful Wrigley Field was the keynote of the Cubs advertising campaign. As for us, we had a real problem attracting people to Comiskey because of the neighborhood. We lived in a dirty, industrial section of Chicago where muggings were a too frequent occurrence. People were fearful of the area.

Veeck turned his attention to this problem and authorized some $150,000 to paint the outside wall of the ballpark a glistening white. Almost everyone ridiculed the idea, saying they'd give it thirty days before graffiti destroyed the esthetic looks.

Everyone but Bill was surprised that it never happened. Those white walls remained sparkling clean and untouched. It was almost like the neighborhood bad boys took personal pride in the walls' cleanliness. Bill always felt the media exaggerated the area's problems. He was convinced it wasn't nearly as bad as its published reputation. He was smart enough to know that perception is the fact, and, true or not, he needed to do more to dispel questions relating to public fear and apathy toward the neighborhood. He created what he termed an "Isle of Light," and practically overnight there was as much light outside the park on a night game as there was inside. Something was definitely working because attendance jumped higher and higher as the season progressed. Was it the play of the team? Perhaps, but some of the credit had to be given to Bill's insight and the internal and external moves he made to improve conditions for the fans.

During each game, Bill would walk through the stands sitting and talking with the fans. He could almost always be found in the bleachers. The last three innings, however, had to be spent in the press box. That was his routine and it seldom changed.

Another thing that rarely changed was Bill's wardrobe. The open white sport shirt, minus any hint of a tie, was his trademark. I used to kid him about always wearing a navy blue gabardine suit. I even accused him of not having a second suit, let alone one of another color or style. He laughed and one day showed me his closet, a full rack lined with navy blue gabardine suits. I asked him why. He told me, with his usual smile, they were "easily interchangeable."

HANK GREENBERG: A MAN TO REMEMBER

It quickly became obvious to me that, other than Mary Frances, nobody knew Bill better than Hank Greenberg. Once I had gotten the stardust out of my eyes, I realized Hank was a warm, genuine human being. He was quietly confident, affluent, but not obviously so, and he was a delight to be around. The first time I met Hank was at spring training in Sarasota, Florida. I listened in awe as he told some stories about his playing days. I remembered Hank hit fifty-nine home runs one year while with the Detroit Tigers and never again came within ten of that record year. I just had to ask him what happened that wondrous year. He told me that, for some reason he will never understand, the baseball looked like it was a watermelon. He said the ball just seemed to hang there and say, "Hit me."

Hank and I got to know each other better on the tennis court. I had been playing for quite a while and had won a couple of club and community championships. Bill told me Hank was a really good player, so when Hank asked me to be his partner for a game he set up at Sarasota's Colony Resort and Tennis Complex, I jumped at the chance. We played against a couple of teaching pros, and, although we were beaten that day, we more than held our own. That was the first of many tennis outings I shared with Hank, both singles and doubles. Hank had become a very successful stockbroker in Los Angeles, and his son made a name as a professional sports agent.

Hank knew Bill inside and out. He understood all his pluses, and even a few minuses. He was a calming influence on Bill and one of the few people Bill would listen to. Bill was stubborn and very dogmatic. He would go through the motions of being a good listener, but when the conversation was over, you realized he couldn't be swayed and was intent on doing it his way. To Bill's credit, when it involved baseball, he was right more often than not.

Bill could always rely on the loyal support of people like Hank, but to have the mayor of Chicago in his corner meant quite a bit. Mayor Richard J. Daley lived only a few blocks from Comiskey Park and had been a fan and regular attendee of games for years. The mayor loved what was happening on the South Side. He credited Bill with the success of the team and the enthusiasm it generated throughout the city. Everyone, it seemed, was reveling in the excitement. The taxi drivers, waiters and waitresses, hoteliers, theatre and restaurant owners, and retail stores were enjoying a field day. Revenues were up everywhere, and Bill represented only good things. People would stop us on the streets and wish Bill well. Cab drivers would roll down their windows to yell hello or say, "Go get 'em Bill." If he ran for Governor of Illinois at that time, he would have won hands down.

WHITE SOX MARKETING PROGRAM

The team had a great marketing program; i.e., let Bill make appearances and make friends. As long as he was able to get out and speak to the people, he was a smash hit. The man was indefatigable. He booked himself for an average of two speeches a night, and oftentimes extended that to as many as four. He spoke somewhere almost every night, and distance was never a factor.

Bill would drive to Joliet, to Elgin, even to Peoria if he knew at least fifty people would show up to hear him. Chicago was not Miami or Los Angeles. We had first class winter weather but, once committed, Bill always made it. People loved his stories and as many times as I heard them, I still laughed along with the rest of the crowd. When the booking got so heavy or the distances so great that it was a physical impossibility to cover them all personally, Bill had a few stand-ins. Most of the time he called on Dizzy Trout, the former Detroit Tigers pitching star, who was also gifted with a great sense of humor. Once in a while, he'd hit me to pick up the slack, and over the winter season I probably made eight or ten such talks, paraphrasing Bill's material as much as I could.

His stories about his days with the St. Louis Browns were always a hit. First, he'd give the big buildup by explaining how poor attendance was at the time. Then he'd talk about the man who called with a party of six asking what time the game started.

"What time would you like it to start?" Bill would respond. Then the guy would ask about the availability of good seats and Bill would say, "What about second base, we're not using it."

On the speaking circuit, Bill spoke the language of the people. There was no innuendo, no second agenda. He was simple, but direct. He was there to promote the White Sox, to build enthusiasm, and to sell tickets.

LUCKY SEATS

At the games, Bill was big on door prizes. The "Lucky Seats" promotion is legendary. Rather than give out an item to everyone who comes through the gates, or the first 10,000 or 20,000 fans, Bill focused on one lucky person. A lucky ticket would be placed under one seat in the park. If that person found the lucky ticket, he or she would win not 1 or 10 or 100, let's say, cupcakes, but 10,000 packages of cupcakes.

Something in this quantity couldn't be picked up at will-call, it had to be delivered – and delivered it was. We would go out of our way to be present for such deliveries. It took about five minutes for the sheer size of the prize to really hit the winning person. After all, 10,000 cupcakes are a lot of cupcakes. When they began filling all the rooms in the winner's home, we would watch the panic set in. People would literally run down the street screaming and begging people to take some cupcakes off their hands.

I once witnessed the delivery of 1,000 pounds of nuts and bolts to a lucky ticket holder's home. The truck just dumped them in their driveway. Sheer hysteria for the winner, and us.

Bill's theory was simple: if everyone in the park got a package of cupcakes, it was nice, but so what? When 10,000 cupcakes were delivered to one person, some 50,000 people would hear about it. Other deliveries included a thousand cans of beer or soda pop to one family – and always the same frantic reaction. Sure, there were games when the team gave away hats, bats, wrist bands, flags, T-shirts, gloves, roses, and so on to the first 20,000 to enter the field. Bill would have given away his third base coach if he thought it would enhance attendance. His thinking was sound and very basic; no matter how good your team is, you're not going to win every game. What's important is making it fun, win or lose. Send the fans home convinced they had a great evening even if the Sox get blown out. It sure made sense to me. You could learn a lot being close to that man.

Then, there were the special nights. The Sox hosted Chicago's cab drivers, teachers, nurses, waiters and waitresses, hotel concierges and elevator conductors. On Mother's Day, the team opened the gates to any woman who could show a picture of a child – might even be her own. That day saw about 4,000 mothers enter. As part of National Dairy Week, the team gave away all kinds of dairy products. But to top off the entertainment, there was a milking contest on the field, with Sox players competing against their opponents. Obviously, it was Bill's idea. But while the fans were having a ball, Bill was a nervous wreck. Sox second baseman, Nellie Fox, was stuck with a temperamental cow that kept kicking wildly. It looked like he would get hit at any moment. Nellie was only the cornerstone of the team. Losing him to a Veeckian stunt like this would have been a disaster. Luckily, he got the best of the cow.

THE ELEPHANT WALK

With Bill's imaginative mind always on alert for something new and different, you couldn't help but start thinking like him. During the course of the season, my agency had been retained to promote the Chicago engagement of the Cristiani Bros. Circus. The circus was to erect its tents in Grant Park adjacent to the downtown area. At that time, the Cristiani Bros. Circus was about as big as they come, with the possible exception of the Ringling Bros. and Barnum & Bailey outfit.

I got the idea to tie the circus and the White Sox together and pitched the thought to Bill. Ever the showman, he loved the idea of doing a complete circus parade around the inside of the ballyard before the game started. It was a cinch to gain major media coverage for both organizations, and the fans would surely enjoy an extra bonus. I cleared the idea with the circus management and proceeded to make the logistical arrangements to transport the entire circus to Comiskey Park.

The transport alone garnered lots of exposure. By four o'clock in the afternoon, the entire circus was in position to make its grand entrance into the ballyard. The sequence of appearance for all Cristiani parades had the elephants lead the way. The main entry onto the field itself was through a gate in center field. Once the elephants were in position, it became clear to everyone that there was no way they could make it through the gate. The ceiling was simply too low. The staff, both Sox and circus, began to scurry around in search of an answer. The stunt had been heavily promoted in advance and the fans were expecting to see a show. This was a problem we just didn't anticipate. I was a basket case. I could already see tomorrow's sports headline, "Circus stunt bombs at Sox Park."

I called Bill seeking a solution. He asked me to put the head of his maintenance crew on the phone. After the call, men with shovels appeared out of nowhere. Bill decided we ought to dig a trench six feet deep and wide enough to enable the elephants and the wagons hauling other animals to pass through. It worked. The elephants strolled onto the field to great applause, followed by lions and tigers, bareback riders, high flyers, and clowns. They all marched around the park to the musical accompaniment of the circus band. Taking up the rear of the parade was a giant calliope on wheels.

Talk about a big hit. The next morning's papers were full of pictures. From that day to the day they tore the old ballpark down, that center field entry way, which had been used hundreds of times for many different promotions, was referred to as "The Elephant Walk."

THE EXPLODING SCOREBOARD

The best promotional gimmick Bill ever came up with was the exploding scoreboard. It's now common for ballparks to have fireworks shooting from the top of their scoreboard after a home run or victory, but again Bill was the man behind the trend. Because it's not the kind of idea that just develops overnight, my natural curiosity spurred me to ask Bill how he came up with it. Over a steak dinner and a few beers, he told me he was watching a play by William Saroyan, in which a pinball machine played a key role. An actor in the production had been playing the machine through most of the play, and, just before the final curtain, the guy hit the jackpot and the machine exploded with all types of visual effects and loud music. It hit Bill right then, and he transposed the idea to the scoreboard and wrapped it around home runs. He actually came up with the concept shortly after he sold the Indians. When he pitched it to them, the team turned a deaf ear to the idea. Bill filed it away and unveiled it with the White Sox.

The scoreboard was built by Charlie Gibbs of Spencer Advertising Co., who helped Bill design it at a cost of $350,000. The board was loaded with ten mortars that fired Roman candles. With it came attendant bombs, rockets, and colored strobe lights that flashed on and off. The board promised an element of surprise, as the tape controlling all the gadgetry was designed never to repeat itself. There were an infinite number of patterns. Not only did the lights on the board go off and on, but also moved up and down while circular images spun 'round and 'round and smoke poured out of the top. Adding to the fun was the musical background piped throughout the park with a powerful, specially constructed P.A. system. It, too, could play musical versions of hundreds of tunes. Bill's favorite was an excerpt from Handel's *Messiah*. He loved the segment that played "Hallelujah" over and over again, as the home run hitter circled the bases.

Upon its debut, the scoreboard was the talk of the baseball world, and Bill's name was further sealed in immortality. The scoreboard actually cost the White Sox nothing. Both the team and the Spencer agency sold advertising space on the board, which covered the cost nicely. The same was true of most, if not all, White Sox promotions involving giveaways. Invariably, they were paid for by manufacturers seeking exposure, or some sponsor with a similar motive.

When it came to promotions, Bill always had a purpose. If the Sox chose to give away 500 or 1,000 tickets to a group or organization, Bill made sure the tickets were good seats, and the games involved noteworthy opponents like the New York Yankees. Ever the savvy marketing man, he'd say, "You give nothing unless you give your best."

A 50,000-PIECE ORCHESTRA

I gradually got better at recognizing when Bill was on to a new idea. I saw that magic in his face just before he asked me what I thought of a 50,000-piece orchestra. It didn't take a mental giant to see where he was going with this thought.

"Wow, Bill, what a great idea," I said. He asked me if I thought it was practical. After about two minutes of thought, I said, "Sure." Then he asked me to make it happen. While he was often the creator, Bill relied on support troops for the actual implementation of his schemes. He didn't like to get tied down with details. And that's how I inherited "Music Night at Sox Park."

Working closely with the Sox in-house staff, my staff and I went to work on the promotional bare bones of the idea. "Music Night" was to be an event where fans brought musical instruments to the ballpark. Those without instruments would not be admitted. We agreed that it could be a kazoo, pair of spoons, or a singing comb, but hoped some fans would show up with the genuine article.

We began scouring the country for the most unusual instruments that could be used in a giant parade inside the ballpark, just prior to the game. Baseball was very sensitive to its traditions about interrupting the game, but was willing to approve anything in good taste before the game started. Within a few weeks, we had located a fifty-foot-long trumpet, the largest cello and violin combination anyone had ever seen, and a piano so large it took a giant flatbed truck to move it. We also lined up dozens of other crazy and impossibly funny items of instrumentation.

When "Music Night" arrived, it drew a full house – each fan toting one instrument or another. In the corner of the White Sox dugout, we stashed the night's big secret, the surprise that was surely going to make this night one to remember. The key moment was the home team half of the seventh inning, or the seventh inning stretch. All the baseball action stopped, and a small man dressed in white tie and tails emerged from the dugout. He was introduced as the conductor of the Chicago Symphony Orchestra. The tiny man climbed a three-step ladder that had been placed on home plate. He faced the crowd, raised his baton and proceeded to lead the throng of more than 46,000 fans in a moving rendition of "Take Me Out to the Ball Game."

One of those joining in song was popular White Sox announcer, Harry Caray. When Bill overheard Harry's passionately off-key version of the tune, a new tradition was born. From that point on, Harry served as musical conductor at the park, and he carried on the tradition when he moved across town to the Cubs' broadcast booth.

With Sherman Lollar catching, Luis Aparicio at shortstop, Nellie Fox at second base, and Jim Landis in center field, that great White Sox defense of 1959 was highlighted by strength up the middle. The rest of the defensive line-up included Earl Torgeson at first base, Bubba Phillips at third, Jim

McAnany in right field, and Al Smith in left. With these reliable gloves behind them, the pitching staff thrived all season. Early Wynn posted twenty-two wins, Bob Shaw had eighteen, Billy Pierce collected fourteen, and Dick Donovan added nine wins of his own. The Sox bullpen that year was just as tough with Barry Latman, Gerry Staley, Turk Lown, and Ray Moore. The contribution of role players like Johnny Callison, "Jungle" Jim Rivera, Larry Doby, Norm Cash, Del Ennis, J.C. Martin, and Sammy Esposito just added to the club's arsenal. Still, Bill yearned for more power.

I'M YOUR NEW HOME RUN HITTER

On Saturdays, I would often join Bill on his walk around the park. Hank would tag along as well, when he was in town. Sooner or later, the conversation would revert back to the need to acquire a power hitter. This went on week after week. I sometimes thought Bill would trade his soul for a guy who could consistently hit the ball out of the park. After hearing him mull over this dilemma time and time again, I finally offered Bill a solution.

Over a period of several years, I was considered one of Chicago's best softball players. As part of the Windy City Professional Softball League, I had been playing in various stadiums across the city since I was eighteen. Although it was only one or two dollars, fans would actually pay to watch the games, the majority of which were played at the North Town Currency Exchange Stadium on Devon and McCormick. I had played for North Town Currency, for Feuer Boilers, and at least one other team whose name I cannot remember. My forte was always the long ball. In the course of a season, I'd hit more than my share of home runs over the fence or over the outfielders' heads. In short, I was a proven power hitter.

Of course, I was accustomed to hitting a sixteen-inch softball, a game played almost exclusively in Chicago. In my mind, however, I couldn't see any gigantic difference between hitting a sixteen-inch softball and hitting a regular-sized baseball. Then again, no one ever accused me of being too bright.

Anyway, as the summer wore on, I kept haranguing Bill about the fact that he really didn't have to look very far for his power-hitting savior. He already had one. I could do the job. Each time I'd float my proposition, Bill would good-naturedly laugh, pat me on the head and give me a knowing look that told me to knock it off. On a most eventful Saturday, however, Bill, Dizzy Trout, and I were walking and talking our way around the park when we backed into the same lament. I started to repeat my often-reiterated theme and, to my amazement, in a moment of pure disgust, Bill turned to me and said, "OK, I've heard this chop suey enough. Go get a bat!"

For a moment, I couldn't believe he had said it. He was really going to give me a shot. Bill turned to Dizzy Trout, a former all-star pitcher for the Detroit Tigers, who was headed for the Hall of Fame in Cooperstown, and said, "Diz, throw him a few." Now, in all fairness, it must be told that Dizzy had been retired from baseball for at least three years and was sporting an oversized mid-section. He was not exactly in his baseball prime. Was I scared? Not me. I was too stupid to be frightened.

I grabbed a bat that seemed about the right weight and length and stepped into the batter's box in fabled Comiskey Park. Diz threw me eleven pitches. I never saw any of them. The ball just kept buzzing past and I kept swinging at air. When it was over, I hung my head and practically crawled away from the plate. Never again did I mention my so-called hitting prowess. I had seen the light, and there was a difference between softball and baseball. It was a chasm far too wide for me to cross.

WE WIN THE PENNANT AND HOST HUNDREDS OF MEDIA

On the field, the Sox carried on without me. They also kept winning, and toward the end of the season, Bill got his wish. The team acquired the heavy-hitting Ted "Big Klu" Kluszewski from the Cincinnati Reds. On Tuesday night, September 22, White Sox fans went gloriously mad when the team won its first American League championship in many moons. Thousands of Chicagoans reacted in brief panic when the city's air raid sirens sounded at about 10:30 p.m., just as the Sox clinched the pennant in a victory against the Indians in Cleveland.

The team plane landed at Midway Airport a little after 2 a.m. the following morning, and Sox players waded into one of the wildest receptions the city had ever seen. About 25,000 to 30,000 people had gathered to meet the team at Midway. The players were greeted with an ovation so loud it drowned out the sound of landing and departing planes. The revelry swept over the entire South Side and the din lasted until the break of dawn.

That night, Bill was in Bloomington, Illinois, making a speech for one of our television sponsors. Dizzy Trout was with him, and as soon as they got the news, they headed to Midway to join the festivities. Dizzy then picked up Mary Frances and brought her to Midway, where the crowd swarmed around her and Bill. Mayor Daley eventually dispatched a squad car to rescue them from the hysteria.

Doris and I watched the game on TV, and, the moment it was over, we dressed and headed to the airport. By the time we arrived, it was impossible to make it through the crowd to try to get close to either the plane or the Veecks, so we simply screamed and hollered like everyone else.

The airport crowd was determined to catch a glimpse of their heroes. They hung from rooftops, telephone poles, trucks, and buses, waving wildly at any sight of team members. When little Luis Aparicio, our gifted shortstop and the man who started the double play that ended the clinching game, got off the plane, the familiar chant of "Go-Go-Sox" rumbled through the terminal. One homemade sign held high recommended manager Al Lopez for president. It was a scene not easy to forget. After all, forty years is a long time to wait, and who knew when the next pennant would be coming.

The next day, Mayor Daley, caught up in the tide of celebration himself, brushed off reporters' questions regarding the air raid siren going off. He said it was "authorized by the city council."

One of the interesting asides to the final game was the fact that our so-called powerless team realized back-to-back home runs by Al Smith and Jim Rivera in the sixth inning. Early Wynn won the Cy Young award that year, and Nelson Fox was named the league's Most Valuable Player.

Before the start of the World Series, Bill threw the largest party the LaSalle Hotel had ever seen. The buffet was beyond comprehension, and the open bar catered to all, including reporters and photographers who came from the far corners of the earth.

The distribution of World Series tickets could not have been handled in a fairer manner. The fans got all the tickets above and beyond the league's normal commitments; sixty-five percent of the tickets went to South Siders who had been our regular customers. With all the concern about being fair to the team's real fans, Bill, in his daily rounds of the bleachers, had come to know most of the regulars. A month before we finally won the pennant, he began compiling the names of bleacher fans who were coming to almost every game. In all, he accumulated a list of about 3,000 people, and he made sure each of them received the opportunity to purchase some tickets. Then, not to leave out the big shots, Bill conceived the idea of having some of Chicago's key citizens draw names out of a bushel basket. Fair enough.

I think Francis Scott Key rolled over in his grave when Nat "King" Cole officially opened the World Series by bungling the words to the "Star-Spangled Banner." He ad-libbed his way through it, and somehow got away with it, but I never let him forget it. Nat was a personal friend from my old Chez Paree days.

The acquisition of Big Klu certainly paid off in the opening game of the World Series. Playing first base, he rocked Comiskey Park with two giant home runs that helped the White Sox take the first game.

That was where the magic seemed to end for the Sox. The rest of the series didn't go quite so well, and we lost the series four games to two.

Somehow, winning the World Series didn't seem as important as having the White Sox win their first pennant in forty years. For a team with no power, they had exceeded everyone's expectations. That winter, when Bill was tearing around Chicagoland making speeches as a buildup to the 1960 season, he loved to tell everyone just how the team won without power. "We scored runs," he'd say, "with the fastest man on the team, Luis Aparicio, leading off and taking a walk. Then Luis would steal second base and Nellie Fox would drive him in with a base hit. After that, we'd wait until the team batted around and Luis came back to the plate." The typical White Sox rally, he cracked, "consisted of two bloopers, an error, a passed ball, a couple of bases on balls, and, with luck, a hit batsman." Most of our wins came late in the game. The team won thirty-five games by one run. "We really smashed the opposition," he'd say, "and that's how we won the pennant."

Because Bill was his own best marketing tool, the way in which the team related to the press was quite distinct from the days of the Comiskey ownership. This obviously created some adjustment on the part of Ed Short, who had served as the White Sox in-house press chief for years. Ed was well-known and well-liked by the sportswriters. In the past, he had been the first point of contact for media persons seeking information. With his open door policy and constant availability, Bill quickly became the media's first stop.

PR TAKES A NEW DIRECTION

Compared to Ed, I was still new to the organization and had been careful not to step on his toes – making sure to bring him in on all plans and activities involving the press. It wasn't until early in 1960, right after we won the pennant, that I really sat down with Ed to talk about the role of public relations and the larger marketing scheme of the Sox organization.

Obviously, we had just capped off a wildly successful season, during which we drew well over a million patrons. In fact, it was the best attendance figure in team history. Still, I felt we had not yet scratched the surface. My sales pitch to Ed was simply that the Chicago area had a population of over six million people, and, if you considered season ticket holders and real White Sox regulars, we played to 250,000 of those people five times. We did it, I added, with a winning team and almost a full page of sports coverage seven days a week.

Ed was accustomed to that kind of coverage, so he didn't bat an eye. "If we wanted to purchase that amount of media space," I said, "we could never afford it." My point was that all his efforts to this point had been directed towards the sportswriters and the sports pages, even though we knew we were going to get that coverage anyway. Beat writers like Joe Goddard and Bill Jauss were assigned by their editors to cover the team. These papers covered the team not because they loved the Sox, but because they knew Sox fans buy the papers and want to read material about their team.

"Eddie," I said, "let's start concentrating on making placements off the sports pages, where we may find some new customers. Let's start directing some of our material towards women. Let's do some features on the athlete's families. Let's write about their idiosyncrasies, their superstitions, their diets, their wives' fashions, and their charitable activities. Let's go after the gossip columns, and the Saturday and Sunday special sections. What do you say, Ed?"

He thought for a moment and rather quickly responded, "We can't do it. Every sportswriter will get ticked off and might give the team a hard time."

Back and forth we went. I tried my best to convince him otherwise, but it was useless. After quietly thanking Eddie, I went out and did it anyway. We never lost a sports page article, but we did gain heaps of exposure in the rest of the paper. I like to think this strategy helped the team's attendance rise even higher in 1960.

It was that same line of thought that brought me to Bill and Mary Frances one day for a discussion about their hosting their own radio and television shows. Bill asked me if I could sell it to the stations. With his popularity, I felt I could have made him manager of any station in town.

Earlier, Bill had spoken of his luck in finding me; now it was my good fortune to find someone like Sis Atlass. Sis was a pint-sized dynamo who had beaucoup savvy when it came to broadcasting. Her father was Les Atlass, who owned WBBM radio, and her Uncle Ralph was the principal at WIND radio. Even before our work with the White Sox, I knew how fortunate I was to have Sis on my staff. But it wasn't until we sat down to discuss a program format for Mr. and Mrs. Veeck for both radio and television that her technical broadcast know-how jumped out at me.

Part of our discussions involved the availability of both Mary Frances and Bill. Would Bill by-pass a couple of speeches each week to do the show? Could Mary Frances be away from the children long enough for rehearsal, as well as the show itself? When these questions were answered affirmatively, Sis and I proceeded to sell the show to local radio and television stations. Of course, it was a talk show with guests. I appointed Sis the show's producer and it turned out to be well-organized and entertaining. Mary Frances was a pillar of strength, and Bill, with his spark for current events and one-of-a-kind humor, made it a lot of fun.

The following year, we repeated the two shows and, in addition, with the White Sox as our partner and with Bill's enthusiastic support, Sis and I wrote, produced, and sold a one-hour television show scheduled for each Saturday morning prior to a home game. It was a program built around teenagers who played baseball and wanted to improve their skills. Each show focused on another position on the diamond. If the highlighted position were catching, our key guest of the day was Sherm Lollar, and, depending which enemy team was in town, we tried to obtain their catcher as well. I remember when Yogi Berra did the show with Sherm. We brought in youngsters from the Babe Ruth League who were thirteen, fourteen, and fifteen, and taught them the finer points of each position. Imagine having Early Wynn and Billy Pierce show you how to properly throw a curve ball? The kids fought for the opportunity to be on the show, and the stars were more than cooperative and generous with their time. The show ran for twenty-six weeks.

Bill Veeck was always an iron man. His upper torso was incredibly strong, but the leg continued to cause him problems. I never knew whether it was the continued growth of the fungus infection or his stubborn refusal to pay proper attention to his stump, but doctors would periodically remove another piece of the leg until they finally removed the knee itself.

Strangely, it wasn't the leg that forced Bill to sell the White Sox and retire from baseball, but a nagging cold. No matter how fierce the Chicago winter got, Bill went without an overcoat, opting instead for his typical navy sport coat over an open-collared white sport shirt. He also continued his murderous schedule of speeches with total disdain for the weather. Incredibly, at least to him, he caught a cold. He never considered taking a day off. He was on the road day after day. His cold got worse and he began a wracking cough. As part of the same condition, he started passing out in the middle of the day.

The hospital originally diagnosed his condition as lung cancer. Tests later showed that his incessant deep cough had smashed some of the blood vessels at the top of his skull, causing his blackout spells. He finally gave up driving himself and had Dizzy Trout get him to his speaking appointments. He lived in fear that he would pass out during a speaking engagement or on our TV show. Bill was stubborn, but he was nobody's fool. The doctors made it eminently clear to him that to continue to actively run the ball club was a serious threat to his life. He was confined to the apartment for several months, where he soon developed a guilt complex about being absentee management.

It wasn't long before he sold the White Sox to Art Allyn, Jr., the son of his former investor. Bill called and asked me to please stay with Arthur and help him however I could.

THERE'S NO SUCH THING AS "OFF THE RECORD"

The A.C. Allyn Company, in addition to its new ownership position in the Chicago White Sox, was a holding company with diversified corporate properties. The company was large, and I was certain Mr. Allyn was sophisticated with every aspect of his business. As his public relations counsel, however, I did have one concern. Despite his success, his exposure was relatively limited to the financial media. With his new baseball acquisition, that situation had just changed dramatically.

In our first meeting, I explained to Mr. Allyn that the press could now be counted on to hang on every word he spoke. I asked that he remember there is no such thing as "off the record." I also stressed he be careful with his choice of words. In the four or five years that I remained his counsel, there were only one or two occasions when he did not heed that advice, and in those cases he paid the price.

While I continued to enjoy my work with the Sox, I missed Bill's presence around the team, and I certainly wasn't the only one. Prophetically, the last line in Bill's first book, _Veeck as in Wreck_, reads, "Sometime, somewhere, there will be a club no one really wants. And then Ole Will will come wandering along to laugh some more. Look for me under the arc lights, boys. I'll be back."

CHAPTER 7

Old Peg Leg Comes Back _____

Suddenly there was a team no one wanted, and "The Most Exclusive Men's Club in America," the owners of major-league baseball teams, were not going to let Bill Veeck have it.

From 1961 to 1965, the White Sox still played baseball at Comiskey Park, but it just wasn't fun anymore. Before he left, Bill Veeck, in his search for power hitters, had traded away the team's future.

Of course, you know what they say about hindsight. Today, it actually seems funny to me that three of the younger players Bill traded away blossomed into tremendous home run hitters for their respective teams. Johnny Callison and Norm Cash really made it big, and Earl Battey wasn't far behind. The White Sox, meanwhile, sank deeper in the standings.

Working with the A.C. Allyn group of executives on their various corporate holdings, like Eastman Oil Company, was a very interesting assignment, but the old enthusiasm and energy for the White Sox was long gone. I was not at all unhappy about leaving the team in 1965.

Mary Frances and Bill, with five of their six children – Mike, Gregory, Marya, Lisa, and Julie (their sixth, Chris, was born shortly thereafter) – moved to Easton, Maryland. They found a twenty-one-room home on sixteen acres, replete with a three-bedroom guest house, two-bedroom coach house, greenhouse, barn, and two boathouses. The quiet serenity of this home seemed like the perfect spot for Bill's recuperation, but it also seemed like an ideal last stop on what had been a long and adventurous journey for Bill and Mary Frances.

Mary Frances had been in the publicity business when she and Bill met in 1949. She was publicity director for the Ice Capades. She had done some modeling previous to that, and had graduated from Carnegic Tech. She and Bill married in 1950.

At times, their life seemed like something out of a travel guide book. After Bill sold the Cleveland Indians, he and Mary Frances bought a ranch outside of Tucson, Arizona, where their son, Mike, was born in 1951. That same year, Bill bought the St. Louis Browns and they moved into an apartment that he had built right into the ballpark.

In 1953, Bill tried to move the Browns to Baltimore and the American League not only turned him down, but literally kicked him out of the league. The Veecks hired a moving van many times over the next ten years. The traveling family went from Los Angeles to a ranch in New Mexico, then back to Cleveland before coming to Chicago and the White Sox in '59, and then on to Easton.

Before he left Chicago, Bill and I actually went into business together. During his two years with the Sox, many manufacturers and corporations were anxious to capitalize on his popularity and creativity. Bill was frequently approached about heading public relations departments for different companies. Unfortunately, his White Sox contract and his ardent responsibility to his investors made that impossible.

However, Bill thought that if he was a part of an outside PR agency, it might be possible to direct this potential business there. We quickly formed Cushman and Veeck Public Relations and had high hopes for its future. Though we maintained the company for more than twenty years, Bill's sudden illness prohibited this business venture from ever reaching its full potential.

When he first moved, Bill discouraged people from visiting him in Easton. As soon as we were given the green light, I went to see him. After so long a hiatus, I didn't know what to expect, but was pleasantly surprised to find him looking quite healthy. He was spending most of his time writing and building furniture. I never thought he had the patience for such intricate work, but his dexterity with tools was amazing. Bill had also gotten into gardening in a big way, and he gave me a five-cent tour of his greenhouse. He was clearly feeling better, and, although he was busy with his new interests, his mind was definitely back on baseball.

Word seemed to spread rapidly that he was on the road to recovery. People wanted to see for themselves. Friends from the media and from baseball began paying him visits, mostly at his invitation. People would pop in for a day or two, and Bill wasn't always consistent about notifying Mary Frances. She had her hands full, basically running a B & B, with minimum advance reservations.

On my visit, Bill craved news from Chicago. He was full of questions about the city, the team, the Allyns, and the press. Despite the questions, he already seemed on top of things. I had a feeling he read the Chicago papers regularly.

I continued to visit Bill periodically, and on one visit in the early '70s, he told me about a young ball player in Easton he'd been keeping his eye on. I hadn't seen Bill that excited about a prospect in a long time. I asked him the kid's name, and he said, "Harold Baines." A perennial major league all-star, Harold Baines is currently over forty years old and has played in the big leagues for over twenty years.

In the meantime, Arthur Allyn had sold the White Sox to his brother, John. Not long after John took over, there were rumblings heard even as far away as Easton that the team would soon be for sale. Bill was hale and hearty once again and felt that familiar itch to get back into baseball.

A group of Chicago business people were considering buying the club and approached Bill about operating the team. Anyone who really knew Bill had to be aware that he wasn't about to operate someone else's baseball team. Besides, the last time I had seen him in Easton, he told me he was negotiating a deal with Jerry Hoffberger, owner of the Baltimore Orioles. After almost a year of, "We're just waiting to sign the papers," Hoffberger pulled the plug for some reason, and the deal went down the drain. Needless to say, Bill was both disappointed and ticked off at this missed opportunity. But at the same time, other options were presenting themselves.

Leo Breen, the vice president and treasurer of the White Sox, let it be known to one of Bill's close friends, Andy McKenna, that not only did John Allyn want to sell the White Sox, he _had_ to sell.

Andy passed the news to Bill, and, in the summer of 1974, Bill flew to Chicago to meet with John Allyn. He was told the team was available for $10 million, but the ballpark and adjoining property would take the price to $13.5 million. Bill told me later that he left that meeting telling John Allyn $10 million was all he had. Things went from bad to worse for the Sox, and by September, Bill received word that half a million dollars' worth of salary checks to players were floating. Mr. Allyn could not cover them.

BETWEEN A ROCK AND A HARD PLACE

Two major problems were wrapped around this untenable situation. First, if the players were not paid, they immediately became free agents. Second, a group in Seattle was ready to step in, provide the cash and take the team to the West Coast. Some will recall the American League had given Seattle an expansion team in 1969, and then moved the team out the following year. Seattle had filed a king-sized lawsuit against baseball, and, if the league could work it out so the White Sox could casually end up in Seattle, all their legal problems would likely be over.

The league offered John Allyn a loan in return for an option to buy the team, with enough time to negotiate with the financial interests in Seattle. Anyone familiar with the inner workings of baseball would be aware that Charley Finley was chomping at the bit to move his Oakland Athletics to Chicago, which coincidentally just happened to be where Mr. Finley's insurance business was based. The whole scenario was tailor-made for the league. Everyone would be happy, except the city would lose the White Sox. John Allyn was between a rock and a hard place. If he gave the league the option and the sale to Seattle didn't fly, then he would be forced to operate back in Chicago, with the entire populace aware that he tried to move the club away from Chicago – not the way to win friends and influence people.

No slouch when it came to being aware of what's going on, Bill called John Allyn and they met in Chicago late in September. John told Bill he needed $500,000 before the end of the week. If Bill could come up with it, John said he would give him an option to buy the club for $10 million, including the park and real estate.

Up to this point in the negotiations, nothing had leaked to the press. A press conference was held, the announcement was made, and the city went wild. Everyone remembered Bill and they remembered 1959 as the year he brought the White Sox their first pennant in forty years. New hope was born.

Bill was seen as an even bigger hero when people learned the details of his takeover, including the fact that Seattle was waiting in the wings. He had saved the White Sox from leaving town.

To complete the deal, all Bill needed was a money syndicate from whom to recruit the purchase price. Between Andy McKenna and myself, along with Bill's longtime backers, the money started to flow in. Phil Frye, the son of Sidney Frye, who was one of Bill's financial backers in '59, was not

118

only Bill's legal counsel, but became an investor. Both Sidney and Phil were with the law firm of Schiff, Hardin & Waite. Johnny Johnson, publisher of *Ebony* magazine, became an investor. I brought in Lee Stern, who was a commodities broker and the owner of the Sting, a professional soccer team in Chicago. Lee contacted businessmen Fred Brzozowski and Harvey Jaunich. Together, they invested $500,000.

I scraped up a couple of bucks myself and joined the fray as an investor. There was Andy McKenna, Cindy Pritzker, Tom Weinberg, Fred Friedlob, and Bill's nephew, Fred Krehbiel. Hank Greenberg was a partner from the moment of conception. Calls were coming in from every corner of the country. In what seemed like a couple of days, the entire $10 million was sold out.

On the night Bill informed everyone we were financially covered, I got a call from my friend and neighbor, Jack Gould. He asked if he could buy a piece of the team. I told him I was really sorry, but we were committed. He pleaded with me to ask Bill to somehow squeeze him in. I reiterated our pleasant problem, but promised to call Bill and ask. I phoned Bill and he asked me how well I knew Jack. "Was he a friend?" I told him he was, and Bill granted the request. He did want to know how much Jack was prepared to invest: I called Jack and gave him the good news, then asked him how big a piece he wanted to buy. He said he was in for $300,000.

We scrambled to get all the financials together because baseball's winter meetings were almost upon us. Knowing he wanted to make a flock of trades once he took over, Bill asked John Allyn to request a meeting with the league to approve the sale of the team. Coincidentally, without the league's approval, no advance tickets could be put on the market. That meant no advance ticket sale, and so began what was not only the greatest run-around in the history of baseball, but any sports enterprise.

This strong-armed game was orchestrated by what Bill referred to as the most exclusive men's club in America; the owners of major-league baseball teams. They were determined to keep Bill from getting back into the game, and equally determined that the White Sox go to Seattle. But they never bothered to tell Mayor Richard Daley about the plot.

The first meeting Bill was able to arrange with the league took place in an airport hotel in Cleveland. The league sent Bud Selig, who is now the commissioner of baseball, but at that time was owner of the Milwaukee ball club, and Ted Bonda. They acted as an advisory committee ostensibly to listen to the details of the sale. Without going into too much detail, the outcome of that meeting was the duo telling Bill he was badly under-capitalized. They accepted the fact that he actually had the $10 million, but refused to accept the fact that Bill could make a profit with an attendance of one million fans. The White Sox were showing a $5 million loss carry-forward that Bill wanted to capitalize on. To do that, he had to show a continuity of ownership, so John Allyn agreed to retain twenty percent of the club. That changed the figures from $10 million to $8 million.

The second part of the harangue was over the stock debentures that Bill was issuing to the investors. Selig insisted that debentures were a debt and not a capital investment. So 'round and 'round the discussion went, and Bill told me it was really heating up. His position was that he had purchased his other teams with the same type of financing, and no one objected. Why now? The owners seemed to be saying Bill was not with the times, that too much had changed from the old swinging stunt days and that kind of stuff just would not work anymore.

Despite this flurry, John Allyn was able to arrange a meeting for Bill with the owners the following week, again in Cleveland. The meeting was pleasant and businesslike, and Bill was given the opportunity to explain his position in detail. Shortly after the meeting, a committee came to Bill's hotel room and told him he had been turned down by a vote of 8-3-1 against. It would have taken nine votes in favor to gain approval. Bill was certain that New York, Baltimore, and Chicago were the three teams voting for him, and that Kansas City had been the one to abstain. However, if Bill could raise another $1.2 million in capital, change from debentures to preferred stock, and not use the sale of the ballpark as a vehicle for raising more investment capital, he was told that the vote could be reversed the following week in Florida. The bottom line was, they would give Bill four days, including a weekend, to make the changes. Just about an impossible task for anyone. But Bill wasn't just anyone.

It would take a Herculean effort by the attorneys to redo all the vast paperwork, but how was Bill to obtain the additional funds without watering down the deal he had sold to the investors? In the midst of this drama (or trauma, depending on whose side you were on), Mayor Daley went on local television and told the citizens of Chicago that it had now become a personal challenge. The mayor not only lived within walking distance of the ballpark, he was a lifelong Sox fan, and no one was about to walk in and take away this beloved team and a valuable part of Chicago's economy, as long as he was mayor.

While this rush of activity was going on, Bill was getting calls from the Seattle press telling him the deal to bring the Sox to Seattle was all but complete. Apparently Danny Kaye, the Hollywood star, led a financial syndicate that was already in Florida with their cash in hand, just waiting to be told that the league had finalized the Veeck turndown.

On top of the league's demand for an additional $1.2 million, Bill was realizing several fallouts from among his original money group. He was now short more than $1.5 million. Like the charging cavalry, Chicagoans including Gene Fanning, Howard Miller, Pat O'Malley, and the sons of the three men on the commodities market came forward. Nephew Fred Krehbiel upped his ante and things were looking better. Still short and reticent to cut what he had promised his investors, Veeck finally took the funds from his own equity position. He had been given fifteen percent of the deal, amounting to over $800,000 for putting the deal together, and he was sharing that with Hank Greenberg, Rudie Schaffer, and Paul Richards, but the bulk of it was Bill's. In addition, he was personally investing about half a million dollars, which made him the single largest stockholder.

THE WAY THIS GAME PLAYED OUT

The timing was touch and go with the Schiff firm. Many of their staff worked through the weekend to turn out an enormous amount of work. Somehow it got done and Bill, backed by his attorneys, checked into a Florida hotel and awaited word to come to the conference room. After getting the call, they hurried downstairs. Led by Bud Selig and John Fetzer of the Detroit Tigers, six members of the franchise committee came into the room. The Veeck team made its presentation, and the committee was stunned. It seemed quite clear that Veeck had done what the other owners felt was the impossible. The committee reviewed every document and spent more than an hour studying the paperwork. Then they left without any type of commitment. It took two-and-a-half hours before our group received a response.

The vote went 8-3-1 for Veeck, but it was once again short of the nine votes he needed for acceptance. Bill told me he and Mary Frances could not believe the vindictiveness. But it wasn't over yet. Mr. Fetzer and Lee McPhail, owners of the Detroit Tigers and Minnesota Twins, were uneasy about the way this game played out.

Bill got word later that both men took the floor on his behalf, saying Bill had complied with everything that had been requested of him. In good conscience, they argued, he could not be turned down. They insisted on another vote and got it. The result, ten for and two against. True or not, Bill was told the two negative votes came from Charley Finley of the Oakland Athletics and Gene Autry of the Anaheim Angels.

The ongoing saga had been front-page news in Chicago, stirring up quite a bit of renewed enthusiasm for the team. Bill had his hands full pulling the deal together, and I had all I could handle with the myriad of media queries coming in. It was now clear that the team would continue to reside in Chicago, and Bill Veeck was indeed the savior. And so the fun began all over again.

Bill literally started immediately. He took a desk in the lobby of the Florida hotel and made himself available for trades and interviews. Before the meeting closed, he had concluded four trades, and Chicago was once again getting ready to sing, "Na Na Na Na . . . Na Na Na Na . . . Hey Hey."

Yes, he was back and looking great. Bill was now sixty-two years old and, by his own admission, having difficulty both seeing and hearing. The old drive and enthusiasm were very evident, but I think he knew it was his chance for a last hurrah. Just acquiring the team, with all the legal mumbo jumbo, had taken a lot out of him. Nevertheless, he moved into White Sox Park and immediately changed the name back to Comiskey Park. He felt he owed the family that recognition. Next, he removed the door to his office and made the opening much larger. He wanted it understood that anyone coming to the ballpark who wanted to see him could just walk on in. And he meant anyone.

He brought back the same telephone technique where anyone could reach him. His old friend and confidant, Rudie Schaffer, was back, and that meant Bill could concentrate on baseball. Rudie had complete control of the business side, including tickets, concessions, hiring and firing of staff, and most elements involving numbers and money.

One of baseball's most respected gentlemen, Roland Hemond, joined Bill as general manager. Roland knew baseball, and was well-liked by almost every owner and general manager in the game. Between him and Bill, they had solid contacts with every team, which made talking trades simple. Bill pulled off another coup by enticing Paul Richards out of retirement in Waxahachie, Texas, to join the team as manager. Paul Richards was part of the old Go-Go White Sox, the successful teams of an earlier era. He brought back a lot of fond memories to the fans.

Just hearing the name Waxahachie brings back some not so fond memories for me. Sometime in 1943, I was on my first solo cross-country flight out of Corsicana, Texas. Just as I passed over Waxahachie, my single-engine primary trainer began spouting black oil, and I watched the oil temperature gauge going up into the danger area. I was flying at about 5,000 feet and realized that I was going down.

All that training they drum into your head as a young pilot started to kick in. Look for a large, open field. If it's plowed, be sure to land down furrow. Try to land in the first thirty percent of the field and watch out for electrical wires. That's what was racing through my head as I headed down. The engine died and I came in dead stick, but made the landing with no additional problems. A farmer came running over and allowed me to use his phone to call the base. I was a hotshot pilot with only forty hours in the air at the time.

When Paul Richards came up from Waxahachie, everyone was excited about spring training. Hopes were high and Chicago fans were dreaming of a return to the pennant-winning year. Every young player was a surefire phenom, especially for the first two or three weeks before the spring games began.

The mood on the street in Chicago was a throwback to Veeck's first takeover, only much warmer. Bill still talked about baseball being an escape from the everyday problems of life. He wanted everyone who came to a game to go home feeling as though they had had a good time. Again, the fans stopped him in the streets with words of encouragement. Cab drivers kept honking their horns at Bill to attract his attention and yell their usual, "Go get 'em, Bill." Whenever we rode taxis together, he would ride in the front seat, while I stretched out in the back. With one leg, the law allowed him to ride in front.

In the pennant-winning year, Bill and Mary Frances lived in the Shoreland Hotel. This time, Bill's only specification to her was that they please find a place within fifteen or twenty minutes of the ballpark. Mary Frances found an apartment in Hyde Park with five bedrooms overlooking the city and the lake. The apartment was close enough so that she and the kids could see the exploding scoreboard go off periodically when one of our players hit a home run. Mary Frances never lost a step in resuming her former role of hostess to the many guests and media folks, who partook of Bill's hospitality at dinner before each game in the refurbished Bard's Room. She built an excellent rapport with the press and was quick to provide Bill with sound ideas in answer to any real or anticipated problems that he faced.

The White Sox marketing effort picked up right where it left off in 1960. It was like *déjà vu* with Bill's schedule set for a minimum of two speeches a night, and sometimes as many as four. He was on the road again and loving it. Along with the speeches came the specialty nights, complete with giveaways. Just for fun, Bill had a shower placed in the center field bleachers and created a "no smoking" section, another feature that proved to be ahead of its time.

Sis Atlass and I quickly got back into the groove of selling the twosome to both radio and television. Our first show was a radio talk show on WMAQ, the NBC affiliate in Chicago. It was slotted at 10 a.m. on Sunday morning and was titled, "Mary Frances and Friend." One thing became abundantly clear as time progressed: we had inherited a lousy ball team. That, coupled with Chicago's atrocious weather, made for management misery. We suffered through 1975. Paul Richards had come onboard for one year as a special favor to Bill and was anxious to return to the relative quiet of Waxahachie. However, before he left the team, we had planned an unusual opening day. What other kind of day would Veeck plan?

It was 1976, and as part of the special events commemorating the birthday of the nation we tried to duplicate the "Spirit of '76." Rudie Schaffer, Richards, and Veeck donned the appropriate costumes, including the white wigs, and proceeded to march out of the dugout with one carrying the oversized flag, and the others beating the drum or playing the fife. It made the front page of the sports section the next day in all Chicago papers.

THE WHITE SOX CARAVAN: REGIONAL MARKETING TOOL

In the off-season, we returned to speech marketing with Veeck once again on his pogo stick, tearing across every sector of Illinois in search of season ticket buyers. He created the White Sox Caravan, where the team's manager and a handful of name players joined him in touring Illinois and northern Indiana. With Bill leading the way, Chicago media traveled with the Caravan. The group made news in every town that they visited. The man was a PR genius. While he spoke about players and the forthcoming season, I was looking for sidebar stories. Between us, we managed to keep the Sox in the news throughout that "non-baseball season," December and January. My concentration was to get coverage off the sports pages and to try to reach more women.

Robert Marcus, who wrote sports and business for the *Chicago Tribune*, said in his column early in September 1976, "If the Sox do get to the million plateau in attendance, it will be the worst White Sox team ever to reach that magic mark. And by all odds, the dullest. That's why I'm more convinced than ever that in a showdown, Bill Veeck could beat P.T. Barnum two out of three falls." Of course, he was right. The team had fifteen designated hitters, without one of these mighty men hitting more than fifteen home runs that year. The defense was abysmal, and the pitching worse. The team needed a first-class makeover.

NETWORK TELEVISION BASEBALL AWARDS PROGRAM

Looking back on the 1960 season, Sis and I concocted an idea that we felt would be good for baseball. This idea was prior to television's Emmy, Tony, and Espy award programs. We were interested in producing a one-hour television special for baseball that would be aired in the off-season. We were convinced that a show featuring all of the baseball annual awards, such as the Rookie of the Year in both leagues, the Most Valuable Player in both leagues, The Cy Young pitcher, the Home Run King, Manager of the Year, the Fireman of the Year (relief pitcher), and a few of lesser import, could be both entertaining and exciting, to a point that it could engender very good ratings in prime time. We took the scheme to Bill and asked his opinion. He thought it was an excellent, creative idea. We asked him who to pitch it to and he suggested the American League president, Mr. William Harridge. He offered to call Mr. Harridge and request an appointment for us.

Sis and I did our homework and started to project some statistics relating to the number of people a show like this could attract as viewers. Even in 1960, the numbers were staggering in size. Would a network buy the idea, and could it be sold to sponsors? In our minds, it was a lead-pipe cinch. Yes, even for prime time. What about presenters? We listed a group of baseball's living heroes who were in the Baseball Hall of Fame as potentials. Then we discovered that the Baseball Writers Association actually made the selection on the basis of a national vote among their members. With this in mind, we offered an option, selecting members of the Writers Association as presenters. Sis and I felt as though we had all our ducks in a row, and it was time to keep that appointment in New York with Mr. Harridge.

We shared the presentation between us, and the league president listened attentively. I don't think he was enamored with either Sis or myself, but out

125

of respect for Bill Veeck, he did give us every courtesy. When we finished, he stood up and quietly said he recognized we had put a great deal of time into the idea and thought the production through quite clearly, but baseball just couldn't possibly allow it to happen. He went on to explain that it was the Baseball Writers Association that made the selections and we couldn't take it away from them. We then reminded him that we had suggested the Writers Association would select the presenters from within their organization. No, he was convinced that the writers would not go for the idea and besides, he liked the current situation with the press making periodic announcements throughout the winter months. He thanked us for coming and asked us not to slam the door on the way out. We felt he had been shortsighted and simply resisted change. As it turned out, we were just a couple of years ahead of the trend.

Back home, Bill found himself what he termed a "secret weapon." His name was Gene Bossard. No, he wasn't a twenty-game winning pitcher or a forty-home run hitter; he was the groundskeeper. With Gene's help, they would shape the infield depending upon which team the White Sox were playing. If the team was quick on the bases, he would have Gene soak the baselines to slow them down. If they liked to bunt and had the speed to match, Gene would slope the baselines so that the ball would roll foul. If the opposition had good runners, the infield grass was cut very short, so the ball got to our infielders in time for them to throw out the runners. If the visiting team was heavy-footed, we could afford to let the grass grow long to slow up the ball and give our fielders an easier play. Bill felt that Bossard was worth about two runs per game. He liked to joke about the infield grass sometimes being as tall as a wheat field.

MARIACHI BAND IN COMISKEY PARK

Whether or not this strategy would boost the team's performance, we were still determined to put on a good show for each game, even if that meant bringing a show to the park before the game started. The Cushman agency had landed the account representing the Mexican National Tourist Council. Our responsibility was to promote tourism to Mexico from within the United States. It was an account near and dear to my heart, and Cher Patric Cox was assigned as account supervisor. At one of our staff meetings, the suggestion was made to have a Mexican night at Comiskey. Cher and I jumped all over the idea and, after fleshing it out with some specifics, decided to bring it to Bill.

126

Always open to anything that might make a game more fun, Bill gave us the go-ahead. All the concession stands featured Mexican food that night. We flew in the Mexican Folkloric Ballet to perform before the game started. Several Mexican community groups were invited to dance in the infield with their colorful costumes, and we located an authentic mariachi band to play. As the highlight of the evening, we had the team emerge from the dugout to take the field wearing giant sombreros instead of their usual baseball caps.

Much of Chicago's Hispanic community turned out to celebrate with us, and the front page of the sport section the next morning, in both the *Chicago Tribune* and *Sun-Times*, was loaded with full-color pictures of the evening. The Associated Press carried the story and pictures across the country. Veeck was making news again.

Whenever Bill came to our agency office, there was always an aura of excitement among the staff. He would move from office to office saying hello to each account executive. He made sure to spend time in the production room and always had a "*kibitz*" for each of the secretaries. The staff looked at Bill as a true celebrity, and one or two got up enough courage to ask for his autograph. He made a point of saying thank you to everyone who even remotely had anything to do with the team's PR campaign.

Bill was still a star, despite running a ball club that commanded fewer than 5,000 fans per game in 1975, and he finished well into the red again in 1976. It was a bad team with bad numbers, and most Chicagoans were saying that buying the team was a bad investment.

At the start of spring training 1977, Las Vegas and the so-called smart money had the Sox penciled in to fill the cellar – last place. The gamblers all said, "No pitching, no hitting, no fans."

There was a reunion of spirit with veterans like Ralph Garr and Dave Duncan, and nervous excitement among the many rookies as they ran through stretching exercises on the field. It was a time for friendly chatter and a lot of kidding about who did what during the winter. The boys of summer were back. The media was ducking us.

Bob Lemon was fifty-six and fresh off his induction to Baseball's Hall of Fame. He was unquestionably one of the game's greatest pitchers in a career that spanned twenty years. In nine years, he won 186 games, more than enough to qualify him to teach young pitchers and lead our ball club.

That spring, I was permitted to sit in the dugout during pre-game batting and fielding practice. Every non-player had to vacate once the game was underway. Occasionally, I felt like pinching myself to be sure it was really me sitting there, sharing conversation with some of baseball's best players. For the moment, the practice of public relations was forgotten. I was an eight-year-old kid again, but instead of throwing rubber balls against a brick wall, I was practically sitting on the field watching real-life baseball heroes do their stuff.

Bill Veeck stood not far from the batter's cage where his new acquisition, Richie Zisk, was pounding the baseball out of the park. Bill remarked to everyone close by, "He can swing that bat. Richie will be important to the team this year, because last year we established the record for leaving more men on base with only one out or more." Later, Bill let me know Zisk was Polish, and Chicago is predominantly Polish, which just may have helped us a bit at the box office.

It seemed like the entire team gathered around that cage every time Zisk got in there. The kidding was always fast and furious. Zisk smashed one out of sight, and Sox center fielder Chet Lemon whispered in amazement, "Lord have mercy."

The Sox had traded what many considered the two best relief pitchers in the league, Rich Gossage and Terry Forster, to Pittsburgh for Richie Zisk. With the trade, Sox management placed a big burden on Zisk's powerful shoulders. They counted on him to make people forget about the team's woeful 1976 record of sixty-four wins and ninety-seven losses, second worst in the majors.

"RENT A PLAYER"

Zisk was the first in Veeck's plan to build a team with a "rent a player" concept. Actually, it was already becoming abundantly clear that, with the advent of the Messerschmidt Decision, the case brought by pitcher Andy Messerschmidt that essentially allowed players to test the market through free agency, the White Sox did not have a fat enough wallet to compete for topflight players. The best we could hope for was to pick up a player of Zisk's caliber for one year. That's why Bill labeled this type of transaction, "rent a player."

Zisk was a good-looking young man who was obviously quite powerful. He stood about six feet two inches. I met him right away, as I needed to build a biography on him to supply to media people. He told me he weighed 210 and needed to drop 10 pounds during spring training. He had done nothing strenuous during the winter. Zisk had taken it easy with only light workouts, free of weight lifting, in a nearby health spa. He told me how exhausted players get playing a 162-game schedule.

Coincidentally, he also said, "In case you haven't noticed, I'm carrying your basic Polish legs, which aren't going to steal many bases and which will not look great in those new White Sox uniforms."

Zisk was referring to the zany outfits the team had introduced the previous year, much to the chagrin of most baseball hard-liners who only relate to Yankee pinstripes. The uniforms were probably an outgrowth of a moment of madness between Bill and Mary Frances. Bill claimed she designed them. They were indeed unusual, coming in clam-digger lengths, shorts, and what might be termed regular baseball pants. The shirts had a distinct softball league look and came in both navy blue and white. The players wore them, but unhappily.

If you believe that any publicity is good publicity, then the uniforms were a bang-up success. They caused quite a stir. Not being from that school of thought, I put out the releases and kept my opinion to myself. The media had a good time with the whole thing, most of them being gentle in their criticism. Ultimately, there was just too much flak from players and good-natured ribbing from the press. Finally, the uniforms quietly disappeared.

When Zisk said the team would be better this year, he had no idea how right he was. He felt his presence in the lineup would offer added protection to players like George Orta and Ralph Garr, because opposing pitchers would not be able to pitch around them. Though Zisk recognized he would have to make adjustments coming over from the National League, he felt he had the advantage because American League pitchers didn't know his hitting style. He told me he had always been a dead low-ball hitter and now, most of his home runs were coming from high pitches.

The other player Bill brought to the squad was Oscar Gamble. Gamble, formerly of the Yankees, was another respected home run hitter. He swung from the left side. With Chet Lemon in center field, the White Sox now had an outfield that could compete with the best in the league.

Bill had one more major move up his sleeve. He landed Eric Soderholm to take over third base. Soderholm had plenty of pop in his bat, and this new trio gave the Sox solid hitters for numbers three, four, and five in the line-up. The funny part was that even with the enthusiasm the trades engendered, no one, least of all me, seriously considered the Sox a genuine threat to win the pennant.

PROMOTIONS AND OFF-SPORTS PAGE PUBLICITY: WORTH THE EFFORT

The season opened and, to the city's great surprise, the team jumped out into first place. More importantly, they continued to win, and fans steadily returned to 35th Street. Before long, crowds were pouring into Comiskey Park as they had in 1959.

But these were not the old die-hard, "I remember the pennant year" fans; these were, instead, thousands of new Sox-loving rooters. The endless stream of promotions – Bat Day, Greek Day, Beer Case Stacking Day, Jacket Day, Cushion Days, Sun Hat Ladies' Day, and Golf Day – that hadn't drawn flies in the two previous years, now brought thousands of cheering, singing supporters. The publicity we poured out, as we had done in '75 and '76, that baseball was fun again on Chicago's South Side, was paying off. But, we realized it was paying off because the team was winning.

On the pure dollars-and-cents business side of baseball, past experience shows that a good promotion brings in from 5,000 to 6,000 extra fans. With fifty-one home date promotions scheduled, we could count on an extra 250,000 fans for the year. In addition, the club tried to find sponsors to help defray the cost of its promotions. Bat Day is a particularly strong draw and each bat costs one dollar. That makes it a non-breakeven promotion. Coca-Cola became a Bat Day sponsor. In baseball, during the years in question, tickets sold for between two and five dollars, and forty cents off the top goes to the visiting club. Then it costs the team about thirty cents per patron to pay ticket takers, car parkers, ushers, and security people to put the fan in his or her seat. If the team had to pay for the giveaway there would be nothing left. We provided our sponsors with visibility through our broadcast facilities as a *quid pro quo*.

I was working hard on making national media placements to establish an aura of prestige and to gain increased recognition for Bill, as though he needed more credentials. For his part, Bill was not too interested in national press coverage because, ever the salesman, he realized that a story in a national magazine or a piece on national television would not sell many tickets in Chicago. He knew there was a secondary benefit to national stories, but they never really turned him on.

Despite the team's early success, we noticed something about the local sports pages. Every day, we would see stories on the Cubs on the front page of the sports section, while the Sox stories would run on page two or three. We expected this from the *Tribune*, because they owned the Cubs. Bill was reluctant to address this with either newspaper. I wasn't quite so shy. I mentioned this to Kup at the *Sun-Times*, and he used the item in his column to raise the question of whether there was a bias in favor of the Cubs. Back-checking the daily papers since the start of the season, I was able to pretty fairly ascertain that the White Sox were receiving one column inch of space for every two-and-a-half inches allocated to the Chicago Cubs. That included the entire paper, not just the sport pages.

Bill was eminently fair in his analysis of the situation. He credited the media with recognizing that a good portion of their regular subscribers lived on Chicago's North Side, as did most of their sportswriters. Wrigley Field was simply more convenient to them – at least until the Sox began looking like genuine winners.

By mid-summer, it was clear the team was on a serious roll. The scoreboard was exploding almost every night as our big hitters did their best to smash the opposition. The word was out that the Sox, a dead cinch for last place and a team full of no names, was in first place. The national press called the Sox the most incredible team of the year. It really was like the old days, with the city in a frenzy over this team that had come from nowhere. The fans decorated the outfield walls with giant bed sheet banners and home run targets. Nancy Faust played the organ with her own attack melodies, which the crowds quickly picked up. The fans lifted the players onto their shoulders and proudly marched them around the field.

THE PRESS BOX: NEUTRAL TERRITORY

I'd sit in the press box and revel as each enemy pitcher was knocked out of the box. With every win, the media coverage grew and the attendance swelled. There was something special about what was happening. Bill explained it like this: "We, the White Sox, we're like the poor kids from down on the corner . . . without uniforms, without shoes, playing with bats wrapped in black tire tape . . . and we're beating the kids from the rich neighborhoods with all their expensive equipment. The Sox are fashionable now because we are the unquestioned underdogs, and people like to see the giants toppled." He called it, "The rags to riches story. If not riches, from rags to respectability." As for me, it took all my self-control not to stand up and scream every time our players smacked a fastball over the fence. It was contrary to my personality to hold things in. After an early season outburst in the press box, Bill quietly whispered in my ear, "Up here, we are supposed to be neutral. Aaron, try to control yourself."

Among our many new fans were women. Bill had done everything he could think of to encourage them to come to Comiskey Park. He was convinced that more women were becoming fans of baseball – not just enjoying the show, but becoming more knowledgeable about the game. Bill was certain women would one day break into the major leagues. I was certain that if he could find one who could play, he'd sign her.

Bill was sincere about this. He said the game was a natural one for women because size wasn't important, and there was a minimum of physical contact. He told me that when he was with the Milwaukee team (Bill owned a minor league team in Milwaukee before joining the Indians), he tried to sign Babe Didrikson, who was a remarkable athlete.

More recently, Bill had gotten a call from Satchel Paige, who was pitching for the House of David. Satch had seen a girl he was certain could make it as a second base player in the majors. Bill took a look and decided she could run and she could throw, but he wasn't sure she could hit. Satchel's response to that was, "If she can hit off me, then you know she can hit." Bill actually tried to sign her but she decided the time wasn't right – that baseball wasn't ready to accept a female player.

Sox management wasn't known for holding many staff meetings, but early in the year, with key staff personnel present, there was a discussion about the need for a new White Sox logo. Bill gave me the responsibility to explore various art concepts and come back to him with some graphics. We used our staff artists and some freelance talent to finally gather a representative group of drawings that looked like they had potential. In about thirty minutes, with Rudie Schaffer, Roland Hemond, Bill, and myself present, we selected a logo that has stood the test of time. It was used on every piece of White Sox literature, including their annual direct mail advance ticket brochure, on television, print ads, players' handbook, advance schedule, and on almost every piece of souvenir clothing sold inside the park and in department stores. At that time, vanity phone numbers were just being introduced. We latched onto "Call Sox" and promoted the number or letters extensively.

Another exciting addition to the team that year was Jimmy Piersall. The former Red Sox outfielder was hired to do color commentary alongside Harry Caray, who handled the play-by-play on television. Jimmy had a reputation as a hot-tempered and somewhat troublesome ball player, but no one could deny his thorough knowledge of the game. As one of the best defensive outfielders in the game, he brought great credibility into the broadcast booth.

Was he excitable? On one occasion in mid-summer, he was the object of an incredibly vociferous attack by a fan sitting a couple of aisles below the broadcast booth. The fan was particularly obnoxious, using more than his share of four-letter words. Jimmy took the harangue through several innings, and finally, in a heated exchange, climbed down off the broadcast booth to physically defend his honor, which he handled with aplomb.

It was a raucous scene, with security diving in to break up the fight. Even Bill dashed over to help out. Yes, Piersall was excitable, but there was another side to Jimmy. Jimmy loved to play tennis in Sarasota during spring training, and, more than once, I shared a singles court with him. He was a perfect gentleman and genuinely considerate of people when he wasn't working as a broadcaster. On the mike, Jimmy called each play exactly as he saw it, without giving excuses for poor performances by the opponents or our players. He was a knowledgeable critic and never hesitated to face a player he criticized.

After hanging onto first place for most of the '77 season, the team hit the skids around Labor Day and finished the year in third place. That magical year the White Sox drew 1,650,000 people through the turnstiles, more than any season in the team's sixty-seven-year history. It was a true love affair between the city's fans and their baseball team. Many called it the miracle on 35th Street. The record shows that Chicago had one of its worst rainy Septembers that year. But on Fan Appreciation Day, they again turned out in throngs in hopes of winning one of the myriad of prizes, or perhaps to offer a farewell or a sign of appreciation to the players who had made the year so special.

Long after the game ended and the fans were filing out toward their cars, you could still hear the strains of "Auld Lang Syne" coming from Nancy Faust's organ.

The crowning blow to our investment group came a couple of years later when Bill told us he was unable to sign our first-round draft choices. He was astounded that kids right out of high school, with no minor league experience, were demanding $250,000 to sign. There was simply no way we could afford to pay that kind of price, which meant we had to pass on the future buildup of the team.

It was a hard pill to swallow, but the board of directors agreed with Bill that it didn't make sense to continue operating under these circumstances. In 1980, we folded our tent and sold out to Jerry Reinsdorf, the current owner of the Sox.

Bill made sure that every investor came away with more than a fair return on his or her capital investment. Our return had been an average of twenty percent per year. Almost every investor who put up money with Bill in 1975 did so in an effort to keep the team in Chicago. Few, if any, expected to collect major profits. We sold the team for $22 million and had difficulty understanding why anyone would pay that much for the White Sox. Recently, the team has been valued at about $190 million.

Bill Veeck died January 2, 1986, at age seventy-two. His health had been deteriorating for years. In addition to his wonderful family, he left a legacy of innovation in baseball. He will forever be remembered for the exploding scoreboard, for his unusual marketing concepts, for the names that we now see on almost every player's shirt, for his role in helping sell the designated hitter to the American League, and for his native ability to capture a city's love and whip up its enthusiasm for a baseball team. Bill was a classy guy and a good friend. To this day, I think of him fondly and miss him dearly.

CHAPTER 8

The Troubled King of Toys _____

From Kissy Doll to Mr. Machine and Mouse Trap,
it was a roller coaster ride.

In 1960, the *Saturday Evening Post* dubbed Marvin Glass "The Troubled King of Toys." He was, without question, the reigning genius in an immensely lucrative industry that he helped create.

At that time, the toy industry raked in almost $2 billion a year. It was a savagely competitive jungle, where only the fittest survived. The most knowledgeable combatants on this creative battlefield agreed on one thing: Marvin Glass – a forty-five-year-old Chicagoan who measured five feet five inches, weighed 127 pounds, and slumped through life with the pained expression of a depressed dachshund – was the most important and prolific independent designer and idea man in the field.

It was mid-winter when I received my first call from Mr. Glass. I had heard the name before but, as is the case with many potential new clients, I knew nothing of his business. Within a few hours, I was anxiously plowing through four inches of snow on my way to learn, among other things, that the Glass office and his apartment were located in a sleazy downtown hotel at the corner of Ohio and Rush Streets.

Before gaining entry to the office, I was carefully scrutinized through a small peephole in a steel door. Once inside, I was ushered through three more doors, each of which was locked. I felt like I was entering Fort Knox.

I remember Mr. Glass being courteous but subdued at that first meeting.

We sat for hours discussing the toy design industry and his role in it. It was quickly obvious his lack of national recognition outside his field bothered him. He was almost sad in describing his feelings, and wondered if I could help change this apparent lack of respect.

Though I was at least fifteen years his junior, we talked philosophically that day about his life and goals. I had been told Glass was brilliant, but was also very dogmatic, and at times could even be a tyrant. I quickly came to the conclusion we would have difficulty working together, because he was used to an entire staff of "yes" men. I felt I was the antithesis of that. I told him so and that was the first time I saw him smile. He said being told he was wrong might be a welcome change. Without either of us realizing it, we left that meeting and began what would be an eighteen-year business relationship. But this wasn't a typical business relationship. After all, this was the King of Toys.

In fact, Marvin must have fired me ten times. I resigned the account at least that many times. From beginning to end, it was a wild roller coaster ride. Though we often disagreed, nothing ever weakened the deep respect we held for each other.

I believe Marvin was the best read and most intelligent person with whom I ever had the privilege of working. He may also have been the most tortured. To Marvin, who read Plato and Aristotle, and worshipped Beethoven, the daily reminder that he was not advancing anything but his bank account was reason enough for him to spend many of his waking hours hating himself. He never slept more than four or five hours a night, and he once told me he dreaded sleeping longer because it's like being dead. He constantly berated himself and was forever frustrated that he never wrote a book or a play, or relieved anyone's suffering for an hour.

Marvin was deep into psychotherapy and felt that many of his problems stemmed from his early years. I knew he was born in Evanston, Illinois, in 1914. His parents came from Germany and Marvin told me their marriage was, at best, rocky. His father, an engineer, was a tall man who never could understand why Marvin turned out to be so puny.

As a kid, Marvin was a dreamer, and his dreams seemed to manifest themselves in toys. For as far back as he could remember, he was inventing unusual toys made from whatever he could find. Public school for him was a disaster, and the private military academy his parents eventually sent him to was even worse. He was a loner who remained somewhat withdrawn from society so he could spend more time creating.

As an adult, there never seemed to be any middle ground. He was either in the pit of despair or at the peak of the mountain. I sometimes felt he actually enjoyed suffering. He smoked three packs of cigarettes a day, plus at least a dozen long, black, and expensive cigars. He was definitely a hypochondriac, believing every headache was symptomatic of a brain tumor. He never understood the concept of a vacation, but on rare occasions made it to Las Vegas for a weekend.

Marvin received his undergraduate degree from the University of Chicago in 1935 and, by the time I met him, he had already experienced plenty of ups and downs professionally. He made a fairly big splash with Tiny Town Theatre, a product he developed in partnership with his friend, Joe Nudelman. Tiny Town Theatre was a projector in which kids could insert and illuminate comic strips. The two men sold the idea for $500, and the manufacturer eventually made $30,000. That was the first and last time Marvin sold an idea outright. From then on, he preferred a royalty arrangement.

His next successful invention was a toy-lined plastic bar that hung on baby cribs. After that came Hingies, a set of animated cutout figures. With Hingies, Marvin was able to build franchise agreements with the creators of Mickey Mouse, Blondie, and several other famous cartoon characters. He took his share of the $94,000 profit, bought out his partners, and set himself up under the firm name Marvin Glass and Associates. Within the toy industry, he was quickly developing the reputation of a prodigy.

Marvin's stock continued to rise with the introduction of his Catholic Weather Chapel. This little structure contained a moisture gauge that caused a Sacred Heart to appear as a sign of good weather to come. To ward off adverse conditions, Saint Barbara, protectress against disasters of nature, materialized. The Chapel netted Marvin enough profit to record his first million. On the downside, Marvin turned around and invested most of his limited fortune in an idea that involved stained glass picture windows. To support its sales, he bought and launched a nationwide advertising barrage that began one Sunday before Christmas. Within a week, the scope of the disaster was plain.

In debt up to his ears, Marvin borrowed from friends to start fresh. With another toy designer, Eddy Goldfarb, he created the Busy Biddy Chicken. When pressed, the chicken unburdened itself of five marbles, one at a time. These peculiar poultry retailed for thirty-nine cents and Marvin's company netted over $300,000 dollars. Goldfarb went to work for Marvin and together they created the Yakkity-Yak Teeth, a motorized set of dentures. When wound, the motor made the teeth click. They sold the product's license to H. Fishlove and Co., which sold more than three million sets of teeth at one dollar retail. The Glass company's take was $84,000.

While these creations were widely popular, it was the Tic Toy Clock that brought a real sense of pride to Marvin. Designed in 1959, it was a large open-faced timepiece with multi-colored plastic parts that could be dismantled and put back together again. The toy needed to be rewound every twelve hours, but kept reasonably good time. Marvin's ingenuity with the Tic Toy Clock helped lure millions of children into an act of self-education, while simultaneously satisfying a common childhood desire to take a clock apart and rebuild it just to see what makes it tick.

Long before Christmas of that year, more than $2 million worth of the clocks had been sold. Marvin must have told me a hundred times, "A toy is the only thing measured down to a kid's size. A toy helps a child cope with reality. We may not be pushing back the frontiers of science, but we may put into the hands of children the tools that will help them push back the frontiers."

NATIONAL AWARENESS BRINGS INCREASED RESPECT

Among Marvin's senior partners: Jeffrey Breslow, Burt Meyers, Gordon Barlowe, Gunar Licitis, Reuben Terzian, Art Nuemann, and John Parks, no one could understand Marvin's motivation in developing a public relations program for his company. It seemed fairly obvious to me. If Marvin wanted an audience to demonstrate his latest toy product, he was forced to go to the manufacturers rather than having them come to him. And, despite Marvin's proven credibility, none of these companies were willing to place the Glass name and logo on their boxes.

Marvin's top men apparently felt additional recognition, awareness, and respect were not key elements in increasing their business. They were wrong. Within one year of beginning the PR program, there was a tremendous change in attitude on the part of all Glass customers, and a sudden growth in the sales of Glass products.

There were several solid reasons behind the company's surge in prestige. First, toys were hot, and the industry's rise in volume brought plenty of media attention. Second, with a new emphasis on the use of plastics, toys had increased in size, and with this increase came a larger package and a higher price. Third, Marvin, with a little help from his PR agency, had established his company as the unquestioned leader in independent toy design. Lastly, Marvin proved to be an outstanding interview. His fearlessness and unabashed honesty with the media made him readily quotable, whether responding to questions relating to toy safety or discussing toys as an educational medium. He always said, "There is no such thing as a safe toy. A simple rubber ball in the wrong place is a threat to safety."

Marvin also spoke against the grain on the procedure of testing products in order to discover what goes into a good one. "You cannot write a great novel, paint a great painting, or compose a great symphony with product testing. Neither can you create a great toy that way." Marvin always felt tests were unfair. "Too much depends on who's doing the testing, what questions are asked, and what the kids in the test are like," he'd say. "A child doesn't know what he wants anyway. Believe me when I say that what appeals to me appeals to a child."

To understand the mercurial world where Marvin flowered and launched one popular product after another, it is necessary to examine the forces of the day. To begin with, the stakes were high, and getting higher. From 1960 to 1965, toy sales increased more than sixty percent. At that time, there were more than 2,500 American firms that were considered toy manufacturers. However, the mortality rate among these companies, even then, was steep. Today, with all the mergers and acquisitions that have occurred, the total number of manufacturers is nowhere near that number. Only a few hundred hang on more or less permanently, and many of these are over-extended and under-financed. It is a fashion business nearly void of reliable statistics.

Attempting to determine public tastes in toys is equally elusive, because toy purchasers and users are rarely identical. Marvin liked to say a parent buys a toy because it's what they would like to play with, but any effort to read this mood and capitalize by getting ahead of the market is like stepping into the unknown. Marvin often likened this to producing a Broadway show. Anything goes. In one interview, Marvin said, "Kids are ultraconservative. They are too insecure to be innovators. Instead they are imitators. If it is to work as a toy, it must be something that the child has seen before and can understand and manipulate."

The change in size from toys like Busy Biddy Chicken and Yakkity-Yak Teeth helped spur some of Marvin's most successful creations. Along came bigger toys like Mr. Machine, Robot Commando, King Zor, Kissy

Doll, Odd Ogg, Bop the Beatle, Golferino, My Mixer, Penny the Poodle, Dandy the Lion, Jungle Hunt, and Raz-Ma-Tazz Piano. It was an era that brought great attention to the Glass company with major feature story placements in prominent national publications like *Time, Newsweek, Business Week, Fortune,* the *Saturday Evening Post,* the *New York Times,* the *Washington Post,* and the *Wall Street Journal.* The *Journal* story, a front-page, right-hand column placement, was truly unusual because Marvin Glass and Associates was not a public company. His hometown paper, the *Chicago Tribune,* published the Glass story with a full-color cover on its Sunday magazine section. All this national exposure was for a company that had previously only been covered by the national toy trade magazines.

Marvin was on a great high and very much in the manic stage. He could feel the attitudinal change in his clients. They were thrilled and honored by the prospect of being invited to the Glass offices to view a particular toy in progress.

The question most often asked by the media was, "Where did this idea come from?" Talking about his first really big hit, Mr. Machine, Marvin likened it to modern man. "It's transparent, screams, and makes a lot of motion without doing anything," he'd say. The idea for Mr. Machine actually came from the often-fortuitous combination of accident and inspiration. Marvin was talking on the phone to one of his ex-wives, and she was being particularly belligerent. She told him the reason for their marital split was that he was nothing but a machine. Marvin told me that when he hung up the phone with her he went directly to the studio. It was 4 a.m., and he created his first mock-up of Mr. Machine, which he always considered an autobiographical toy.

He was addicted to work and expected everyone on his staff to share that same philosophy. Staffers would work eighty to ninety hours a week and were used to Marvin calling a project meeting whenever he got an idea, which was frequently in the middle of the night. It was at such a meeting that the idea for Robot Commando was born.

Marvin had just finished reading George Orwell's novel, *1984,* when he had a vision of a friendly big brother, an invincible machine that would move at a child's command and protect him. After much debate and swapping of ideas, the project was code-named C-42-A. C was for Commando, 42 was its project number, and A represented its position as a top priority. For two feverish weeks, the staff labored night and day. It wasn't easy to figure out how to cram the necessary motors and working parts into the toy's plastic shell. The shell was repeatedly altered to provide for new gears and electrical connections. The final model had two motors, one for movement, the other for the cannon arms and a missile-firing head. The toy's flashing eyes looked sinister in semi-darkness but not in daylight, and they were a drain on the batteries. It was just too complicated.

Drawing an analogy to automobile manufacturers, each year brings a new innovation, and each innovation costs the consumer hundreds of dollars added to the base price of the new car. In toy design, Marvin liked to point out that each major innovation needs to be added at a cost of perhaps ten cents. Not an easy chore.

Designing the project took a full year and had involved solutions of 6,400 separate mechanical and engineering problems. When Marvin accepted the final model, he called it the Robot Commando and made his telephone call to the president of Ideal Toy Company in New York.

The previous year, Marvin had sold Ideal Toys on that autobiographical robot, Mr. Machine. It was all the rage that Christmas, grossing more than $7 million in retail sales. It was so popular that Ideal couldn't make it fast enough to satisfy demand. Now Marvin Glass had another idea, and Lionel Weintraub, Ideal's president and CEO, was itching to see it.

Once through the security envelope, Marvin greeted Weintraub at his office, offered his visitor a chair, and brought out another of his innovations in the toy industry: a confidential disclosure agreement. By signing it, Weintraub would guarantee that, if he did not buy the toy he was about to be shown, Ideal would not make another like it. Weintraub signed.

Marvin, the showman, opened a curtain, and standing at center stage was a small device of futuristic automation – something out of Space Odyssey. Marvin scooped it up and put it on the floor. From the robot's back extended a long cord with a microphone attached. Marvin shouted into the microphone, "Robot Commando!" The thing stirred to life. It hummed and buzzed, and its eyes began to move as if in a penetrating, searching gaze. I watched Weintraub stand transfixed as Marvin shouted commands into the microphone. The robot marched around the room, fired rockets, and hurled plastic grenades. Weintraub was sold, and as an Ideal product, Robot Commando turned out to be the toy sensation of the year.

With Marvin's continued dominance in his field, he was convinced more and more people were willing to buy their children one good toy rather than a lot of inexpensive ones. He no longer saw children as inarticulate about their wants. Instead, they – not their parents – were becoming the driving forces behind any successful toy. When kids said, "Buy me that," they would get it.

Despite this transformation in buying power, Marvin stood firm on his feelings about educational toys. "A toy is for fun," he'd say. "If it teaches a child something, so much the better." He believed kids needed a catharsis, so he made toys he hoped would make children laugh. He often said, "The best thing for a child to play with is another child, and the next best thing is a toy, especially one that can play back."

Kissy Doll was one toy designed with this theory in mind. Marvin said, "Kids have been kissing dolls for thousands of years, it's about time the dolls reciprocated." King Zor wasn't quite as affectionate. This three-foot-long toy dinosaur, inspired by Marvin's recollection of the legend of St. George and the Dragon, looked terrifying. Zor carried six plastic prehistoric rocks on his back and a red bull's-eye on his tail. A child would fire a dart at the target, and a perfect strike would cause Zor to lunge toward St. George and launch one of his projectiles with a primordial roar. The designers figured Zor offered children (mainly boys) an outlet for their combative instincts, and a chance to feel like a knight fighting an evil dragon. It was another runaway best seller.

Marvin did not believe in marketing a toy for a specific age range. "As soon as a parent sees a toy labeled for five- to seven-year-olds, for example, he or she tends to underestimate or overestimate the mentality of the child."

With that type of attitude, Marvin made things easier on his staff. From a business standpoint, the real difficulty in toy design is to come up with a toy that's tough enough to withstand a child's play and simple enough to produce, but is still sophisticated enough for children to find appealing. In working with Marvin, I saw firsthand that it could sometimes take up to five years to work out the kinks in a product.

The epic of his Ric-O-Shay pistol, which retailed for what was, at that time, a sensationally high $3.98, and sold 1,003,000 units in its first eight months, began two years prior to its appearance on toy store shelves. At that time, operators who sold their toy weapons at $.29 to $1.50, and rarely added a new wrinkle, had long-dominated the toy gun business. Late in 1957, a $3.00 gun that could be fired like a real pistol hit the market. Heavily advertised on television, it sold like crazy.

For Glass, this was startling intelligence, and he and his colleagues debated the problem in one staff meeting after another. What could a gun be made to do? It could make a bang or even shoot bullets, but that was old stuff. Could it make a ricochet noise? Marvin, who spent hours each week scouting western movies on television, thought the ricochet was the answer. After several failed attempts by staff engineers and electrical technicians, which spanned almost two years, they finally came up with the perfect sound. That sound was inspired by the popular TV show "Gunsmoke." The staff was clever enough to tape-record the ricochet of a gun heard on the show, then play it through an oscilloscope and observe its vibrations.

ADDING SIZZLE TO THE SELL

When the gun was perfected, Marvin put a call into Jack Holden, director of new products for Hubley Manufacturing Co. of Lancaster, Pennsylvania, the country's oldest and biggest toy gun maker. Holden agreed to a meeting, at which he willingly signed Marvin's disclosure agreement and had his first peek at the gun. He wanted to try it himself, but Marvin refused. Holden was told he had to assemble Hubley's board chairman, president, and six other key officials before Marvin would let him demonstrate the gun and its sound.

Holden brought the men to Marvin's office, where they sat silently at a conference table while Marvin wielded his gun in the middle of the room. "Gentlemen," Marvin declared, "the Ric-O-Shay." With that, he fired. The men around the table smiled. Marvin, with sweat pouring into his eyes, moved about the room, ducking behind chairs, and firing away like a TV cowboy. Then, as shouts of "that's it" filled the room, Marvin gently placed the gun on the table.

The Hubley Company quickly signed an agreement, advancing Marvin an initial $50,000 against a 10.9 percent royalty on each gun sold. When the finished product was demonstrated at the Toy Show before an assembly of retailers, this often-cynical audience did something that nobody could recall their doing before – they applauded. A few years later, in the wake of President Kennedy's assassination, Marvin vowed never to design a gun again.

CLIENTS NEED TO SHOW COURAGE AND SPEAK OUT

With the myriad of diversified toy products being constantly developed by the Glass firm, plus the idiosyncrasies and verbal gifts of Mr. Glass, the Cushman firm had a field day maintaining a continuum of national and international media placements. Marvin and his newest toy designs were now in demand by media everywhere.

Because of his outspoken position on toy safety and his negative outlook on toys as an educational vehicle, we were providing public relations counseling in addition to pre-sell publicity.

In 1971, Marvin's designs accounted for about $175 million of the toy industry's $3.6 billion retail sales, or about five percent. Success brought the need for expansion, and the firm chose to construct a building that could house the company's more than one hundred model makers, engineers, designers, and audio specialists. But this wasn't just any space. While still residing in the downtrodden Alexandria Hotel, a virtual citadel of business rose from the ground at the corner of LaSalle and Chicago Avenues. Practically windowless, the muscular stone structure was designed with high-level security in mind.

After the company moved into its new headquarters, visitors were greeted at the menacing iron front gate by a closed-circuit television camera. Once inside the building's perpetually locked doors, they found security personnel maintaining a heavy presence. Getting into Marvin's personal office, which was lavishly furnished with original paintings and Tiffany glass, involved a series of clearances. The designers' work cubicles and the machine shop were considered off limits to most visitors. Exceptional visitors, usually meaning a representative of a major national publication, would be taken on a hurried tour of the building, with white sheets covering next season's toys in progress. Even internal windows were covered over to prevent workmen who periodically remodeled the facility from spying. Marvin's ideas were worth millions, and he was determined to safeguard them.

While Marvin was ferociously protective of his company's ideas and image, he didn't seem as concerned with how others might view his personal life. He was an eccentric, and there really was nothing common about his everyday existence.

Although he had been divorced four times, twice from the same woman, Marvin always prided himself on his sexual prowess. Few would have mistaken him for handsome, yet in all the years we worked together, he had that subtle knack for attracting the most beautiful women.

Unquestionably, his gift of gab made him fascinating to women, particularly younger women. His unlimited generosity simply added to his appeal. We sat together on a flight to New York for another toy fair and were served by a gorgeous blonde stewardess. Her name was Dixie and she was truly stunning. Despite Marvin's uneasiness on planes, he was obviously attracted to Dixie. At one point, he leaned over and told me he was going to have dinner with her that night. I laughed out loud and told him to forget it. I said she's probably married or engaged or, at the very least, has a ton of men at her beck and call.

Marvin took this as a challenge, and before I knew it, the two of them were holding hands and she had agreed to dine with him that evening in New York. The man was smooth.

For years, between marriages, Marvin dated a *Playboy* centerfold. Doris and I spent many evenings out with Marvin and this young woman, who, despite the stereotype, was extremely intelligent. However, the favorite topic of conversation was Marvin's insatiable sexual appetite and his amazing ability to satisfy any woman.

According to Marvin, he was quite an accomplished lover. He said he owed his past marital troubles to the fact that he loved the chase. Once he had won over a woman, he'd tell me, and she had agreed to become his wife, it spelled the end of any sexual relationship between them. Marvin told me that once married, he could never share the same bed.

Marvin's professional relationships were certainly more healthy and long-lasting than many of his personal relationships. Pauline was his secretary, administrative assistant, and an all-around anchor of support. She was an Oriental beauty with brains to match, and reminded me of the Dragon Lady from the popular cartoon, "Terry and the Pirates."

She was his unheralded confidante. Wherever and whenever there was a job to be done outside the shop, Marvin called on Pauline. She was with him for years and definitely went beyond the call of duty, right down to the selection of his clothes. Pauline not only shopped for Marvin, she helped maintain his Evanston mansion. She made reservations for deluxe hotels, first-class flights, limousines, theatres, and restaurants. With the top brass of the toy industry regularly coming to see "King" Marvin, Pauline would step in and plan their evening's entertainment. She was always busy and always under the gun, but always kind, considerate, and soft-spoken.

With Pauline's help, Marvin's extravagant home was now a true show palace. It was built to fit the manner of the elegant bachelor and studded with original paintings by Picasso, Chagall, Dali, and Rouault. It also boasted a sauna, large pool with liquor dispensers along the back wall, and two chefs. Marvin's favorite personal chef was Poy Tom, an outstanding practitioner of gourmet Chinese cuisine.

Poy Tom was more than capable of preparing a first-class menu for large groups of guests to one of Marvin's many dinner parties. It was fairly common for Marvin to host many of the nation's top toy executives at his home. Pauline would routinely hostess these evenings and assure perfection. By midnight, she'd be on her way home while the men were invited to the lower level of Marvin's home for a swim in the pool.

I attended a good many of those parties, which often led to my fiercest battles with Marvin. These were based on the fact that the executives down in the pool were soon joined by a bevy of *Playboy* bunnies. I simply did not want to participate at that level, and it drove Marvin crazy. I never claimed to be a prude, but Doris and I were newly married. He absolutely refused to believe in fidelity and could never understand, or respect, my reticence. It actually upset him deeply. By the next morning, however, all the harsh words were forgotten.

SUCCESS BREEDS SUCCESS

While a bit unusual at times, these casual evenings gave me great exposure (pun intended) to the leaders of major toy companies. Marvin was wonderful, enthusiastically recommending my company to other toy executives. They were familiar with the incredible coverage we had landed for Marvin. Ultimately, Aaron Cushman & Associates, Inc., represented toy clients that included Ideal Toy Company, Topper Toys, A.C. Gilbert Company, Fundimensions, Whitman Publishing Co., Hubley, Hasbro, and Merry Manufacturing Co.

At different times over the years, I've been shocked at the *naïveté* of corporate executives with regard to the mystic area of public relations. Their complete lack of realistic comprehension as to exactly what professional practitioners can accomplish on their behalf is probably tied to their perception of those few public relations people who would sell an exaggerated emphasis on their own personal media contacts and their ability to guarantee placements. One such example of this is an experience we encountered with the Topper Toy Company.

UNDERSTANDING YOUR CLIENT'S EXPECTATIONS

Topper was the largest toy company in gross volume sales in the early '70s. As a small, but growing, agency you can imagine our excitement when the president and CEO of Topper Toys invited the Cushman agency to Elizabeth, New Jersey, to discuss our retention as their agency of record. Marvin briefed me on Topper's marketing direction and offered me a bit of information about the gentlemen whom we were to meet. The company was marketing large plastic toys in giant packages through supermarkets, at which time was a very unique approach. The CEO was a refugee from Nazi Germany and a brilliant engineer.

I made the trip to Topper with Lee Block, a senior vice president of our firm and a marvelously capable PR man. To our delight, the meeting went well. We left with a new account and the largest annual fee we had to date. We returned from New Jersey as conquering heroes. Our entire staff greeted us with wild applause, and a good amount of backslapping.

Over the next three months, Lee and I made the trip to Elizabeth several times to present our creative plan for approval. The leadership of Topper unanimously praised our plan. Before leaving this time, we asked for permission to announce the fact that our company had been retained. Lee drafted a simple two-paragraph press release, and we forwarded it to Topper for approval. With approval obtained, we proceeded to release the story to all of the toy trade publications.

By that time, we had built many solid relationships within the toy trades and, in particular, with one editor named Anis Amory. Amory phoned me as soon as the release hit his desk. "Aaron," he said, "I have been waiting for an opportunity to do a major story on your company, and this Topper announcement gives me the right vehicle." I immediately expressed my thanks and appreciation.

Amory's story broke the very next week. Its lead read, "Topper Toys of Elizabeth, N.J., which last year had gross volume sales of $80 million and returned a dividend of X per share, today announced the selection of Aaron D. Cushman & Associates as their public relations agency." The story went on and on about Topper and also extolled our virtues and experience within the industry. An hour later, a Topper executive was on the phone. I could tell he was upset from the tone of his voice. "Did you see the story?" he asked. And, "Was it the press release that you issued?"

I told him indeed I had seen the story and, no, it was not the story we had issued. But, I pointed out, it was certainly positive. I couldn't understand what was troubling him, but before I could utter another word he said, "You're fired!"

After a short pause, I asked him why he was troubled by the story. "If you cannot control what the press prints," he said, "we don't want you." I tried to explain to him that we are a factual information source, but once that information is in the hands of the media, it is their prerogative to print it or not, and to embellish it or not. We cannot, nor can any other PR organization, I continued, control what actually goes into the public domain. It was no use.

I hung up the phone and sat at my desk, feeling absolutely desolate. In my frustration, I put my head in my hands and bent forward on the desk. Lee had sensed something was wrong and came into my office at that moment. He took one look at me and knew immediately what had happened. I confirmed it in a cracking voice and Lee broke down crying. He told me he just couldn't take this type of irrational action by any client. He told me that was it, he was getting out of the business.

A month later, Lee kept his word and our company was a two-time loser. Topper was gone and so was Lee Block, one of my best men. Lee went back to the hospital-medical field where he had started and has made his mark within that burgeoning industry. To this day, I miss his solid professional counsel and his friendship.

I'm not sure if the leaders at Topper learned anything from this experience, but it taught me to be very aware of what others might consider the role of public relations to be. I believe, in the long run, it helped me to better connect with clients, to ensure that, while we are learning how their business works, they are being given a clear understanding of how our business works as well.

NOTHING REPLACES SHOWMANSHIP

Marvin was different. Although he'd rant and rave about my uselessness every now and then, he really understood the score from the start. He capitalized on our resources, and we made the most of his talent. He always had a flair for the dramatic. He was a showman every step of the way, including those times when he was forced to bring his designs to the manufacturing companies. For effect, Marvin carried his toys to prospective buyers in a gorgeous mahogany box that he chained to his wrist. When he opened the box, it was like magic, and he only got better at it.

He once created a black doll when they were almost unheard of. This wasn't a white doll painted black; it was designed after Marvin conducted a search for a black model. He emphasized accuracy.

Feeling confident with the finished product, Marvin asked me to conduct a market study analyzing the potential market size for this doll. Once armed with statistics that indicated its potential, Marvin invited key leaders in the toy industry to view the doll. After those leaders signed the usual disclosure agreements, the room went dark. Then, two small spotlights popped on to display the doll and the model on rotating pedestals, each dressed exactly the same.

On other occasions, Marvin really threw himself into the sales pitch, getting down on the floor and playing with his creations. He was known to say, "Any man who doesn't enjoy playing with toys should get out of this business."

The highlight of each year's planning and production was the trip to the New York Toy Fair. Held each year at 200 Fifth Avenue, where almost all the major toy companies had their permanent show rooms, the Toy Fair brought together all the buyers of the national retail stores and chains. The major buyers from companies like Sears, K-Mart, Toys "R" Us, and Wal-Mart were always given the first opportunity to view new products and invited one week prior to the formal opening of the Fair.

The Glass entourage planned to attend with the key buyers – and an entourage it was. Marvin sent Pauline ahead, usually with his Chinese cook, Poy Tom, to prepare his suite and arrange all his clothes. In addition to most of his eight partners, Marvin liked to travel with his psychiatrist, his banker, his attorney, his public relations counsel, and his current amour. It was quite a group.

By the morning of the first day, rumors of various product successes were already swirling in Marvin's suite. We always stayed at the swank Regency Hotel on Park Avenue, where he was given true celebrity treatment. The phone in his suite was ringing by 7:30 a.m. On the other end was the president of one toy company or another telling Marvin the product he licensed to them was the talk of the show.

By 10 a.m., having received at least ten calls, each excitedly proclaiming their company had a runaway winner, Marvin was beside himself. He couldn't wait for the limousine to arrive and carry him and his entourage to the fair. Indeed, his arrival at the fair had the aura of the "Second Coming."

From showroom to showroom, Marvin was hailed as the messiah of toys. The proverbial red carpet was rolled out for him. He was greeted at the entrance to each showroom by the president and product development manager, and guided into their private offices where he was waited upon like royalty. Each CEO proclaimed that his Glass product was selling at a rate of so many millions and their largest problem, their only problem, was keeping up with demand.

It was no wonder that as we left one showroom for another, with the cheers still ringing in his ears, Marvin would stop in the corridor, lift up his arms and shout, "I am the greatest!" In this manic state, he would continue for several hours, proclaiming over and over, "*Sieg Heil* . . . I am *der Fuehrer.*" To the senior man in each company who relied on the Glass company to fill their new product needs, Marvin was truly a savior and worth every dime paid to him in royalties. Many junior members of these manufacturing companies smirked behind Marvin's back and chuckled at the idiosyncrasies of the man and the size of his traveling ensemble. Between showroom visits, we managed to get him to two or three interviews each day.

By the end of the second full day at the show, observers could begin to see the mental about-face taking place. Marvin was getting bored with the adulation and the repetitive backslapping. The depressive side of his personality began to appear. Nothing pleased him. Whatever Broadway show Pauline selected for the evening's entertainment wasn't good enough. The limo driver wasn't parked where he should be. The restaurant selection was terrible, and the table even worse. Traffic was miserable and he definitely didn't approve of the television commercial being used by one or two of his clients. When entertaining buyers or being entertained by buyers, Marvin was able to disguise his true feelings. He'd save his outbursts for our return to the Regency. The first few days in New York were delightful; now everything was a nightmare.

By the third night, most of Marvin's group had fled either to an early slumber or some other more pleasant activity. But for Marvin, this night was apparently reserved for attacking PR. He and I sat at the bar in the Regency and he began his tirade by exclaiming, "Why do I need you? Look at all I've accomplished by myself! Besides, where was *Time* magazine? I should be this week's cover story!"

He was unhappy with the interview he'd done with The Associated Press. "A waste of my time," he said. Nobody reads their stuff anyway. And the local television show is a "so-what." Who cares? Even though I pointed out to him that the AP story meant a wire service placement that would appear in several hundred papers, and that the local television show interview just happened to be in prime time when every buyer from every department store was locked in a New York hotel room, it was to no avail. He was dead set on railing against PR, his lack of interest in it, and its unimportance to him.

When the attack got personal, I stood up, looked him right in the eye and said, "Marvin, you are full of shit, and I don't intend to sit here and let you vent your spleen on me. Goodnight." I turned and headed for the elevator. The morning after was always the same. At breakfast, he would stop by my table and quietly apologize for his attitude the night before. By morning, I, too, had cooled down and realized it was all part of his being a manic-depressive. As the years passed, I got better at seeing his tirades coming and learned to beg off early before things got hostile. But I also learned that, with Marvin, you couldn't always avoid trouble. If only Phil Donahue knew the trouble he avoided.

For weeks, I had been making calls to major national and syndicated television talk shows that might be interested in booking Marvin as a guest. The producer of the "Phil Donahue Show" was quite receptive to the idea. He was aware of the exposure Marvin had been receiving recently and thought we could work something out. At that time, the show originated out of Dayton, Ohio, but was syndicated on several stations throughout the Midwest. At one point in our discussions, Phil Donahue got on the phone and told me if I could deliver Marvin Glass with some of his toy products, he was prepared to devote his entire one-hour show to Marvin. I told him I would check the date with Marvin and get right back to him.

KNOW YOUR CLIENT'S SHORTCOMINGS

This was big, but Marvin hated to fly. Most of his interviews were either done in his Chicago office, at his home in Evanston, or by phone. Except for the New York Toy Fair, he rarely traveled anywhere, particularly if it meant flying. But I asked him anyway, hoping his ego would help him overcome his fear. Yes, he would do the show. I couldn't believe it.

I asked if he understood that the show was done live from Dayton and would require our traveling there with several product designs. Yes, he understood and was still willing to do it. I went on to explain to Marvin that because he was scheduled to do the entire show that day, Donahue would have no backup if we failed to show. Marvin assured me he would make the show and told me not to worry. With his assurance, I called Donahue and confirmed the appearance.

In order to be on time, we had to take a 7 a.m. nonstop to Dayton. Knowing Marvin, I tried to cover every base in advance. First, I sent him a written memo that included a list of suggested items to take with us. Then I called Pauline to make sure he had it on his calendar. Then I personally called his driver and outlined the timing. To make the 7 a.m. flight we would have to leave Marvin's home in Evanston no later than 6:30 a.m. I planned to arrive at his home at 6 a.m. I rang the doorbell at 6 a.m. sharp, and that's when the nightmare began.

No one answered the door. After three or four tries, I decided to knock on the back door. After more knocking, the back door began to open, slowly revealing the concerned face of Poy Tom. In one hand, which was raised high over his head, Poy Tom held a large, menacing meat cleaver.

"Poy, it's me, Aaron," I practically whispered in fear.

"What you want? What you want?" he kept demanding, while frantically rubbing sleep from his eyes.

For what seemed like ten minutes, we danced back and forth – me proclaiming that I had to get Mr. Glass up and Poy telling me, "Missa Glass, boss man, him sleeping." Feeling the time burning away, I gathered enough bravado to push past Poy and his meat cleaver and make my way into the house. As I got to the bottom of the stairs, Marvin suddenly appeared at the top. He was still in his pajamas, looking like an unmade bed. "Jesus, Marv," I said in disappointment. "Today is the Donahue Show. Please don't tell me you forgot. We have fifteen minutes to get the hell out of here and head for the airport."

Marvin looked at me like he'd never even heard of Phil Donahue. He proceeded to tell me he had a bad night, felt lousy, and couldn't possibly make it. I was furious, but held it in and focused on the mission of getting him out of there. I reiterated the whole situation, telling him we couldn't leave Donahue high and dry with no other guest as backup. "For the sake of your own reputation," I implored him, "let's get on the road."

He eventually agreed to at least try to make the plane. I practically dressed and shaved him myself. Fortunately, the driver was on time and the limousine was already packed with the necessary toys. We piled into the car and I told the driver we had eighteen minutes to get to O'Hare. I told him I was counting on him to go like hell, to fly if necessary. Forget about getting any tickets; I would take personal responsibility.

He stepped on it. We shot up Dempster Street at about seventy-five miles an hour, but that only lasted about two miles. I looked up and could see we were crawling and there was no traffic in sight. I was sitting directly behind the driver and gave him a not so gentle nudge to get it moving. We were back up to cruising speed, but again began to slow a few minutes later. I was starting to lose it and screamed at the driver, "What the hell are you doing? Get this car in gear." Again our speed climbed dramatically before gradually slowing. I leaned over the front seat and saw Marvin pulling the driver's leg off the pedal.

At 7:05 a.m. we pulled up in front of the terminal and Marvin smirked, "Gee, I'm sorry but we missed the plane."

"Like hell," I said, jumping out of the car. I began running down the terminal like a raving madman. As I reached the gate, I could see our plane pulling away from the terminal. I climbed all over the poor gate attendant. I begged, screamed, and cajoled for him to please bring that plane back. I made it sound like a life or death situation. If Mr. Glass didn't get on that plane, the world would come to an abrupt halt. Marvin and the others had arrived at the gate by then and were quiet and disbelieving bystanders to the unfolding drama. The gate person looked at me as though I was totally berserk, yet to my utter amazement, he proceeded to call the plane back.

Remember that this was the early '70s. I doubt this would happen today. The craziest part of the story is that the airline had to kick four first class passengers off the plane in order to accommodate our group. Glass was so impressed with the entire scene, and with his feeling of omnipotence, that he quietly got on-board and never said another adverse word the entire trip. We made it to the studio on time and the show came off without a glitch. Marvin was his usual charming and literate self, and Mr. Donahue never knew how close he came to having sixty minutes of empty airtime.

About six months after this episode, Marvin called to tell me he had gotten *Time* magazine. He went on to say, "And I did it without you." I told him that was wonderful news and then asked just how he had done it. Apparently *Time* had contacted Marvin directly to express an interest in doing a story on him. "They knew all about me," Marvin explained. "They had seen much of the nationwide coverage I had received." I told him how pleased I was to know what a great PR man he had become. The funny part was he really believed that he had done it on his own.

In all the time we spent together, one of our most interesting adventures occurred when the British toy industry named Marvin Glass as the "Brighton Toy Man of the Year." With this declaration came an invitation to attend the Brighton Toy Fair and to be honored at a black-tie dinner.

Marvin was overcome with emotion when he learned he was actually receiving international recognition for his accomplishments. Realizing the business potential this brought, let alone the personal ego boost, drove him to a level of excitement that I had never seen before. It was only after the initial enthusiasm wore off that he realized accepting this honor meant a transatlantic flight. It took him weeks to come to grips with this, and he ultimately decided to go.

Now came the question of who would accompany him on this trip. Surprisingly, his first selection was his psychiatrist. Marvin viewed this as a life-threatening flight over the ocean. He was sure he'd need some help.

He decided he'd need his PR man as well. This was certainly a major media story in need of professional handling. With another member of Marvin's staff along as well, we boarded British Air and settled into our first class seats.

Marvin had agonized over this trip for weeks. He was white-knuckling it from the start, but I became angry when the psychiatrist handed Marvin a gas mask not long after take-off. It would put him to sleep for the entire flight. I begged Marvin not to do it, but the doctor insisted. With Marvin incessantly mumbling in fits of terror, the eight-hour ride was horrible.

PROTECT YOUR CLIENT

Aside from my concern for Marvin's general health, I realized there was a good chance a strong media contingent would meet us at the airport in London. I didn't want the King of Toys coming down the ramp in a stupor. Unfortunately, that's exactly what happened. Marvin could hardly walk. I told the media it had been a difficult flight for him, but he would be fine in the morning. It took him almost forty-eight hours to recover.

Luckily, by the evening of the dinner he was one hundred percent and raring to go. Riding in a Rolls Royce, we drove from London to Brighton, where Marvin was feted at a gala reception for British toy VIP's and several high-ranking government officials. Then came the moment.

It was a page right out of the coronation of a British king or queen. Royally garbed ushers, replete in their red robes and white wigs, led us to the dining room. As the door to the dining room opened to reveal almost 1,000 guests, the royal spokesman stomped his golden staff and proclaimed, "Me Lords and Ladies, pray rise for the right honorable Mr. Marvin Glass."

As one, the entire room jumped to its feet and applauded. Marvin was ceremoniously led down the aisle to his position at the head of the table. For just an instant, I looked at his face and it was radiant. At that moment, all the weariness and worry surrounding the trip was forgotten and all was well in his world.

I was seated five or six places to Marvin's left, and I couldn't help but notice that no one was touching the food that had been placed in front of each position. A kindly woman on my right leaned over and whispered in my ear, "For heaven's sake, please ask Mr. Glass to begin or else no one may eat." I scribbled a quick note and handed it to Marvin. He got the idea. Being the non-eater he was, everyone could have gone hungry were it not for that woman.

In 1970, Marvin made the coup of his career when he enticed Anson Isaacson to join his firm as managing partner. Anson had formerly served as vice president of product development for Ideal Toys in New York and was the man with whom Marvin and his staff worked closest on some of his most successful products.

Anson had also been CEO of A.C. Gilbert Co., an old-line and well-respected company whose claim to fame was The Erector Set and The Chemistry Set. Anson and I had a long-standing relationship. When he was named top man at A.C. Gilbert, he retained my company as public relations counsel.

Anson was smart, knowledgeable, courageous, and very straightforward. There was no double talk. You knew exactly where he stood. Perhaps most importantly, he was respected within the industry and among all of Marvin's staff. Anson was calm and collected, an interesting change from the often frenetic Marvin.

THE MARKETING OF A SUICIDE

The marketing of a suicide is the way some corporate executives responded to the news that Anson and Marvin had struck a deal with daredevil motorcyclist Evil Knievel. "We wanted to sell things that excite the imagination of the public," Anson said at the time. "And this does it." He was referring to the announcement that Knievel was preparing to jump the Snake River Canyon in Twin Falls, Idaho, in September of that year. From the commercial side, Knievel's great leap over the mile-wide canyon was shaping up as the hottest media event since the Billie Jean King/Bobby Riggs tennis match.

The Glass Company had purchased the international rights to Knievel's name. At least fifteen companies expected to cash in on the Knievel craze, and nine had actually acquired rights to manufacture Knievel toys and accessories. These items ranged from watches, radios, and hobby kits to motorcycle-like accessories for bicycles and images printed on tank tops and other boys' clothing. Anson estimated that manufacturers of Knievel products would capture $200 million in gross revenues that year. Marvin Glass and Associates would collect five to ten percent in royalties, and Knievel himself would receive about half of that.

Several Evil Knievel toys took off quickly, especially Ideal Toys' red, white, and blue "Sky Cycle," a miniature motorcycle modeled after the one Knievel intended to use in the jump. The twelve-inch-high, battery-powered cycle – with rider – could jump a variety of hurdles and came equipped with trailer, toolbox, and accessories. The Glass company received a $100,000 advance against royalties on this product in 1972. With a retail price of about $14, the cycle was expected to earn $18 to $25 million.

Top Rank Productions, Inc., of New York had acquired the closed-circuit television rights worldwide for the Knievel jump and expected $11 million to come from broadcast rights with two million viewers in the U.S., Britain, Puerto Rico, and Latin America. They even spoke of a possible motion picture tie-in. Of Top Rank's total take, sixty percent would flow back to Glass and Knievel. The jump did indeed come off, although unsuccessfully. Knievel came away without serious injury. The media coverage was close to being overkill.

While the daredevil was quite astounding, Evil Knievel the man left a lot to be desired. His personality often mirrored the image of his reckless jumps. There were moments when he could be a courteous gentleman, but they were rare. In my experience, words like demanding, inconsiderate, and overbearing paint a more accurate picture. Nevertheless, thanks to the ingenuity and creativity of the Glass organization, and the marketing savvy of Anson Isaacson, everyone holding a Knievel license was enjoying expansive sales. I'd like to believe that we had something to do with the product's success.

In the midst of the 1972 Toy Show, with the Ideal Toy Company display room jammed with dozens of buyers, I went into Lionel Weintraub's private office to extend my congratulations. Lionel was seated at his desk, his head in his hands, his eyes closed. He was mumbling quietly to himself.

"Are you okay?" I asked.

"I've got a $25 million headache," he responded. "I'm sitting here trying to figure out what I have to do next year to replace the $25 million in sales we will achieve through the Knievel motorcycle this year. I know my board of directors and stockholders will soon be asking me that question, and I don't have the answer yet."

This struck me as a peculiar way to react to success. I quickly realized it's just part of the ups and downs of the toy industry. It probably also serves as one good reason why the CEO is paid so well.

Marvin's successes have more than compensated for his failures. Two of his toys, Ideal's Mouse Trap and Louis Marx's Rock 'em Sock 'em Robots, have ranked among the industry's top ten sellers for years.

As the first three-dimensional game, Mouse Trap changed the course of the children's game industry. Prior to Mouse Trap, games had to have dice and spinners and something to push around a board. Mouse Trap has a marble that goes through all kinds of gyrations, down steps, and through chutes, all just to push a plastic, three-ounce cage over a mouse. It has inspired several generations of games in the three-dimensional category.

Marvin loved to tell the story of how Mouse Trap came about. An acquaintance of his was in the exterminating business, and one day he described to Marvin the ways in which he caught rats. Marvin was fascinated, and a short time later picked up a book of Rube Goldberg's crazy, often three-dimensional, inventions. Marvin simply put the two concepts together and went to work on Mouse Trap.

Marvin suffered through several months of serious illness before he died in January 1974. Throughout his illness, Anson kept the company rolling along. Upon Marvin's death, Anson was named president and CEO of Glass and Associates.

Anson was particularly strong in arranging licensing agreements with Disney and major motion picture studios. He led the company through several years of growth and continued prosperity. On more than one occasion, he sent me to the West Coast to open negotiations for a licensing agreement. On one particular trip, I phoned Anson from Los Angeles the night before my return to offer him an update. He asked me to be brief because he was in a meeting. Then he suggested I come home early and fill him in on the details in person.

I hopped the red-eye that evening and called my son, Gary, asking if he would please meet me at the airport. Gary was a recent college graduate and had joined our firm as an account executive. We planned to drive from the airport to our office, despite the fact that I was feeling tired after being up all night.

My plane was about thirty minutes late, but after finding Gary and grabbing a cup of coffee, we headed for downtown. Traffic was uncharacteristically light that morning. We seemed to be off the expressway and in the Loop in no time. We were riding up LaSalle Street and at Chicago Avenue passed the Glass office building. At that moment I had a sudden change of plan. "As long as we're right here," I told Gary, "it might be smart to stop and see Anson now." I thought we might catch him before his day got too busy, so Gary made a U-turn on LaSalle and we pulled into the Glass parking lot.

Everything seemed quite normal as Gary and I walked to the building's steel front gate and faced the closed circuit television camera. We were buzzed in and started up the stairs to the reception desk when all hell seemed to break loose.

Pop. Pop. Pop. The sound of gunfire pierced the air. I was accustomed to hearing so many unusual sounds in this building that I let the thought pass. The screams that followed were not rehearsed. They were hysterical, and all too real.

I pushed Gary down and crouched next to him on the stairs. We laid there for what seemed like a few minutes. Suddenly, policemen with guns drawn dashed past us on their way up the stairs. One officer bent low and whispered, "Are you hurt?" We shook our heads "no" and he continued up the stairs.

I vaguely remember telling Gary to get outside and wait for me. I slowly climbed the stairs. I can still hear the people crying and screaming. When I reached the landing, blood was everywhere. Pauline came to me crying. Through her sobbing she said, "Anson is dead."

No one seemed sure what had happened, but it was obvious several people had been shot and most of those were dead. I stood there for just a moment and then it hit me. Had I arrived thirty seconds sooner, my son and I would have been sitting with Anson in his office. A police officer asked me to leave and I went back down those terrifying stairs to where Gary was waiting.

By the time we reached our office, I had stopped shaking. We turned on the television news and the story was on the air. The details were still fuzzy, but by morning the newspapers had put the pieces together. Albert Keller, a troubled electronics specialist who had been in the Glass organization for four years, had stormed through the firm's executive offices on that fateful Tuesday, July 27, 1976, and shot and killed Anson Isaacson, 56, managing partner; Joseph Callan, 54, partner; and Kathy Dunn, 33, a designer. In addition, he wounded Donald Nix and Douglas Montague, then killed himself. It was ironic that the shootings took place in the building where security precautions had been considered fortress-like. With all of the emphasis on protection from the outside, no one ever worried about any threats from the inside.

The one story that I never wanted to write was Anson Isaacson's obituary. I had lost a good friend. On our way back from the funeral, Jeffrey Breslow, the company's newly appointed managing director, fired me. He told me he was sincerely afraid of any further exposure. He specifically mentioned his concern for his immediate family. I knew that after almost eighteen years, it was over.

It had been a magical time. I had watched the Glass Company gain worldwide recognition and respect to the point where companies like Parker Bros., Bradley, and Ideal did incorporate their MGA logo and the phrase, "Designed by Marvin Glass Assoc." on their boxes. Knowing that Cushman & Associates had played a key role in making that happen gave me a great sense of accomplishment.

In succeeding years, I watched the toy trade publications carefully and never do I recall seeing another story on the Glass organization. It is almost as though, from that day on, they ceased to exist.

CHAPTER 9

"What's a Marriott?" _____

*How rare for an outsider to view and be a part of the birth
of a company destined to become the largest of its type in
the entire world. We were architects of their international
public relations program.*

Nippersink and Oakton Manor Resorts were the agency's training ground for the hospitality industry. It was Bob Stein's boutique advertising agency, specializing in hospitality accounts, that brought the Cushman organization to the attention of the Shinderman family, who owned both properties. Nippersink and Oakton Manor were located about a one-hour drive north of Chicago and a similar drive south of Milwaukee. They were the Midwest's answer to upstate New York's Concord and Grossinger Resorts. Those properties were a true learning experience and they laid the groundwork for what became one of the Cushman agency's specialties and real strengths.

It was in the mid 1960s when I first heard the name Marriott. The call came from two media friends who told me that Marriott was sniffing around, looking to find a local public relations agency that had familiarity with hotels. In response to my query, "What's a Marriott?" no one seemed to know. The best answer I could get was that they were a tiny company headquartered somewhere in the East. At that time, any thoughts that this company was destined to become a leading worldwide hospitality organization would have been considered off-the-wall.

Currently, Marriott International has about 1,900 lodging properties located in fifty states and fifty-six countries. They operate and franchise the broadest portfolio of lodging brands in the world, offering travelers more than 350,000 rooms worldwide. According to their annual report, they manage 144 senior living communities across the United States, provide furnished corporate housing, and operate a nationwide network of food distribution centers. They employ close to 150,000 people. There are four corporate subsidiaries of Marriott and each is listed on the New York Stock Exchange.

The initial interview with Jerry Best, director of sales, and Robert Barrie, the hotel's general manager, for what was to become the Chicago Marriott seemed to go well. I quickly learned that Marriott had only three small properties in the Washington, D.C., area and was planning an expansion. Jerry surprised me when he told me they were building a 500-room hotel on the Kennedy Expressway, not far from O'Hare Airport. Chicago had not seen a new hotel of major proportions go up in many years, and certainly nothing of importance near O'Hare. We were competing against several of Chicago's larger PR agencies, but for some reason, all the Marriott executives I spoke with seemed to like the fact that we had not been inculcated with Hilton, Sheraton, or Hyatt operating methods. They were a new breed and welcomed fresh thinking without hearing, "This is how we did it when we worked for Hilton." They were more interested in our local media contacts and political savvy than in any national contacts or experience we may have had. I was happy to get the business, but, to be perfectly honest, I looked at the hotel as a nice, small local account with some probable longevity, but limited growth. I could not have been more wrong.

Once assured that we were indeed Marriott's Chicago representatives, our staff began research and programming. We convinced ourselves that the strategy for our campaign should be built around the fact that the Chicago Marriott would be the first major hotel property to be built in the O'Hare Airport area. Other than a smattering of mob-operated, hot-pillow joints on Mannheim Road, we were to be the first luxury hotel. As the hotel was being finished, we continued both planning and implementing at the same time.

Our almost daily meetings with local management began to disclose some very unusual characteristics. These people really cared. They were motivated like no one I had ever met before. Yes, we had our modest resort experience, and I had done some extensive traveling, but the few Marriott folks I had met were a different breed of cat. They loved what they were doing and absolutely ignored the hours they poured into the job. It was not unusual to find Jerry Best and his sales crew in their office soliciting group convention business late into the evening and on weekends. Doing PR for any hotel will normally eat you alive as far as time is concerned. The Marriott attitude (or affliction) caught up with my people within the first month, and it became clear that any thought of maintaining time sheets was out of the question. Cushman account executives forgot about everything but creating awareness for Marriott in the Chicago market area.

An invitation was extended to visit their headquarters in Washington and to view their existing three hotel properties. I jumped at the opportunity. Walking with the general managers through each hotel, I was impressed with their open enthusiasm and dedication. There was a sense of pride cohesive with not only what was said, but with what was done. In other hotels, I had seen executives who spotted a scrap of paper or a cigarette butt on the lobby floor direct a bellman or reception clerk: "Please pick that up." At Marriott, the general manager bent over and removed the object himself. I saw no evidence of rank or overactive ego involved. They really cared, and I found it refreshing.

Our first releases provided an architect's rendering of the 500-room hotel and listed all its amenities. Aside from the indoor-outdoor pool, what appeared to be of most interest to the local media was the 22,000 square feet of banquet, reception, convention, exhibit, and conference rooms plus the twelve conference suites. The press kit elicited the same response from every media recipient: "What's a Marriott?" "Who are these people?" It was never clearer that the PR equation was applicable here, and if we expected the media to carry our message, we first had to convince them of the quality of our product.

EXPOSURE = AWARENESS = SALES

No question about it, Marriott had absolutely zero awareness in the Chicago market. Hundreds of thousands of cars drove past the hotel every day and people asked, "Wonder what they are building over there?" The hotel was almost complete, but there was limited signage. I insisted that every "doubting Thomas" reporter be taken for a tour – no easy assignment with the hotel at least thirty-five to forty-five minutes from the Downtown Loop. We were determined and pleaded our case to each reporter and city desk until they relented. Clearly anyone could see that they were looking at a $75 to $100 million investment, and that deserved the time to investigate further. Once on the property, our case was made and it became an "open sesame" to publicity, depending upon our ability to create newsworthy activity.

The results were incredible. They far exceeded anyone's expectations. We were in the papers almost every day between actual news, special features, column notes, and photographs. We interviewed every employee searching for the unusual. As a matter of fact, when the call for employment went out, over 2,000 people responded and formed a line over a block long at the employee entrance. We parlayed that into newspaper back page pictures and the ten o'clock television news. The hotel utilized at least fifty large globe lights to brighten its entry, driveway, and parking lot. At Halloween, we painted smiling pumpkin faces on each globe and the photo made print. The contrast between the sheer luxury of lobby carpeting and immense chandeliers, versus workmen taking their lunch break clad in overalls and sitting on the floor propped against a wall became a photographic opportunity upon which we capitalized. Every radio and television talk show in the Chicago area was targeted. Our biggest problem was literally dragging different management personnel away from the hotel long enough to do interviews.

Mr. J. Willard Marriott, Sr., came to see the hotel the day before opening and I met him for the first time. Prior to his arrival, I don't think I had met a single Marriott staffer who wasn't eager to tell me that the entire Marriott success story had begun with one nine-seat A&W Root Beer stand in Washington, D.C. Research showed that Mr. Marriott had come from Salt Lake City, Utah, where he acquired a knowledgeable belief in the Mormon message, which enthrones honest work as a cardinal virtue, and insists on energetic independence, thrift, and the self-respect that comes from providing for family, church, and brothers and sisters in the faith who have been less fortunate.

In 1927, Bill Marriott, with a friend's financial help, bought the A&W Root Beer franchise for Washington, D.C. Needing a location, he rented half a bake shop in the middle of the city, put up a partition and opened for business. A few weeks later, he returned to Salt Lake City to marry Allie Sheets, and she became treasurer of their new enterprise. The story has it that they opened at 9 a.m. and usually fell into bed, exhausted, at one or two the next morning. Root beer sales fell off when the autumn air grew crisp, and Bill decided to sell chili, tamales, and barbecue-beef sandwiches. With Bill waiting on people and Allie in the kitchen doing the cooking, they named their establishment The Hot Shoppe. In the 1930 depression years, while expensive restaurants failed across the country, profits mounted in the bright, clean atmosphere of The Hot Shoppe, where emphasis remained on inexpensive, high-quality food and good service. Mr. Marriott told me that they placed enthusiastic and cheerful people who were interested in and cared about the service they were providing, and thought nothing of working seven, twelve-hour days a week. Without saying that it was in the best Mormon tradition, he did say that he searched for ways to cut his employees in on profits. He said it inspired initiative, industry, and *esprit de corps*. He also said it was just plain good business. I know now that their profit-sharing program had enabled kitchen food handlers and housekeepers to retire after twenty years with $500,000. That profit-sharing program, and their more recent stock purchase plan, have been a material assist in the long-term retention of personnel.

What impressed me the most the day that we toured the back areas of the new Chicago hotel was the time he took with practically every employee. Mr. Marriott appeared to be genuinely interested in their families and personal welfares. He asked questions about their children and their home lives as well as their happiness working for his company. I'm talking about cooks, dishwashers, housekeepers, and bell personnel. Bill Marriott, Sr., was a very special man.

As we approached opening day, Jerry told me that group and convention sales were substantially ahead of projection and that he felt it was primarily due to the extensive publicity which had successfully created awareness within the corporate Chicago market. Flying on an emotional high, we reviewed our invitation list covering media, political leaders throughout the Chicago area, local police and fire personnel, plus the corporate management people who represented potential group business. We were careful to create a separate list for a travel agent party. The main list came to about 5,000 persons and, after coordinating with all departments, received the go-ahead. The affair, held in the grand ballroom, was later termed "The Fire Drill" because of the sheer weight of numbers. Marriott chefs outdid themselves with their lavish and decorative preparations. We helped to organize small group tours, which were led by Marriott administrative personnel as well as Cushman account staff.

Sitting in a cab with Bill Marriott, Jr., en route from O'Hare Field to the Chicago Marriott, he asked me why it was necessary to plan an opening newsmaking stunt. "After investing close to $100 million, I don't understand why I can't just open the door and walk in or routinely cut a ribbon," Mr. Marriott said. I responded with, "Bill, you certainly can do exactly that. But in the nation's second largest market, about all the coverage it will give you are two columns on the real estate page. It's too rudimentary. In Chicago, we must find a way to make the news media sufficiently interested to ensure that they cover the event even though we are located relatively far from their newsrooms. Everything we do to officially open your hotel is designed to provide at least one photograph for the front or back page of each daily paper and thirty seconds of television footage for the evenings news programs."

Marriott had established a tradition of giving an award to the person who had played the most important role in the successful launch of each new hotel property. In Chicago, at a reception for all hotel employees following the opening, Jim Durbin, Marriott Hotel president, announced that the award was being presented to Aaron Cushman for his agency's contribution. The award had heretofore almost always gone to either the GM or the marketing director. I was floored.

WE GO NATIONAL!

Through our months of working together, despite my respect for their professional expertise, I was shocked with their *naïveté* regarding the business of public relations. It was after the opening that I discovered Marriott had never had PR counsel before. Jim Durbin and I sat together for a meeting, at which time I suggested that what had happened in Chicago could easily be repeated in many other cities coinciding with their growth program. Given the opportunity, public relations could play a key role within their marketing mix. I was talking to the brightest, most open-minded CEO, one whom everyone in the company loved. Jim was originally from Texas and had just the slightest drawl. He was about six feet tall and very athletically fit. He was a soft-spoken gentleman who, if provoked, could be hard as nails.

In the next few minutes, I explained to Jim that there were at least five solid reasons for Marriott to develop a marketing-oriented public relations campaign: 1. Because public relations can be a direct assist to the acquisition of more business in existing markets; 2. Because it is a cost-efficient way of opening new markets in concert with advertising; 3. Because of its inherent credibility factor, predicated upon the consumer's continuing belief that whatever is published or broadcast editorially is the truth, it adds strength to the advertising message; 4. Because PR provides strong support toward the recruitment of staff personnel by constantly reminding them, through national hospitality trade publications, exactly what working for Marriott means with its vast benefit programs; and 5. With the high cost of personnel training, PR is one excellent way to encourage retention.

Within another five minutes of questions and answers, Jim bought the idea and hired the Cushman agency. We arrived at a fee structure that we both felt was eminently fair, with incremental fee increases as Marriott added to its number of properties. Without realizing it at that moment, Marriott was the beginning of the establishment of our own national reputation, and ultimately led to creating an award-winning campaign for St. Louis and St. Louis County titled, "St. Louis: The Meeting Place." It also brought the Cushman organization to the attention of many foreign governments interested in utilizing our travel expertise to increase U.S. tourism to their countries.

THE BEGINNING OF A THIRTEEN-YEAR RELATIONSHIP

The very next day, I received a phone call from Tom McCarthy, newly appointed vice president of advertising and public relations. Within a week, I was back in Washington at Marriott headquarters to actively begin a close personal relationship that covered thirteen years and carried us through sixty-five different hotel openings, plus the launch of Marriott's first cruise ships and the opening of their two Great America theme parks. In many ways, the Marriott relationship was the most exciting, rewarding, and enjoyable of any client activity over all the years.

It was the people and their receptivity. McCarthy told me honestly that he knew nothing about public relations. He explained that he had been in hotel sales and that this was a new assignment for him. He openly asked for my help and guidance to learn the PR business. I have never seen any person work harder to master a job. Tom personified the smiling Irishman with the laughter and personality to match. He had the true gift when it came to oral communication, and, if anyone could sell the Brooklyn Bridge, it was Tom McCarthy. I tend to forget the days and nights we worked hard together because of the fun we had. There was the touch of a leprechaun or the devil in Tom, and he was forever playing innocent jokes on various people. We became not just business colleagues, but good friends, a relationship that continued long after both of us had left Marriott.

Before Tom could take me down the hall to make further introductions, the door to his office burst open and big W.W. Bud Grice, vice president of marketing, stuck out his giant hand and said, "Welcome to Marriott, Aaron." People in the know had told me that much of Marriott's initial success in the hotel business could be credited to Bud Grice. Warm and friendly, Bud was sincere when he told me, "We need your expertise." The third member of the marketing team was Al LeFaivre, whom I had met years ago in Chicago. Al was national vice president of sales. We became Marriott Hotel's marketing quartet from that moment and spent many years using our different specialties planning profitable hotel operations for the company.

We, at Cushman, were obsessed with the need to develop a national image of Marriott Hotels. Our program began with a stepped-up publicity effort in Washington and Chicago and spilled over into the national travel and hospitality trade magazines. As we became privy to more and more of Marriott's expansion plans, we started to parlay that information towards gaining national exposure. Initially, we targeted the wire services, and with each major story placement, found ourselves on the receiving end of queries from national magazines. *Business Week* and *Time* did early stories. Shortly thereafter, I wrote a feature story for *Hospitality Magazine* and was subsequently invited to become a regular contributor on the subject of public relations and marketing of hotels. I carried that byline for the next twenty years.

THE MARRIOTT MARKETING QUARTET

Once the real estate site selection people picked their city and exact location, it was time for the Marriott marketing quartet to move in. Marriott was growing rapidly and I soon came to learn the three most important words in hotel people's vocabulary – location, location, location. Tom, Bud, Al, and I traveled to each new city, took up residency in a nearby hotel, carefully toured and scrutinized the cities' demographics and, after two or three days, sat down together to plan exactly what our new property would include. The architecture department of Marriott back in Washington wanted to know approximately how many rooms to build, what amenities to include, how many square feet of meeting room space should be built, how large the grand ballroom should be, and approximately how many suites should be included. Using our individual backgrounds, we pored over the details. Questions of population make-up, affluence, age groups, corporate offices, government facilities, professional sports franchises, media outlets, transportation, parking, and competition were a few of the factors considered. Each city was different and we knew that ultimately we would have the responsibility for marketing the finished product.

The company spent millions of dollars each year on its training programs. An employee was almost besieged with opportunities to make the most of him or herself. Marriott paid part of the tuition to encourage the acquisition of high-school diplomas or to take job-related college or business school courses. They had a career progression program which enabled ambitious workers to move up to more responsible jobs. Those with special aptitudes were enrolled in their Learning Center, a sort of Management Development University. A *Reader's Digest* article summed up one Marriott employee statement, "If all companies treated their people the way this one does, there would be no employee relations problems – no need for Social Security, Medicare, or anything like that."

Alert to the history of the company when it comes to training, we suggested a public relations frontline training program for all employees who come in contact with hotel guests, no matter how infrequently. This included telephone operators, front desk reception personnel, bellmen, security, concierge, housekeeping, waiters and waitresses, engineering, valet, pool, and spa staff. In a period of ninety minutes, we tried to convey their individual importance in establishing the right image for the property. We emphasized that all the effort by the company and other staff personnel went down the sewer if one member of the Marriott organization had a bad day and transmitted an inhospitable attitude to the guest. The guest will not remember the lavish accommodations, the excellent service, and the fine food if they run into even one sour apple. No matter what the level of their job, we asked them to remember that "You Are Marriott."

Bud Grice and Al LeFaivre handpicked their local directors of marketing and sales for each new property that came on line. Bud, imbued with the emphasis on training, pulled his field staff together as often as possible. At the outside, it was at least every six months and often more frequent. Our properties had a propensity to run occupancy at least ten percent larger than the closest competition, despite a higher rack rate. Knowing this, it wasn't necessary for Bud or Al to push their men too hard. Instead, they both used the public relations success story to add motivation. Tom McCarthy and I were always given as much time as we needed to orally and visually describe local media support for individual hotels and the national coverage as well. The department heads played a role in selecting advertising material, ad sizes, and placement dates, and were therefore

familiar with locally placed advertising. Some were familiar with what
was happening in their local market with respect to PR, but had no idea
as to the volume of awareness being created across the country. They
really got a kick out of viewing the television pickup of many of our
special events.

P.T. BARNUM IS BACK

Imaginativeness is a quintessential quality of the public relations
executive, and at no time is this more evident than when a company wishes
to present something new, but not unusual, to the public. That challenge
faced Marriott Hotels often during our years together. Retracing our steps
as far back as 1880, entire towns were set agog when Phineas Taylor Barnum
created the greatest, gaudiest showbiz extravaganzas that ever marched
from railroad station to fairground. He was the super PR man of his day
and got more publicity for less money than anyone in the world. In 1971,
Hospitality Magazine's entire cover page, in glorious four-color, displayed
a photograph of the Marriott marketing quartet with the headline, "P.T.
Barnum is back." In the article, they said, "Mr. Barnum's modern day
successor is Marriott Hotels, Inc., which, like the master showman, uses
extravagant ideas to make front-page news. Perhaps their greatest success
is how Marriott consistently makes front-page news by jazzing up the dullest
subjects in the business-hotel openings, topping-out ceremonies, and
groundbreakings."

I like to point out that one result of our high-impact publicity campaigns
with openings and groundbreakings is that our sales representatives find a
better reception after prospects have been pre-sold on Marriott's image via
editorial coverage on television and newspapers the day before. They no
longer run into, "What's your company name? Never heard of them."

THE TRIPLE GROUNDBREAKING IN THE SKY

How do you breathe excitement into an earth turning? The receptionist
in my office told me that Bill Marriott, Jr., was on the phone. Not exactly
an everyday occurrence, it got my attention in a hurry. "Hi, Bill," I said and
sat back to listen. "Aaron, we have an unusual situation coming up and I
could use your help. We've selected locations in Kansas City, Denver, and
Newport Beach, California, and would like to hold groundbreaking at each
location as soon as possible. You know it has been our policy to have all
vice presidents attend each groundbreaking, only this time, it could be very

time consuming. I don't like the idea of so many of our key personnel being away from Washington for so long. Is there something you can do to speed things up?" I asked him to give me a few days to think it through and I would call him back.

In our staff brainstorming session, we came up with a plan we called, "The triple groundbreaking in the sky." Simply stated, the plan called for us to race the sun across the country and complete the three special events within one day. Mr. Marriott, Jim Durbin, and Bud Grice loved it, and we began making it happen.

The date was set for May 15, 1973, at which time Marriott was a chain of twenty wholly-owned hotels and nine franchised inns. For the airborne ceremonies, we chartered a Continental Airlines DC 9, with seating configuration for slightly more than one hundred persons. Invitations to take the entire flight were telegraphed by Messrs. Marriott and Durbin to a cross section of carefully selected syndicated writers in Washington, New York, Boston, and Chicago. The twenty national media people who accepted were flown to Washington to catch the charter on its initial heading to Kansas City. Business and civic officials in Kansas City were invited, as were reporters and photographers from the Kansas City dailies and local television news reporters.

Accompanied by a large brass band and a bevy of beautiful girls, everyone boarded the plane for a 9 a.m. takeoff. Timing was critical if we were to cover all three cities before the sun set. My greatest fear that day was that somewhere en route we would run into bad weather. It was a huge risk. Once airborne, we gave guests a forty-five-minute sightseeing tour of their own city while breakfast was served. Tom McCarthy and I had placed Mr. Marriott and Jim Durbin on the aisle seats in the first row and I stationed myself between them and the pilot's cockpit. At the appointed time, the plane came down to 500 feet over the ground, and we proceeded to simulate a bomb run over the exact location of the new hotel. We had a model appear from the rear of the plane carrying a black box with flickering lights and a toggle switch atop a purple pillow. She ceremoniously carried the box down the aisle and placed it in Mr. Marriott's lap. The pilot was in touch with the ground by radio, and as we approached our location, he tapped me on the shoulder and I did likewise to Bill Marriott. As Bill pushed the toggle switch, the plane banked steeply so our passengers had a clear view of the ground. Colored smoke bombs and small size dynamite explosions took place to herald the groundbreaking. Television cameras in the plane and on the ground were shooting footage and every photographer on the plane was having a field day. We quickly circled the field, landed, bid a hasty farewell to our local Kansas City passengers, and were on our way to Denver. Of course, we had cleared the low-level flight with both the tower and the FAA. (The little black box with the flickering lights was simply a prop and had no electrical or remote connection to the ground explosions.)

Denver was simply a repeat performance, only this time we served lunch onboard as our passengers enjoyed their local sightseeing flight. Once again, local officials and media persons had been transported to the airport on special chartered buses and limousines. They signed a guest book, were given press kits and badges, and were escorted to their pre-assigned seats onboard. As soon as our Denver VIP's had deplaned, the national press and host group took off for Newport Beach, California. This time, it was cocktails and *hors d'oeuvres*. I had assigned my top senior account people to cover the details at each city. Joel Feldstein and Dick Stahler carried the load and made it look easy. While I was on the plane taking bows, these two were on the firing line sweating out each tiny detail. McCarthy, an ardent Catholic, had gone to church the Sunday before and prayed for good weather. Someone up there listened because we never saw a cloud.

By 7 p.m., we were in Los Angeles and took our national guests to Chasen's for dinner, before reboarding for the long flight home. Somewhere around 5 a.m., I crawled into bed dead tired. It had been a day to remember.

One direct result of the activity was its provision of an unusual informal and prolonged opportunity for top Marriott officials to have personal contact with local political leaders, opinion makers in the three new markets, local writers, and television anchor persons, plus the multiple members of the national media that were with us all the way. The press took the story of the three new Marriott hotels to readers across the country. Photographers found enough unusual shots to keep their cameras busy. Print and electronic media carried the news that Marriott was planning facilities and resorts in 10 other cities in the U.S., Canada, and Holland. They played heavily on the fact that the new hotels would contribute substantially to the economies of the areas they were entering and made this writer very happy with their reports that characterized the three-city event as "unusual," "innovative," and "supercolossal." The *Boston Herald Advertiser* termed the effort "different and quite impressive" and summed up its results by saying: "There are few people now in the three cities who do not know about the new

Marriott Hotel." Even more gratifying was the next-day report from the national sales office that they were receiving many calls requesting information as to opening dates and whether Marriott would accept group and convention reservations now.

THE "TASK FORCE" IS INTRODUCED

It was true that Marriott had written manuals on practically everything that related to good hotel operations. That included recipes on how to make pancakes and how to clean a room Marriott style. To protect the service and quality of their operation, the company created a "task force" in conjunction with each new property. Management selected the most capable person in every department, regardless of the location of the hotel in which that person was employed. It included the outstanding performer from among restaurant hosts, waiters and waitresses, cooks and dishwashers, housekeepers, bellmen, front desk receptionists, security personnel, doormen, etc. Everyone in the company fought for the prestige that being selected on the "task force" would bring them. It meant that they would be placed on temporary duty at the new hotel approximately ten days to two weeks before opening. Their job was to train the new employees who were to take over when the "task force" went home. Marriott management refused to accept a response to a guest during the opening period like, "Please forgive us because we are new on the job," or "We have only been open a few days." When the door opened for customers, the hotel had to be ready. To prepare the kitchen staff and the wait staff, they fed every employee off the guest menu for a week before opening. It was great guest relations.

GRAND OPENING CHECKLIST

Probably one aspect of being a Virgo has always been my uncontrollable drive for organization and attention to detail. It served me well during two wars, and I found it essential when planning a grand opening. Actually, two checklists were created. One to cover all elements of the opening, and the second to pinpoint the official ceremony. The checklist for Marriott Hotel openings included:

1. Selection of VIP speakers. The entire program is not to exceed thirty minutes and, therefore, speeches need to be correct but short. Other than the Mayor, Senator, or Congressman, who else?

2. Who will introduce the various speakers and gather needed bios?

3. Prepare three-by-five-inch cards for Bud Grice as MC.

4. Complete script outline for MC.

5. Rehearsal set for at least two hours in advance of the opening to provide time for corrections or additions if needed.

6. Arrange transportation for Marriott personnel from the airport to the hotel and back to airport.

7. Nametags to be placed on backs of seats for speakers and those to be introduced.

8. Lapel name tags for guests made out in advance off RSVP cards and arranged in alphabetical order.

9. Provide supply of blank nametags and felt tip pens for those who came without responding.

10. Separate table for press registration. Cushman staff to man and provide press kits.

11. Phone follow-ups to non-responsive city image-makers and unconfirmed media.

12. Place podium in proper location, being certain that it carries the Marriott name and logo.

13. Check out speaker system with engineer. He stands by in case of any problems.

14. Raised platform with steps and carpet, draped and with flowers.

15. Placement of all props needed for program.

16. Arrange seating auditorium style. Not too many to start. Have additional supply handy to fill.

17. How will the buffet be set up? Check out the ballroom for traffic flow. No matter the number of guests, they must have easy access to the food.

18. Check bar set-up. How many? Where will they be located? Are they sufficient in number to comfortably handle the crowd? Are quality brands being served?

19. Guest tours. Where will they convene? Who is responsible for obtaining knowledgeable guides? Who establishes traffic flow and assures that sample rooms and suites are open for viewing?

20. Music. Who hires the band? Who meets with leader and assigns location and timing?

21. Helium-filled balloons. How many people needed to fill? Who will supervise release on cue?

22. Souvenirs. Who to select? How many? When to distribute?

23. Select our own local photographer to cover. Which Cushman staffer

assigned to work with photographer? Pre-establish specific shots we must have, plus at least one major news picture for media distribution.

24. Write and distribute advance request for news coverage and follow-up.

25. Subdivide local newspapers into their integral parts and select specific Marriott personnel for interview, i.e. architect, interior decorating, financial, management, cuisine, and personnel. Who on Cushman staff to service news and photography to any media that didn't attend?

26. Photographer to provide contact sheet of all pictures to Cushman for possible national distribution. Have release ready for signature for those participating in photos.

27. Provide sashes for hostesses who will greet guests. Provide safety pins and set rehearsal time.

28. Parking area. Must be cleared the night before and roped off. Place signs directing traffic flow.

29. Place signs directing guests to ceremony site.

30. Copies of all speeches for working press.

31. Rooms should be pre-registered for VIP guests. Personally check each VIP room in advance.

32. Gift package placed in each VIP room with a press kit and a welcome letter from the GM.

33. Select all personnel who are to carry walkie-talkies and check the equipment for clear operation.

34. What have we forgotten?

The second list covering the ceremony proper was primarily concerned with timing. Sequence of speakers, specific time limits on each, necessary visual props (renderings, flags, etc.), setup for single news photo and television, positioning, sun location, backdrop, and protocol were items covered to come as close as possible to perfection. In every opening, we tried to tie the event as closely as possible to the local environment. We utilized local customs or heritage whenever they would fit our themes naturally. For instance, at the Miami opening we used a dolphin swimming in the hotel pool with a trainer standing at the edge of the area, encouraging the dolphin to crash through a large hoop and break the ribbon with its body.

The second element in every opening was the disappearance of the official key to the entrance of the hotel. Since hotels never close their doors once officially opened, we continually were challenged to find ways to symbolically "throw away" the key. In Miami, the hotel was built with a center tower and two long extensions with two or three levels of rooms. Garo Ypremian, the famed extra point kicker for the Miami professional football team, was recruited to kick a football over the relatively low roof of the hotel extension. To maintain the flow of events, he kicked from the edge of the pool following the ribbon breaking. As the football disappeared over the hotel, a giant inflated balloon in the shape of a football began to rise towards the sky. Slung beneath the helium-filled football was a ten-foot-long replica of the official front door key. It just kept rising into the heavens and has never been heard from since.

LION ON THE LOOSE

In Lincolnshire, Illinois, a posh northern suburb of Chicago, Marriott had built its first resort property replete with its own golf course. Within the hotel, they had constructed a magnificent theatre with tiered seating for several thousand people. The theatre was jammed to capacity with local notables and politicos, along with a smattering of metro daily news reporters and photographers, as we proceeded with our traditional ceremony. This time, Jim Durbin was doing the MC honors and among our guests were the mayors of every village and township within forty miles. Our foil for today was a very large male lion with a magnificent mane that was on a short leash held by his professional trainer. The plot was to have the lion dive through the proverbial hoop and thereby break the ribbon. Next, the lion was provided with a giant platter of raw meat, carefully textured by our chefs to resemble the front door key of the hotel. By devouring the key, the lion resolved our problem of having that key disappear forever.

Most people are familiar with what is said about the best-laid plans of mice and men. When the immovable object meets an irresistible force, unusual things happen. The lion, in his enthusiasm over a free meal and the need to show off for the assembled multitudes, broke loose. He pulled so hard on his leash that the trainer went flying and Jim Durbin ran in search of altitude. The lion ran up the aisle and dashed across several rows of terrified guests. With the trainer in hot pursuit, the lion finally found the exit to the lobby and proceeded to make its way casually toward the reception desk. The screams could be heard for miles. The trainer caught up with his "pet" and the excitement was over. Ah, the travails of a PR man! The Chicago media loved it and even went so far as to accuse us of pre-planning the lion's escape.

The St. Louis hotel was located directly across the street from Lambert Field. Its location gave us our theme and we proceeded to recruit the very first group of TWA stewardesses and their uniforms for display at the opening. A replica of Charles Lindbergh's plane, "The Spirit of St. Louis," was located within the airport terminal on prominent display. The city and the airport administrator agreed to allow us to use the plane, but we had the job of moving it from the terminal to the front of the hotel. Those familiar with the area realize the heavy traffic flow that seldom lets up. The only way we could move the plane was with plenty of manpower, and we did it at 3 a.m. to avoid traffic. It was quite a sight with people pushing Lindy's plane across the road. In this instance, we used a helicopter to break the ribbon.

MOTHER'S DAY IN MEXICO

In Denver, it was a man wearing skis shushing down off a slanted, snow-covered roof to break the ribbon. At Dulles, it was three sky-divers plunging from 8,500 feet and guiding themselves to a tiny island in the hotel's front lake to present the flags of the United States, Virginia, and Marriott to dignitaries for raising. Understanding the local customs in Mexico and adapting our plans accordingly, we selected Mother's Day for our press preview for all Mexican media personnel. Mother's Day is greatly revered in Mexico, so the invitations to view the Paraiso Marriott, our first international property, were addressed to both newsmen and their mothers. About 225 mothers and sons accepted Marriott's hospitality. That venture resulted in the Paraiso carrying a higher number of Mexican guests than any American-operated hotel in Acapulco for several years thereafter.

The U.S. press contingent numbered forty syndicated travel writers. In a heretofore unheard of move, our invitation clearly stated that there would be no briefings, no touring of rooms, and no forced itinerary of any kind. The writers were invited to take advantage of the beach and anything else they might enjoy. It was to be a relaxing three days as guests of Marriott.

In anticipation of their arrival, Tom McCarthy and I spent time at the front door trying desperately to teach our Mexican bell staff what we felt was the proper way to greet incoming guests. It was clear that these young fellows had no experience and needed help. The phone advised us that the press entourage had landed in Acapulco and departed in cabs for our hotel. They were on their way. With time running out, I convinced Tom to let me demonstrate "the correct way" to greet our guests by handling the first taxi load to arrive. As the taxi stopped, I stepped up and, with an overly dramatic flair, proceeded to sweep the door open. As the first person stepped out, I said, "Welcome to Marriott's Paraiso." The guy, whom I immediately recognized as a *Chicago Tribune* editor and friend, looked at me as though I had lost my marbles and said, "Aaron, what the hell are you doing here?" I felt a little foolish, but smiled and said, "It's a small world."

DECOMPRESSION CHAMBER FOR FISHERMEN

McCarthy and I were always searching for fun things to do to enhance the Marriott image and make it everyman's hotel. Just a flicker outside Minneapolis, Marriott had opened another luxury hotel. It was actually located in close proximity to the northern wilds. I watched innumerable men come in the front door dressed in suit and tie like any businessman. These same people rapidly changed into hunting and/or fishing togs (depending on the season) and took off out the back door on their way to the wilderness of northern Minnesota. In about a week, tired, dirty, and bedraggled, they would find their way back to the hotel. We honestly felt that the trauma of jumping from the forest primeval to the luxury of a Marriott was too much strain for the human body to endure. To overcome this problem, we created a decompression chamber for returning fishermen. The hotel erected two pup tents in its pool area and allowed the men to check in. They were provided access to lavish washrooms and showers, and the chefs gave them room service inside the tents. Jim Klobachar, who writes for the *Minneapolis Star Tribune*, insisted on being the first to test the chamber. Jim did a full page of pictures to accompany his story, and for years requested that he be the first to use the decompression chamber at the start of each new fishing season.

200 CARTONS OF CHICKEN FOR JOHN GLENN'S FAMILY

Sixty million people watched their television screens as Lt. Col. John Glenn rode his spacecraft into the uncharted heavens. At Marriott headquarters in Washington, Bud Grice had started his own countdown. As soon as he realized the size of the television viewing audience, he called the advertising agency and told them to get some time on the program. The advertising account supervisor looked at Bud with a grieved expression and said, "We've only got $100,000, and that's the budget for the year." Bud told him to sit tight and keep his eyes glued to his TV set because, somehow, he was going to get Marriott seen on that screen. The rest of the story is still being told around Marriott offices to new employees and visitors.

Looking for inspiration, Grice turned back to the TV set. He found his idea when the camera switched to the home of Mrs. Glenn and the announcer noted a contingency of newsmen had gathered there to report her reaction to the flight. Grice dialed the Marriott kitchen and asked how many cartons of chicken were on hand. He ordered two hundred cartons reserved for pick-up at 11:30. Then he called the garage and asked that one of the panel trucks be washed and that a driver meet him at the kitchen. The duo drove to within one block of the barricade across the street leading to the Glenn home. Grice realized he didn't stand a chance of getting through the police cordon dressed in his business suit, but figured they might let the driver through in his white coat. "When the officer waves you down, just say that you're bringing Mrs. Glenn's lunch," Grice instructed.

The ruse worked and the barrier moved aside. The truck, which was the first unofficial vehicle to be allowed in, pulled up to the curb and three network cameras panned to the white truck with the red and black Marriott crest. As the cartons of chicken were carried up the front walk, the voice-over on television said, "Well, it looks like Bill Marriott has sent lunch for Mrs. Glenn." A second plug came later when other cartons of chicken were distributed to the press corps.

After his successful flight, when the Glenn family came to Washington to visit President Kennedy, Colonel Glenn was asked where he would stay. He answered: "The Marriott took care of my family when I wasn't around. I'll stay there." As the Glenn family walked toward their suite, the astronaut's mother saw two housemen taking down a sign that said Presidential Suite and putting up one that said The John Glenn Suite. It had been pre-arranged, but was too good a picture to pass up. Both wire services sent our pictures nationally to their subscribers, and the Marriott PR program scored another coup. For the price of 200 cartons of chicken, Marriott found itself pictured on television screens all over the world. Somewhere in the shadows lurked a smiling PR man.

The gleaming New Orleans Marriott, thrusting up forty-two stories over the foot of Canal Street, added 1,000 rooms, which represented a thirteen percent increase in the city's total hotel capacity. The excitement within the market area as a result of groundbreaking, topping out, and grand opening resulted in $60 million in convention reservations booked before the hotel opened. The 175 major conventions that had been booked meant approximately 180,000 Marriott guests. The city revenue to be accrued in the areas of dining, shopping, transportation, and sightseeing would have an enormous impact on the entire community. The New Orleans Marriott employed 1,000 persons with an annual payroll of between $4 and $5 million. More than 900 of the employees were from the New Orleans labor force and had been chosen after approximately 10,000 interviews. We played these numbers hard in all our news releases.

Some of the other numbers we used to give the community an idea of the hotel's size include 5,999 cups of coffee served each day, equating to 150 pounds of coffee. The hotel's food and beverage director estimated that, during the first year, over 100,000 dozen eggs and 100,000 milkshakes and pieces of pie would be served. Carrying the numbers game a step further, the hotel had 74,000 pieces of linen, including 30,000 sheets and pillow cases, 12,000 towels, and 12,000 face cloths. The hotel had 38,000 drinking glasses in the supply rooms and 6,000 coffee cups on the property.

Each individual hotel was an entity unto itself. I recognized early that the only way to maintain consistent exposure in the local market was to employ a local agency. I reviewed each city's PR organizations by phone before setting appointments for interviews. Tom and I flew to each city to carefully select the agency we felt had the creativity and capability to handle the Marriott account in their city. We gave no credence to size, but sought people who could cooperate and implement the national program. Before Tom and I left Marriott, we had thirty-one public relations agencies onboard – all supervised by Cushman. To maintain some symmetry and still allow creative input, I wrote a standard operating procedure for all agencies.

LOCAL PUBLIC RELATIONS AGENCY RESPONSIBILITIES:

1. The agency account executive must become an insider. He or she has a need to familiarize himself or herself with every aspect of the property. The first step in accomplishing this familiarity is to attend all staff meetings.

2. A communication channel has to be established within the hotel. PR should meet regularly with department heads, become familiar with them personally, and build confidence.

3. The public relations director should check registration records, corporate and convention sales books, and catering at least once each week. Working well in advance, the PR person can determine newsmaking events booked into the hotel, as well as newsmaking celebrities checking in.

4. Public relations should review personnel records of all employees

looking for the unusual. Some of our most widely placed wire stories came from people features.

5. A current and accurate list of all media market wide should be immediately developed. It should include metropolitan dailies, suburban or community press, radio, Internet, and television assignment editors and anchor people. Nightlife and city magazines, as well as local or regional business publications, should be included. The list should be updated regularly.

6. A six-month public relations plan should be completed and approved by management and Cushman within the first thirty days. It should be budgeted. The plan should require extensive research to confirm or revise the initial research done by the national marketing group. We must be able to identify our potential customers.

7. Creativity is the key ingredient. Local public relations personnel cannot rely upon the physical property or its staff to provide input exclusively. Each Marriott Hotel is a highly salable publicity commodity. It will take the unique talent and experience of the public relations agency staff to maximize idea development and maintain the ongoing exposure level necessary to support the marketing program.

8. The measures of success will not be the time and effort put forth. It can only be based upon implementation and actual publication or broadcast of Marriott publicity material. In short, do not write for management approval. Don't waste your time and the hotel's money distributing information to media unless you can clearly see a strong percentage for acceptance.

9. Train management and department heads to turn over all media inquiries to PR. It is your responsibility to respond rapidly, even in negative situations. Management should be told that you cannot kill a negative story. However, by building positive media relations over the long pull, it's possible to soften the downside.

10. Take every opportunity to have the various media as your guests. Entertain to build contacts for the hotel via lunch, dinner, or an occasional weekend reservation on special occasions.

11. Community relations: Encourage management to participate in civic and business organizations. Set up a speaker's bureau for select department heads and the GM. Encourage their placement on broadcast talk shows. Cooperate with civic leaders and charitable organizations that make requests for an occasional Escape Weekend to give away at a fund-raising affair.

12. Set up promotions and contests with radio stations, newspapers, airlines, car dealers, shopping centers, etc. PR must evaluate the promotion and be assured of a *quid pro quo* as far as value received either editorially or via paid advertising in return for what the hotel is giving. Should be a ratio heavily favorable to Marriott.

13. Take nothing for granted. Merchandise the results of your publicity efforts directly to the sales department so they may use the published material as further confirmation of their sales position when pitching a prospective corporate meeting or convention.

14. Similarly, merchandise reprints of successful publicity to all employees to build pride with community recognition. Employee relations programs will pay dividends with retention.

15. Plan ahead for the opening of your indoor-outdoor pool, the new health club and spa, a new restaurant, and perhaps a new lounge. Support the hotel's marketing efforts in conjunction with special holidays like St. Patrick's Day, Valentine's Day, Mother's Day, Halloween, Thanksgiving, Christmas, and New Year's.

16. Maintain a current supply of press kits and other collateral material at the hotel. There should be a color slide and black and white photo file kept ready for distribution.

17. It is your responsibility to develop a crisis or disaster plan. Situations do occur in hotels, such as people drowning in the pool, a suicide or murder, or even natural disasters such as hurricanes and tornadoes. By having an advance written plan, you may alleviate much of the downside of adverse publicity.

18. Lastly, a written monthly progress report is required. It should be written for local management with a copy to Cushman.

INTERCHANGE OF IDEAS PROGRAM

One of our better ideas created during the years with Marriott called for an interchange of ideas between properties. Since no one has a corner on the idea market, it seemed to make sense to take advantage of every brain at our disposal. Whenever any PR person in the network made a key placement that in my judgment could be duplicated by multiple hotels in their community, I drafted a complete scenario spelling out exactly how the idea developed and what the local PR person did to make the publicity placement. In each case, the PR person involved was credited. Accompanying the detailed one-page outline was a copy of the actual news release and a copy of the newspaper tear sheet. The packet was sent to every local hotel PR person with a request that they try to duplicate the idea in their market. It required me to personally review each news clip that came into our Chicago office and select those that looked promising. Almost immediately, we found that each single placement was being reproduced in one third of all our hotel markets. The local agencies welcomed the added support and relished the national recognition they received via the listed credits. It was a clear win-win situation. Within three months, I found myself issuing one such memo each week. The idea made for a heavy personal workload but it proved to be worth the effort.

For a while, we focused on people features. We found an African American woman employed in the housekeeping department of the Houston Marriott who had been selected to be a member of the United States Olympic Team. She was a high hurdler. United Press International covered the story and it broke with photographs in almost every country in the world. Another find occurred in Boston, where a twenty-one-year-old young lady was employed as a sommelier – reportedly the first female wine stewardess. This time, it was Reuters that carried the story and picture worldwide.

Hubert Roetherdt became a perennial story. He was food and beverage manager of the Chicago hotel when we discovered his hobby – building magnificent ship models. His home was decorated with multiple examples of his work. Everyone who saw the finished product agreed that they were of commercial or even museum quality. Our first placement appeared in the Sunday supplement of the *Chicago Tribune*. Thereafter, each time Hubert was transferred, we sold the same story in each local market. Hubert was transferred so often (because of his expertise) that I laughingly accused the personnel department of just wanting to take advantage of his publicity potential.

Once a year, McCarthy invited all Marriott PR agency principals to a one-day seminar. We had recognized that the proficiency level of individual agencies varied a great deal, depending upon their specific market area. We could not expect the same PR comprehension and performance in secondary cities that we might expect in New York, Chicago, or Los Angeles, despite the fact that we felt we had picked the best agency in each city. The experience and sophistication level differed, in some cases, broadly. Our seminar was an effort to upgrade the understanding and subsequent level of all agencies, and Tom McCarthy looked to our office to establish the timed itinerary. We tried to locate the seminar at different hotels, to give the PR directors an opportunity to view as many properties as possible. Basic PR 101 subjects such as writing technique were avoided, and the seminar stuck to new idea development and challenges relating to creativity. We didn't want to give the impression that the seminar was designed at too low a level to avoid hurting any agency's feelings. The annual get-together helped the idea interchange program by creating more familiarity amongst the participants.

22 KEYS TO SPECIAL EVENTS

So often in public speaking opportunities, someone in the audience who was familiar with the Marriott PR program has asked me to outline the steps we take preparing for and actually implementing special events. It's no secret that many of our activities were designed to provide Marriott recognition of special events. Attention to detail plus creativity is essential. In my mind, there are 22 keys to special events:

1. Communicate: Put everything in writing. So many people are involved that you cannot rely upon oral communication. Be thorough and constantly update revisions in plans so all involved personnel are fully informed.

2. On-site inspection: Creative inspiration begins here. What you do depends upon location, type of facility, surroundings, traffic access, proximity to airport, and distance from media.

3. Creative session: What will you do to make news? Depending upon the property, we have run a wide gamut of events, including hot-air balloons, high divers, helicopters that cut ribbons, parades, marching bands, transcontinental antique automobile races, statuesque beauties, and smooth-swimming dolphins that jump through hoops. Zero in on your stunt idea and measure it from the standpoint of both still photographers and action-inclined television news crews. Your idea must be new and different for your city.

4. First draft: Write the first draft of a complete program. Decide what you want to happen, in what order, over what time period, and make it happen on paper.

5. Guest list: Who do you want and how many? How big should your invitation list be to assure the attendance you desire? Cull your list carefully to eliminate duplication and avoid the wrath of anyone scorned by oversight.

6. Distinguished guests: Make personal or written contact with those who are to participate in the program. Advise them of arrival time, desired speaking time limitations, and special provisions for parking and seating.

7. Invitations: Get them out and let them work for you. Plan to go into the mail at least two weeks in advance. The event will dictate the necessity for an RSVP.

8. Media lists: Limit your invitations to those elements of the media who should be interested and whose coverage will be meaningful to your program. Avoid blanket invitations designed to fill your room and merely look good. Depending upon the significance of the actual event, your list should contain a cross section of persons from top management, byline columnists, feature writers, and city desk coverage of reporters and photographers on assignment.

9. Advance publicity: Use personal contact and short column items plus advance interviews to build interest among the news media. Control your advance release of information, being careful not to give away too much or you may not get coverage at the event. Look carefully at the reporter who cannot attend your function, but would like an advance copy of your press kit. If the story is big enough, he or she just might jump your request for a timed-release date.

10. Final working program: This document should include complete timing of every aspect of the program. It should delegate responsibility to specific individuals. It should cover final details on assembly, location on the property, transportation, hosting guest arrivals, registration, VIP package in rooms, entertainment, music, food and beverage service (there should be easy access to both for guests), security, stage platform, lights, P.A. system, direction signs, reserved seating chart, and a minute-by-minute breakdown of the actual official program.

11. Suppliers and equipment: Cross-check all outside purveyors as to their instructions (in writing). Florists or electrical engineers who arrive the day after don't make a contribution. Decorations, lighting, souvenirs, and menus are in this category.

12. Incidentals: Nametags prepared in advance from RSVP's and alphabetized for easy access, guest book, notepads, and pencils, as well as display publicity material, such as color renderings, need to be on hand.

13. Assignments: The public relations director is in complete charge. However he/she cannot do it alone. You will need hostesses, food and beverage people, security, secretaries, messengers, etc.

14. Photographer: The photographer is a key person. Since everything being done is to provide solid picture opportunities, that photographer should be handled by you and given specific assignments. Do not permit him/her to shoot pictures of their own volition. Review the key shots to be made in advance. Check together for background, lighting, and, if outside, take the angle of the sun into consideration. Avoid blatant commercialism. Introduce the hotel's name discreetly, perhaps in a corner of the key photo.

15. Dress rehearsal: Be objective and search for missing items or problem areas. All elements but the principal speakers should be present.

16. News memo: Request coverage using mail, fax, E-mail, etc., forty-eight hours in advance, with follow-up phone campaign where necessary.

17. The big day arrives: Call early morning staff meeting with all participants. Be sure the final written program is held by all and that everyone clearly understands his or her personal assignments.

18. Execute: Only one person is in charge and that's the PR director. Double-check all elements yourself. If you're watching or enjoying the program, something is wrong.

19. Working press coverage: These are your VIP's and don't forget it. Let management host the governor and his aide. You take care of the media.

20. Press kits: Distribute press kits to all media in attendance. Hand carry kits to no-shows within the city and use electronic communication to out-of-towners. Your photographer's photos require same-day service.

21. Smooth finish: Close your event with lunch, dinner or cocktails, and *hors d'oeuvres*. Provide people with a reason to stay and explore the property.

22. Social hour critique: Relax and learn what did and didn't happen. How did the event come off, and was it effective in accomplishing the hotel's goals? Everything is fresh in people's minds, and under the informal atmosphere, you will get a candid analysis.

When Wilt Chamberlain was in New York to play basketball at Madison Square Garden, he liked to stay at the Essex House across from Central Park. Wilt, as every sports fan in America knows, was well over seven feet tall. To accommodate him, McCarthy and I concocted the idea of having a custom-made, eight-foot-long, king-size bed built. On his next trip, with his permission, we turned the unveiling of the world's largest bed into a media event. *Sports Illustrated* and most of the New York sports pages were there to catch Wilt spread out on his most comfortable bed.

Ever alert for targets of opportunity, we caught the curator of the New

York Zoo checking into the Essex House with a tiger pup. The tiger couldn't have been more than two months old, and its appearance at the front desk immediately drew a crowd. We had the curator register with the tiger, using the animal's paw print for signature. It made the AP wire.

LOS ANGELES IS TOP BANANA

Probably our most lavish and festive grand opening occurred in Los Angeles near the airport. The hotel was something smashing. By far, it was Marriott's most expensive project to date. To capitalize, we did a press tour of nationally syndicated travel writers, and twenty-seven made the trip as our guests. For this special evening, the ballroom contained two giant elevated stages, one on each side of the room. Both were draped, ceiling to floor. As one curtain opened, the black-tie-attired audience of more than 500 persons was invited to dance to the music of Harry James and his orchestra. When the James band took a break, the curtain on the other side opened and there was Bob Crosby and his full orchestra. It was non-stop dance music. Of the more than twenty-five big name Hollywood stars present, Bob Hope and John Wayne carried top billing. In typical fashion, McCarthy and I put our heads together looking for that little something extra. On the phone, we convinced New York's gossip columnist, Hy Gardner, not only to join us in Los Angeles, but also to be prepared to don the costume of our doorman to receive the celebrity guests as they arrived. Under the white helmet and red dress coat with huge white buttons, we were curious to see how many of the stars would recognize him. It was John Wayne who did the double take. Initially, he passed Hy as he stepped from the limousine. He suddenly turned, took a second look, and burst out laughing. They hugged in typical Hollywood fashion.

EUROPE WELCOMES MARRIOTT

Holland was to be home to our first European hotel. The Marriott marketing quartet made several trips abroad, feeling that the customs probably were quite different than those in the U.S. The location of our Amsterdam hotel was in the center of the Liedseplain. It was comparable to New York's Fifth Avenue or Chicago's Michigan Avenue. Everyone connected with the Amsterdam hotel counseled us against using the promotional techniques for which we had become famous in the States. They were convinced that Europeans were far more conservative than Americans were and that the usual flamboyant approach wouldn't work.

On the verge of buying their concept, I finally mediated the discussions by stating that we would play down the groundbreaking, but do something special for the opening. There was considerable trepidation on everyone's part, including mine, when we selected our ribbon-cutting stunt. The hotel was only about ten stories tall. I wanted something dramatic and went in search of a special kind of high diver. In Belgium, I found a man about forty years old, who agreed to take a dive off the hotel's roof into a rubber pool built in the middle of the street in front of the property. The pool was four feet deep, and I wanted assurance that the diver understood the parameters. He not only understood the situation with the ribbon stretched over the top of the pool, but he suggested that we introduce fire in the pool, which he was prepared to dive through. I had never worried about safety in any of our events, but this time my heart was in my throat. It was not an easy plan to sell to the quartet and management, but with increased insurance, they agreed to go ahead. Would the local press and the European syndicates go for the story? On that fateful day, with Jim Durbin and Bud Grice joining me in the nervous wreck department, traffic was stopped and a crowd of about 1,000 gathered. My man did a beautiful swan dive off the roof into the fiery pool and emerged smiling, obviously unhurt. The next day's papers carried a series of three photographs on their front pages. We could not have asked for better coverage. The pressure was off and everyone involved breathed a sigh of relief as we flew home.

HOW TO DIG A HOLE WITHOUT FALLING IN

With so many precedents having been set, it's almost axiomatic that every new hotel shall have a groundbreaking. The trick is to be able to dig that hole, preferably without the traditional shovel, and to avoid tumbling into your own hole and being trapped in the morass of inattention to detail.

There is an art and almost a science to the development and execution of exciting, news-making special events. There is no formula for its creation. Ideas can be as prolific and subject matter as diverse as the capability of the creative thinkers. There are so few true news stories in conjunction with hotels. Facing the facts, only when a new hotel is announced, when it is opened, when management personnel is announced, and, perhaps when a new restaurant is added, is there a semblance of news. Beyond that point, further exposure falls into feature story placement and special events, with the latter providing the wherewithal for a flow of publicity rather than a single placement. The special event could be the difference between a ho-hum attitude on the part of the hotel's prospective customers and the generation of some genuine excitement. It's certainly worth trying for.

Good judgment is a prerequisite, so be selective with the basic idea. Your event should parallel the image you are trying to develop. If you're selling staid conservatism, modern elegance or fun, food, and excitement, your event should be a reflection of the entire marketing approach. Coverage for the sheer weight of it is not the answer.

In Houston, Texas, there was concern that the local populace would misread the quality level of the property principally because its name was unfamiliar in that city, and because the hotel was built with a low-rise profile. To establish its quality construction and high standards of service, a story was placed with the *Houston Post* that took the exact opposite position to the mundane, "See Europe on $5.00 per day." The *Houston Post* article read, "The new Marriott, $150.00 per day, Dahling . . . and worth it." A tone was immediately established and the hotel has gone on to its prestigious position in the community.

Remember your purpose. Assuming media coverage is a prime consideration, don't lose sight of the fact that twenty people (media reps) are your key audience and they represent a readership or viewers of hundreds of thousands of prospective customers. Oftentimes, management gets so involved in the event itself that they may forget its primary purpose. In their enthusiasm to entertain the maximum number of business leaders, management may select a late afternoon time for the ceremonies. This could be disastrous from the standpoint of news coverage. Similarly, the selection of either a Monday or Friday or a weekend for your event simply means your potential for media coverage is substantially reduced. For maximum coverage, counsel management to plan a midweek day and schedule it for the morning. This will permit most media to meet their deadlines. Usually the highlight can be boiled down into two minutes, during which the still photographers and the TV action crews do their thing. The elements that either lead up to or away from those moments are as essential as window dressing.

Whenever the marketing director leaves the company, you can anticipate his or her departure as the beginning of the end for your relationship as public relations counsel. After the tenth year of our Marriott association, Bud Grice was "retired." His contribution to the Marriott success story had been so large that I personally never believed he would be asked to leave. From long, agonizing experience, it was clear to me that every new marketing person wants his or her own team. Regardless of your impact on the company and the agency's positive recognition, sooner or later the new marketing person will have his or her way. If your agency has performed well and continues to do so, the new marketing person will not be credited. It's simply business as usual. It may take time, but the new leader has to find a way to get you out.

Two years later, an ambitious and unscrupulous young man forced Tom McCarthy out. That was a clear sign that our days were numbered. Over the years, Tom and I had had a gentleman's agreement that our agency would not accept another hotel account while we were in Marriott's employ. Our reputation had grown along with Marriott, and we had several offers from other hotel chains and resort properties, all of which I turned down. One year after McCarthy left, I decided it was time for the Cushman agency to move on. There was no sense waiting for the inevitable. Things were never going to be the same, even though we still had Jim Durbin's confidence and a very positive relationship with most hotel GMs and directors of marketing in the field. I loved the company and had loved working with its key men, and it tore my guts out to resign. Marriott was one of our largest accounts at that time with the number of hotels, three cruise ships, two Great America Theme Parks, along with the fact that each of the three Chicago hotels were individual clients. It had been thirteen wonderful years, but it was time to say good-bye.

On February 5, 1997, I was the recipient of the Hospitality Sales and Marketing Association International's highest public relations award. I was presented with the Winthrop W. Grice Award in front of a black-tie crowd of 1,000 at the New York Marriott Marquis and lauded for what they called my "outstanding professionalism during more than fifty years of work in the hospitality and tourism industry." The annual event is the largest and most prominent within the travel industry. Although Bud Grice had been long gone, I couldn't help but think he might be pleased.

CHAPTER 10

"St. Louis: The Meeting Place," and Payola in Mexico _____

More than just a slogan, it was the positive public
relations program that played a major role in the amazing
revitalization of a great city and county.

Marriott was our catalyst, our launching pad into major national PR accounts. Initially, they came from within the travel and tourism business. As soon as I had closed the door on our Marriott relationship, our company released information to the effect that the door was now open for any new prospects. We had sustained our verbal agreement not to accept other hotel chains and that agreement was finished. The staff was in a panic over concern for their jobs. There was no denying we had taken a giant reduction in income, and in many ways it was reminiscent of our earlier days when the banking incident had caused me to resign all entertainment clients. We had a great staff and I didn't want to lose a single person, so I bit the bullet and stood pat, telling everyone that they need not fear for their security. I was confident that the word in the field regarding our capability was strong and that some of the people I had turned down would find us. And that's exactly what happened.

Within two weeks, the calls came with a rush. We quickly heard from Ramada International, Holiday Inns, Best Western, and Quality Inns. In the midst of this happy activity, I received a call from the general manager of the St. Louis Marriott. He had always been a staunch booster and, in addition to his hotel responsibilities, he was serving on a city and county commission to find a public relations agency for St. Louis. On the phone, he explained that the search was on, but he wanted me to be aware that his commission would undoubtedly be prejudiced in favor of any local PR organization. At that time, Aaron D. Cushman & Associates, Inc., did not have a St. Louis office and was therefore considered a foreign corporation. One strike against us. I have always been a risk taker and the proposition was so interesting, I decided to go for it.

In the very first meeting with County Chairman Gene McNary and Project Manager John G. (Jack) Walsh, I did a lot of listening. They explained that the city's average hotel occupancy that year (1977) was less than sixty percent, no new hotel construction was on the horizon, and conditions were generally dormant. They kept emphasizing the need to bring convention business to St. Louis. In my years with Marriott, I had learned a great deal about group and convention business. Without fear of contradiction, I was comfortable taking the expert's position and quietly telling the assembled commission members that they were totally incorrect in evaluating their needs. Apparently every other PR group with whom they had spoken unanimously concurred with their opinion. For a quick moment, the room went deathly silent. My Marriott friend suddenly closed his eyes and, unobserved by anyone at the round table but me, began to slowly shake his head.

I caught the hint but figured, "What the hell?" If I didn't think their position was right, how could I rationalize taking the easy road and agreeing with it. Besides, if we got the business, I knew we could never be successful competing with Chicago for convention business. To fumble around and admit making a mistake would weaken our sales position, and much more importantly, I was convinced I had been correct, even if they did not agree with my position.

"Gentlemen," I said, "I have just spent thirteen years with Marriott Hotels, and I hope you will admit that they were second to none in the sale of group business. It's because of that extensive first-hand experience that I would like to make my position clear. First, I do not believe that you can successfully compete with your existing physical facilities against other Midwestern cities like Chicago. Second, large conventions, were you able to sell them, would fill your downtown hotels but do nothing for outlying properties in the county. Since a portion of your financial support comes from all hotels, large and small, you would create a large schism and considerable dissatisfaction. Lastly and most importantly, corporate meetings represent three times the total revenue that conventions do and, despite the fact that each group may be smaller than a convention, group sales represent three times as many people. Your target should be the enticement of corporate meeting planners, not convention directors."

For several minutes, no one said a word. Mr. McNary then asked me to leave the room for a few minutes while they discussed what they had just heard. In the adjoining anteroom, I was almost ready to pack up my material and leave. It didn't seem logical that this group of seven prominent men, each successful in their own business, was about to be convinced that they had made an error in judgment – particularly by a company that didn't reside in St. Louis. Fifteen minutes later, they invited me back and said, "You're hired."

It was to become the single most successful rebirth of a major city, beginning in 1977 in conjunction with the fiftieth anniversary of Lindbergh's historic flight in the "Spirit of St. Louis." What better opportunity to launch the new spirit of St. Louis, building on all the area's assets and accomplishments? It not only would instill greater pride in St. Louisans, but would also exploit the many advantages of the area, attracting visitors and new business.

It started with in-depth market research to learn what meeting planners needed and wanted in an area, and further, what they thought of St. Louis. Results showed that more often than not, images were either formed on misconceptions of what the city had to offer, or there was no image at all. In fact, the research showed that meeting planners had no antipathy for St. Louis. They did not have negative thoughts about the area. They simply didn't think about St. Louis.

To spread the word that St. Louis had been rebuilt and revitalized by a dramatic infusion of money and leadership, a campaign dubbed, "St. Louis: The Meeting Place" was initiated by the combination of D'Arcy, McManus & Masius (advertising) and Aaron D. Cushman & Associates (public relations). The initial story ideas provided to the press included:

1. Location at the geographic hub of the U.S.

2. Within a three-hour flight or less from any major city in the country

3. Over 390 meeting rooms suited for groups of up to one hundred people located in area hotels

4. Largest corporate headquarters area in the Midwest

5. Eleventh largest Standard Metropolitan Statistical area in this country

6. Second largest auto assembly area

7. An aerospace manufacturing hub of the nation

8. Transportation hub: the second largest rail center in the U.S.; meeting

place of five interstate highways; and the largest inland port in the country.

Within the first eight months, *Hotel/Motel Insider Newsletter* reported hotel occupancy figures rose to eighty-one percent, accompanied by all the attendant advantages of business stimulation. In the first year, the program had revitalized the area's efforts to attract business and leisure travelers. The St. Louis community was enjoying widespread recognition as an even better place to meet than it had been three-quarters of a century ago, when "Meet Me in St. Louis" became the popular refrain of the 1904 World's Fair. St. Louis and its assets have been featured by more than 700 different media since the first publicity placement. Total campaign impressions exceeded 486 million. The scope of media coverage ranges from international wire services and network television to national business, travel and meeting publications, to newspapers in cities throughout the United States. Some of our national magazine placements were in *Business Week, Dun's Review, Forbes, Town & Country,* and *U.S. News & World Report.* Specialty publications like *Advertising Age, American Way, Association Management, Flightime, Hotel & Motel Management, Lodging Hospitality, Meeting News, Medical Meetings, Motor News, Realities, TWA Ambassador, Travel Agent,* and *Travel Weekly* carried articles. In some cases, they were five and six pages in length.

In addition to the *Wall Street Journal,* some of the major story and photo placements came from the *New York Times, Chicago Tribune* and *Chicago Sun-Times, Atlanta Journal, Boston Globe, Cincinnati Enquirer, Cleveland Press, Dallas Morning Star, Louisville Times,* and the *London Times.* The broadcast outlets, both radio and television, were too numerous to list.

By 1979, seeing the success that we were having in media and watching the positive meeting planner reaction, I suggested to Jack Walsh that we package a meeting planner seminar and pinpoint the people we were seeking. After coordinating with the city fathers, an invitation was sent to fifty corporate meeting planners. We encouraged *Meetings and Conventions* magazine to co-sponsor the seminar and to be responsible for the serious elements of the curriculum, while we concentrated on exposing the attendees to the existing array of hotels, fine restaurants, cultural and entertainment features of the city. The combination of publicity and seminar brought St. Louis, city and county, 1.2 million people who spent $294.3 million. The campaign played a key role in accruing an influx of capital investments of over one billion dollars, and a forty-two percent increase in hotel lodging space.

Direct bookings were not the goal of the seminar, but nonetheless, seven of the thirty planners who attended did book following the seminar. Meeting planner seminars became an annual thing with County Supervisor Gene McNary saying, "Once corporate meeting planners are reintroduced to St. Louis, their outdated images of what used to be a conservative community will go right down the river." *Meetings & Conventions* magazine said, "Obviously, there is a seemingly endless list of details involved in the planning of such a seminar program, and Aaron Cushman & Associates, public relations counsel for 'The Meeting Place' campaign, was at the helm as the organizer with Maritz Travel handling transportation and transfers."

Following the second year of the St. Louis campaign, we opened an office in Clayton, Missouri, close to county headquarters. At that time, a most fortunate thing happened when young Tom Amberg sauntered into the Cushman office. I honestly cannot recall who discovered whom, but I quickly found out that Tom had been a journalist working for the *St. Louis Globe Democrat* for the past twelve years. He was one of those fellows one instantly likes. Our initial conversation lasted a couple of days, and I hired him for our St. Louis office. Within four months, Tom was managing our office and doing very well. He was very bright and well-connected in the community, and made great strides in recognizing the differences between his previous job as a newspaperman and his current assignment in PR. We worked side by side for several years, and he was a quick learner. I tried to teach him as much about selling the public relations business as I could during the few days each month I spent in St. Louis. Mostly, he had to grasp the examples of successful campaigns we had conducted for others before he joined the company. Tom Amberg became a great acquisition for the company, and a loyal and trusted friend. Under his guidance, our St. Louis office flourished. He handpicked a marvelous staff of hard-working professionals who contributed to our growth. Among our top people were Mary Nowotny, Jim Telle, Beth Fagan, Doug Arnold, Mark Bretz, David Arns, and Karen Dregley.

It was through Tom's connection in the Missouri governor's office that our company was offered the PR account for the state. To avoid any conflict of interest, we resigned the St. Louis relationship after five great years. Frankly, I was glad to get away from Mr. Walsh. He was a pontifical, political appointee and expected everyone to periodically kiss his rear end. I never could play his game.

Fran Kerchival, another Marriott escapee who had been director of sales at several of their hotels, was a welcome voice. Fran was one of the "fun-loving" guys within the Marriott organization, and we had shared many an evening together. He told me he had just been appointed president of Pickett Suite Hotels. At the moment, they were a non-existent hotel company with their first property under construction in Columbus, Ohio. He described Jim Pickett's plans to build a national chain of all-suites hotels across the U.S. and wanted to know if I was interested in working with him as PR counsel. Before giving him a quick "yes," my only question was regarding Mr. Pickett's ability to finance this would-be chain. Fran was convinced that Mr. Pickett had both the personal bankroll and the financial contacts to cover the long haul. I jumped on his bandwagon with the understanding that representing Pickett in no way was an exclusive relationship. Our company was to be free to work with other hotels that were not competitive. We shook hands and another friendship became a long-term business association. Like the PR business, the hotel industry is a small fraternity.

Shortly before Kerchival's contact, I had interviewed and hired a great young woman. A person who loved media contact, Cher Patric Cox was the perfect account executive for Pickett hotels. She had come to me from Los Angeles, where she had been assistant producer of the Dinah Shore network television show. She was Swedish-Irish, but her knowledge of Yiddish words was astounding. "How come?" I asked. "When you work with the likes of Jerry Lewis, Milton Berle, Jack Leonard, and all the other comedians who played on the 'Dinah Shore Show,' you pick up the Yiddish shtick," she responded. Full of laughs but nobody's fool, Cher had that knack for creativity. When she worked on an assignment, no one gave it more hustle.

Columbus, Ohio, never knew what hit them. Using our Marriott techniques, we went after the area communities with a vengeance. Starting with a local press conference, we began building recognition for the hotel and for Jim Pickett personally. Next came the first architect's drawings and financial information, followed by a barrage of people features and amenity information. Cher and I had an affinity for clever ideas. Watching Spider Dan get arrested after he had climbed Sears Tower in Chicago, we decided to use him in our topping-out ceremony for the Columbus Pickett. Spider Dan climbed skyscrapers without using ropes or other tools and had always drawn a crowd. Only in our case, it was to be legitimate, and he would be under contract.

Most Columbus politicians will remember forever the day that he began his climb up the front wall of the fifteen-story hotel. Located in the heart of the downtown Columbus business district, everything came to a screaming halt as Spider Dan began to gain altitude. Traffic stopped. Uncountable herds of people crowded the street in front of the building, and office workers leaned out their windows to watch the proceedings. Fran and I had protected Pickett with added insurance and I figured if he could climb Sears Tower, one hundred plus floors, he could probably climb our fifteen-story building without incident.

Sure, the Columbus papers were there. However, the interesting media story was the TV coverage. They arrived as he began to go up and didn't leave until he mounted the Pickett flag atop the roof several hours later. The hotel and Spider Dan were on camera for at least four hours. People were beginning to recognize the Pickett name.

Some months later, prior to the grand opening, Cher dashed into my office with an Indiana newspaper in her hand. "I've got our opening stunt," she exclaimed. We had struggled searching for the right idea. In this case, we needed an event that was ultra-conservative and dignified in keeping with the location and the décor of the hotel. We had cast aside every creative thought as not fitting the occasion. With that as background, I wanted to know what had gotten her so excited. "I've contacted the Royal Lipizzan Stallions organization and they have agreed to be the feature at our opening." My comment was, "Great, but what will it cost us?"

"They are scheduled to do a performance the night before within a few hundred miles of Columbus and are happy to play our gig for $5,000. Their normal fee for a show is $25,000. How's that?" Cher asked.

The Lipizzans were perfect for the Pickett. They certainly added the touch of dignity and class that we had searched for. Our agreement called for the stallions to perform their show in the street directly in front of the hotel's entrance. The conclusion of their performance would have all their riders and horses lined up to literally charge through the official opening ribbon, which was to be held by the governor of Ohio, the mayor of Columbus, Jim Pickett, and Fran Kerchival. It was a repeat performance of our topping-out ceremony. This time, the street in front of the hotel was closed by official decree, replete with police barricades. With the advance publicity, thousands came to view the show, including those lucky folks working in adjacent high-rise buildings, who were able to hang out of their windows. Local media coverage was strong, and this time we made the national wire services. Fran, Jim, Cher, and I went on to build and open fifteen hotels in eight years, before Pickett sold out to Guest Quarters. In the end, it was the financial demands required by expansion that Jim Pickett couldn't handle.

During the time that we handled the Pickett account, we had also gone to work for Ramada International out of Phoenix, Arizona. They were in the midst of planning and construction for their Renaissance brand, which was to come on stream within a year. In addition to hundreds of motor hotels around the country, they owned and operated the two Tropicana Hotels in Las Vegas and Atlantic City. Ramada was interested in creating more awareness for these gaming properties. In our initial meeting, all parties concluded that we should begin with the Vegas hotel.

Our first inspection visit indicated that the hotel was in decent shape, but they needed to increase occupancy without reducing room rates. By doing so, they would automatically feel an increase in gaming revenue. Back in Chicago, our crew held several brainstorming sessions searching for answers. After doing some research, one of our conclusions was that people didn't gamble because they didn't know how, and were embarrassed to appear stupid in a casino. Affluent people who could afford to gamble felt this way, as did blue-collar workers. If the hotel could conduct a gaming school open to one and all at no charge, we felt it could be meaningful. Furthermore, we concluded that it gave us the opportunity to conduct a national media tour designed to explain the gaming school concept. Phoenix Ramada thought the idea had merit, then authorized us to proceed to discuss the gaming school idea with the Tropicana manager and the head of gaming. They were reluctant, but conceded it was feasible, and agreed to try it for three months. With their acceptance and cooperation, we began a search of Tropicana gaming personnel to staff our national road show. We needed to find a dealer or pit boss who understood all aspects of every gambling game. Someone who could speak well and be easily understood, and someone whose image would reflect the hotel's quality and elevate the overall image of gambling.

We interviewed at least a dozen people who were admittedly knowledgeable, but couldn't fulfill our other requirements. When Sherry Anderson walked into the room all I could say was, "Wow!" She was six feet tall, blonde with blue eyes, and knockout gorgeous. Was she a beautiful, dumb blonde, or could she be our person? We talked for just five minutes before I realized that Sherry was very bright, quite articulate, and didn't want the job. She had no interest in going on the road to do newspaper and television interviews. She had been a showgirl in the chorus line at the Tropicana before she took a fall off the stage and injured her back. Everyone on the staff thought the world of her, and management trained her to be a dealer. She did that job well and was promoted to pit boss, where she presently worked.

Sherry wasn't interested in an all-expense-paid U.S. tour. She wasn't interested in the publicity that would come her way. She, at a little over thirty, didn't want to be discovered by Hollywood, and she wasn't interested in the additional money that the hotel would pay. I tried for over an hour to convince her that it would be worth her while to make the gaming school happen on the road. No matter what I said, she wasn't buying. About to give up, I got off the personal approach and started talking about what this trip would do for the hotel – how, if successful, it could mean better times for the hotel and its employees. No dumbbell, Sherry was aware of the problems the hotel currently faced, and that's what ultimately got her to say she would do it. She asked me several times if I felt that what she was about to do could really make a difference in Las Vegas.

Sherry was outfitted in a tuxedo. She would have looked good in rags. We packaged a blackjack tabletop of cloth and a similar replica of a craps table to take on the tour. Back in Chicago, the Cushman staff had the job of booking the national tour.

Initially, we were concerned about the acceptance that media might give, so we decided to start Sherry in smaller markets. It would also give her a chance to relax and get familiar with the kind of questions that would be forthcoming. The Tropicana Hotel in Las Vegas opened the first gaming school in town and was amazed at the numbers of people who came. Today, almost every hotel on the strip has its own gaming school open to the public. As for Miss Anderson, she appeared in twenty-seven market cities, including two national television spots. In the twelve months that followed Sherry's tour, gaming revenue at the Tropicana went up eleven percent.

We now had three offices, including St. Louis, and Century City, California. Cushman & Associates was servicing resort properties, including Host Farm and Corral in Lancaster, Pennsylvania; the Dutch Inn, Orlando, Florida; the three resorts owned by Carson in the Chicagoland area; Pheasant Run in St. Charles, Illinois; several properties in Palm Springs, California; and Lodge of the Four Seasons in the Lake of the Ozarks. Some individual properties which the agency serviced included The Four Seasons Hotel, three Downtown Holiday Inns, Hotel 21 East, and Ambassador East and

West in Chicago; the Adams Mark and Ritz Carlton in St. Louis; the Hamilton Hotel in Itasca, Illinois; and Sheraton Hotels in Northbrook and Naperville, Illinois. We also opened the Omni Hotel at the St. Louis Union Station.

By 1991, we were ranked twenty-fifth largest public relations agency in the country. The list included those owned by advertising agencies. That same year, we were ranked twelfth largest independent PR agency nationally, and had grown to become the sixth or seventh largest in Chicago. Our client list included Chrysler, Motorola, Ralston Purina, Serta Mattress, Keebler Cookie Co., Warner Lambert, State of Missouri, Mayo Clinic, Con Agra, Armour Foods, the Association of Chicagoland & Northern Indiana McDonald's, Chicago Federation of Labor, National Root Beer Institute, Orange Crush, Hires Root Beer, Fuzzbuster Radar, Maytag, and Century 21 Real Estate Co., in addition to our hotel and travel destination business.

In 1973, I was accepted into the Society of American Travel Writers (SATW). This was principally a society of journalists, which included travel editors, newspaper and magazine travel writers, and freelance writers. This august group permitted a small percentage of their membership to be public relations people specializing in travel. Most PR people in SATW accepted their second-class citizen role because membership enabled them to build close personal relationships with the writers. Actually, it was a wonderful group of people from every state in the union, and each year we convened in a different part of the world. When SATW accepted an invitation to a convention, whether international or domestic, the convention site could anticipate about $10 million in publicity. That's because our conventions were business and working sessions. We toured the area extensively in search of story material. For years, I served the Society by becoming chairman of one committee after another. I was elected to the board of directors and served two terms for four years. PR members were associate members, and I was elected chairman of the associates' council. The Society honored me with several silver President's Plates, and, as the '90s began, they named me a Marco Polo, their highest award. Of some 1,200 members, there are only twenty-one Marco Polos. The most important aspect of membership has been my ability to know almost every travel writer in this country on a first-name basis. Traveling together for so many years, Doris and I made many good friends, as well as business contacts.

In the beginning, our activity was limited to the entire center of the United States, from Minnesota all the way to the Gulf of Mexico and from

Ohio on the East to Texas on the West. But once we entered into the Caribbean, the agency covered clients in Barbados, Palmas Del Mar, Puerto Rico, Mullet Bay, Jamaica, and the Bahamas. International destinations included the governments of Sweden, South Korea, Singapore, Cayman Islands, Canada, and Mexico. Some say our eleven-year relationship was a world record for length of retention by Mexico. Officially, our client was the Mexican National Tourist Council and former President Miguel Aleman headed it.

At the outset, I sent Phil Hoffman and Cher Patric Cox to Berlitz to learn Spanish. I made the mistake of not going myself. Through the Acapulco Marriott adventure, I had picked up enough Spanish to get by socially, in restaurants and traveling, but I could not hold a conversation or understand what our Mexican colleagues were saying. Even though Phil and Cher became proficient, I was not comfortable unless our meetings were in English.

Twice each year, President Aleman called a meeting in New York, and all agencies were required to attend and prepare a progress report. *El Presidente* was my client. I was in his employ, and his English was better than my Spanish, so we had to converse in English. Language limitations always kept me embarrassed in his presence. In July, our sixth year together, I quietly asked Señor Aleman if I could have a moment with him in private after the business meeting. He motioned me to follow him as we left the conference room, and he led me into his private office. "Now, Mister Cushman, tell me what is on your mind," he asked.

"Mr. President," I started, "the government of Canada has inquired as to my company's availability to undertake a public relations program for them. I have studied all aspects of a possible campaign to see if there is a competitive element that might be detrimental to Mexico. I have looked at the markets carefully and find them to be quite different; each requires its own individual approach. I'm certain you can understand my desire to work with Canada in addition to your country, but I would never commit without discussing the situation with you and hopefully receiving your blessing."

President Aleman looked right into my eyes as he put his hand through his greying hair. For about a minute, he said nothing. Mentally, I was reviewing his options. He could say "no" or "yes" or, heaven forbid, "you are fired." I knew he and the work-a-day leadership of the Mexican National Tourist Council were very pleased with what we had accomplished on their behalf, and I hoped he liked my honesty. After what seemed an eternity, he said, "Mr. Cushman, I give you my approval, but please don't tell anyone."

Mexico had forty-one tourist destinations, and Cher, Phil, and I visited every one. There is no way you can sell a product without being totally familiar with it. If we were to write editorial material for U.S. media consumption, we had to know our stuff. It seemed like we were on the road forever, which reminds me of something that occurred during the Marriott days. One of my senior men came to me and said that he was aware that I took all the good trips to Europe, South America, and the Caribbean while he was traveling to Omaha, St. Louis, Louisville, etc. I told him he was right and asked if he would like to take the good trips for a while.

Actuality and what is in the eye of the beholder are often times quite different. What he didn't realize is that the so-called good trips called for a long jet flight, sometimes at odd hours, a taxi ride to your meeting, several hours or perhaps days locked in a hotel meeting room, a taxi ride back to the airport, and the return trip home. Little if anything is seen of the local area, and there is even less time for sleep. It took eighteen months for him to come back to me and ask, "Do you think you can find someone else to take the good trips?"

For Mexico, we used our travel page contacts to make quick major placements in magazines like *Conde Nast Traveler* and *Travel & Leisure*. Next we approached syndicated travel columnists who worked primarily out of New York, Los Angeles, and San Francisco. In the first three years with Mexico, we organized one national SATW convention in Mexico City with pre- and post-trips to Acapulco and Puerto Vallarta. Over 250 writers came back with stories and pictures. SATW is subdivided into five geographic chapters, and we had two chapters come to Guadalajara for regional meetings. In retrospect, our initial approach to encouraging more Americans to visit Mexico was concentrated in the travel sections. Quite a mundane approach. Then we got talking about peripheral publications and that led to a giant effort toward special interest publications. We began listing areas and they seemed to go on infinitely. There was tennis and golf, swimming, snorkeling, scuba, and fishing. There were the beaches, weather, flora and fauna, history of ancient civilizations, history of Jews in Mexico, architecture, archeology, private aircraft, boating, costumes, food peculiar to Mexico, the unusual insurance and real estate government regulations, silver and gold mining, crafts, and even medical publications. Once the categories were reasonably complete, we began fleshing out the numbers of magazines within each category. Our list came to several hundred to be added to our travel list.

Phil put together a media tour of seven magazine editors from within the medical field. When discussing medical questions in Mexico with Americans, all conversation began and ended with "The Touristas." Our *gringos* (U.S. citizens) were told to fear the water in Mexico and be careful of what they ate. Practically no one was familiar with Mexico's first rate hospitals and the fact that they had a quality medical school in Guadalajara. Phil convinced these editors that they owed it to their readers (mostly physicians) to examine Mexican medical facilities first-hand. We were well aware that doctors were among the major traveling groups in the U.S., and, with modest educational seminars, they were able to write off the expense of a trip. Mexico wanted more medical group meetings, and we felt that the media tour was a step in the right direction.

One by one, we attacked each special interest group of magazines using different approaches. The volume of publicity was overwhelming. The Mexican National Tourist Council had never seen such vast coverage, and tourism was up in response. Our company was cleared to go national with our material.

Rumor had always persisted that to do business with Mexico meant that you were forced into kickbacks. In the first two years everything was clean as a whistle. Suddenly, the PR group head who handled the West Coast wanted a meeting in our Chicago office. He was Mexico City's primary PR contact at that time and had been involved in the interview process when we were selected. I had no doubt that he was well-connected in Mexico and had been for many years before we came into the picture. The PR representative gave no reason for his trip from Los Angeles to Chicago, but indicated it was hush-hush.

After the handshakes and coffee, he got right down to business. "Mexico is asking all PR representatives in the U.S. to return ten percent of their monthly fee," he said. I sat there dumbfounded. Why now, after over two years of working together? It didn't make sense. To top it off, he told me to avoid being too obvious, Mexico requested that the funds be sent to his office in Los Angeles and he was to hand-carry the envelopes to Mexico City.

I was fuming inside, but proud of myself for maintaining my composure. I listened and told him I would think about it and give him a call. Without mincing words, he let me know that the kickback was mandatory if we were to retain the business.

When he left, I closed the door to my office and sat back to think. I certainly didn't want to lose the Mexican business, but on the other hand, I had never been a party to this kind of activity, and I didn't want to start now. It looked like another one of those, "say good-bye" client situations. But before kissing it off, I was determined to hear it straight from the horse's mouth. I was going to Mexico.

The Director General of the Mexican National Tourist Council was Señor Moreno, and I requested a meeting with him personally. Of course, he wanted to know the subject matter, and I simply said it was personal and I would discuss it with him face to face. I did tell him I was coming at my own expense.

Two days later, I sat in his office in Mexico City asking myself how to broach this very tender subject. There was just no way to soft-pedal what I had been told, so I gave it to him straight. I wanted to know if those orders had indeed come from the top, meaning from him.

Moreno glared at me across his desk. He was apparently in shock. Was it because of my frankness or because he was completely in the dark? He spoke very softly and slowly in perfect English and asked me who had given me this information. His face was flushed, and he was obviously angry. "I have never given those instructions to anyone. I am furious that someone in our employ would make this kind of allegation, and I shall handle that situation quickly. Mr. Cushman, be assured that we have no intention of changing our method of how we work together financially. Thank you for taking your personal time to bring this to my attention." I took the next plane home and the question was never raised again during our eleven-year tenure with Mexico.

CHAPTER 11

Crisis Communications:
Every Situation is Different ____

*The most carefully laid plans must constantly be
re-evaluated and refined, and planning is just the beginning.*

We had cut our eyeteeth on crisis and disaster problems, going back to my covering air crashes with the Strategic Air Command. Since those early days, the company had been thrust into at least forty different crisis situations, and none were ever the same. Still, in the big scheme of things, the two most important lessons learned from all of these experiences were: first, even the most carefully laid plans must constantly be re-evaluated and refined, and, second, planning is just the beginning. Since every crisis is different, it's a mistake to assume that any plan will provide all the answers. The best defense is staying on your toes. "Been there, done that," doesn't really apply.

Every example I could think of emphasized the dissimilarity of crisis circumstances and the differences in planning that are necessary. Take the case of Hygrade Hot Dogs headquartered near Detroit, Michigan. A frantic CEO contacted us to explain that *Consumer Reports* magazine had done a story alleging the discovery of rodent hairs and other impurities in many branded hot dog products. Because Hygrade Ball Park Franks is among the largest producers, they got hit the hardest. Before the ink on the story was dry, cancellations came pouring in from concerned distributors. On the phone, the CEO said, "If this trend continues much longer, it could put us out of business."

By the next morning, we were in his office reading the article and starting the creative juices flowing. The tour of the plant was clear evidence that it was spotless stainless steel and that every precaution had been taken to protect the consumer and guarantee a fresh, wholesome product. We mutually decided to open the plant to all media and encourage their unsuppressed investigation. The local papers, the wire services, the food trades, and the grocery trades were encouraged to take a look for themselves. Our counsel was to forego any legal action against the publication to avoid prolonging the agony. Continued negative exposure would not be helpful. Within four weeks, the downward slide of the sales curve stopped and began to reverse itself.

With Marriott, we had lived through a series of crisis situations that occurred in different cities in the U.S. In Houston, on a Saturday night with the main ballroom jammed to capacity, a tornado literally tore the roof off. Fortunately no one was injured, but several cars in the parking lot were demolished. By having built a history of positive press relations within the Houston community, we were able to minimize the publicity damage.

At the Marriott on the Kennedy Expressway in Chicago, police pulled off a major drug bust. As is their custom, police normally display the volume of drugs and/or weapons found at the site. Knowing the media interest in exactly that picture, we convinced the police to remove all evidence from the hotel, take it to the local police station, and invite the media to take pictures there. Marriott had a single credit in the story.

At other hotel properties, we were notified of a drowning in the pool (an infrequent occurrence), an occasional suicide, and, on very rare occasions, a murder. In each case, we made an effort to minimize the exposure after explaining to each GM that we did not have the power to kill the story.

The Four Seasons Resort at the Lake of the Ozarks is a sprawling multi-acre luxury property. A gas explosion destroyed twenty-four rooms and killed one guest. It was a true disaster and the media climbed all over the story. The resort received a number of convention cancellations as soon as the word got out. Our staff was on location within three hours and, within reason, kept the fallout to as little as possible.

On a sleepy August afternoon in the Midwest, one of our clients made an unpleasant discovery. Samples of feed grain purchased from a local supplier showed traces of chlordane, a suspected carcinogen. Portions of the grain shipment had been fed to livestock used in the company's production of items for human consumption. According to Mary Nowotny, our account supervisor, they were fortunate that no contaminated product entered the processing cycle and that no one was injured or made ill as a result of the contamination. An aggressive quality assurance team detected the contamination and saved consumers who could have been at risk, as well as thousands of dollars' worth of finished product that would have had to be destroyed. Perhaps more seriously, the company's record of safe product production might have been challenged. Even in the absence of these dire consequences, the close call constituted a crisis.

When the crisis arose, our job as crisis management consultants was to maintain the client's credibility and integrity, squelch rumors by correcting inaccuracies, counter employee concern with assurances of product safety and production stability, and contain media exposure as much as possible.

RUSH-HOUR, RAPID-TRANSIT, ELEVATED TRAIN CRASH

Probably the most horrible tragedy in which the agency was ever involved occurred in Chicago, when a rush-hour, rapid-transit, elevated train crashed into the rear of another train stopped at a station. Over 135 passengers were seriously injured and several deaths resulted.

The crisis was complicated because so many thousands of people were riding various trains at that particular time en route to their homes, and families were unsure as to which specific trains were involved in the accident. That single disaster taught our agency a number of lessons. Our client was Louis A. Weiss Memorial Hospital, which happened to be closest to the site of the crash, and hence received most of the injured. The pre-existing disaster plan immediately went into effect, and all doctors and nurses away from the hospital were recalled. Beds and rooms were made ready and, when the hospital ran out of rooms, beds were set up in corridors.

Our responsibility was to obtain names and addresses of each victim and notify families and next of kin. What we did not anticipate was the crush of hundreds of people who jammed the hospital's lobby pleading and demanding to know if their loved one was among the dead or injured. Before and after lists were posted in the lobby, the crowd overwhelmed the staff. Our single most valuable lesson came from the realization that because of the thousands of incoming calls, we were unable to make an outside call. All the lines were jammed, and we had not set aside a private phone for just such an emergency.

Within fifteen minutes of the crash, the media were all over us. They demanded information, which we had as yet not accumulated. Some insisted on speaking to victims, and several photographers were caught by security sneaking up the back stairs, attempting to photograph injured victims.

Shortly after the crisis ended, I approached both major Chicago newspapers and the network affiliate television stations' management and requested a meeting to review media behavior during the emergency. The outcome of those meetings resulted in the creation of a committee of five members of the media and myself to write a set of rules and media guidelines designed to protect the privacy of hospital patients. That booklet, which is still in existence, limits media access to patients and hospitals.

NEO-NAZIS PLAN TO INVADE SKOKIE, ILLINOIS

In the spring of 1978, when the village of Skokie, Illinois, hired the Cushman public relations agency, we both got more than we bargained for. Our initial assignment was to create an awareness throughout Illinois, and perhaps the nation, that Skokie was an excellent municipality with diversified ethnic families, a favorable tax base, cultural and artistic emphasis, and a lifestyle bolstered by a wide range of municipal services not usually found in most communities of its size. The timing turned out to be very fortuitous.

Our program had been underway several months, and we had just finished a presentation to Mayor Albert Smith and the village commission for a coordinated, marketing-oriented communications campaign, combining all the resources of the village under one planning umbrella. We called the program "Skokie Spirit." We received enthusiastic approval, but before we could begin to roll it out, the morning newspapers exploded the surprise story of an impending Nazi march.

The papers, both the *Chicago Tribune* and *Sun-Times*, used the largest and blackest type font I had seen since the papers announced the end of World War II. Frank Collins, leader of the American Neo-Nazi Party, had made an announcement at a press conference that his group intended to march in front of the Skokie Village Hall on Saturday, June 25. It took everyone by surprise.

Skokie was a community of 69,000 people; thirty-nine percent were Jewish and Skokie was the current home of 7,500 survivors of World War II concentration camps. Collins had obviously picked his target carefully and with malice aforethought. If he wanted national attention, he was about to receive even more than he anticipated.

Although the Neo-Nazi-planned demonstration garnered major front-page headlines almost daily, village officials could not neglect their normal daily business of running the community. At their request, we became the central communications resource for all queries. A Cushman team of account executives, headed by Senior Vice President Richard Stahler, was briefed on the facts and allegations. Richard lived in nearby Morton Grove and was familiar with the Skokie area.

Almost immediately, calls began coming in from every state in the nation. Television, radio, and newspaper reporters wanted up-to-the-minute information about the status of the demonstration and Skokie's legal battle to block the march.

As the official link between the village and all media, our ability to communicate effectively was critical in this extraordinary situation. To avoid jeopardizing ongoing legal proceedings or inciting Frank Collins into any form of retaliatory action, attorneys evaluated all written or oral statements disseminated on behalf of the village.

From the moment Collins announced his intention to march in Skokie, the village began its legal battle to block his entry. Each new court action resulted in a flurry of speculation and questions. The agency's account team logged over 1,000 calls in two months. Sometimes our response to litigation had to be ready in a few hours, if not minutes.

UNHAPPY MEDIA PEOPLE

Media representatives were not always happy about dealing with a public relations firm on what they considered to be a major news story. In fact, some were quite hostile and challenged our right to be the sole communications source. Reporters felt that the village, which normally answered calls on routine matters, was hiding behind our firm. When we explained that the village could not respond to the heavy volume of phone calls pouring in and still run itself, most reporters understood. We emphasized that we spoke for the village and could provide the kind of instantaneous response that village political leaders could not.

Skokie was not a nine-to-five public relations challenge. We were on call twenty-four hours a day. Cushman account team's home phone numbers were made available to reporters. Night shift personnel had the same access to current information, as did those on the day shift.

From the beginning, we counseled the village to keep as low a profile as possible considering that the Nazi threat had become an international issue. We responded to questions and, when appropriate, conducted press conferences to update our position. We made no effort to seek publicity. Village officials were asked to appear on talk shows and news programs, but declined. We refused to give Frank Collins and his supporters a public forum.

Many of the phone calls came from concerned citizens who wanted to offer suggestions on handling the demonstration. Suggestions ranged from ignoring the Nazis, to requesting that the media cease coverage, to dressing people as clowns and forming a circle around the Nazis. We counseled the village not to plan any organized response to the Nazis. Skokie's concerns were solely to ensure security on the day of the march and to provide accurate and factual coverage of the event.

SKOKIE SPIRIT

When controversy on the impending demonstration reached a crescendo, the village unveiled "Skokie Spirit." Deflecting attention from the march was not easy. By appropriate timing of the announcement, we were able to capitalize on Skokie's newsworthiness and still focus attention on the positive aspects of the village.

The emotional situation got so hot that the governor called out the National Guard to supplement the local police force and the sheriff's officers. A decision was made that if the Nazi rally took place, police would not allow spectators to drive within one square mile of the rally site and that all local autos in that area would be searched. Bonnie Pechter, spokesman for the militant Jewish Defense League headquartered in New York, said 1,000 JDL members would come to Chicago to confront the Nazis at the Federal Building. "Why? Because we want to let them know we are there," she said. "We want to give them a little preview, let them know what's waiting for them if they march in Skokie."

Sammy Davis, Jr., called the proposed Nazi rally "horrible" and "despicable." Davis added, "I am speaking as a black Jew myself, and I have been one for the past twenty-four years." He also told a press group in McCormick Place, where he was starring in *Stop the World, I Want to Get Off,* "But from every bad comes some good. It's bringing Jews and blacks closer together," and the Jewish targets of the Nazi rally now have "the supportiveness of the entire community of good people."

"I've been to Dachau," said Davis. "I've been picketed by the Nazi party in the past and probably will be in the future."

In Skokie, Mayor Albert J. Smith said, "Although recent developments hopefully will result in the cancellation of the planned Nazi demonstration, the village of Skokie must go ahead with plans to deal with that event." He said approximately 300 police officers and Illinois National Guardsmen would be on hand to keep the peace.

The Skokie police said spectators who arrived on foot would not be searched and those wearing helmets would not be prevented from doing so. "We may have a large number of motorcycle riders that day," said police Sgt. Michael Burns with a slight smile.

Collins and his colleagues continued making scurrilous remarks with anti-Semitic overtones to the press. I had my hands full trying to keep well-meaning private citizens and various organizations, Jewish and gentile, from making emotional statements, which the press was eager to pick up. With over 200 media from all over the world now in Skokie, desperately fighting for any scrap of information to meet their next deadline, private people had microphones, cameras, and note pads thrust in their faces, and were asked what should be done and what they would do.

THE NAZIS BACK OFF

Fortunately, Collins and his band of Nazis backed off, and their Skokie march was cancelled. We prepared statements for political and religious leaders, who expressed relief. "What has happened is now history," said Mayor Smith. "But I would be remiss if I did not express the gratitude of every Skokie resident for the magnificent outpouring of support we received from both Christians and Jews from around the world. Today we look forward to a return to peace and tranquility, a hallmark of the Skokie lifestyle. We are proud of our village's unwavering stand on the issue."

The pressure was off, but we thought of the thousands of people, some peaceful and some apparently bent on violence, ready to pour into town from all over the nation. Add that to the thousands of law enforcement officials and troops rolling in to set up a security perimeter, and we realized the tension-filled atmosphere. Local phone calls reflected a new trend; callers were disturbed by all this hate and all these outsiders using their town, stomping across the private perspectives and cherished memories of their own community. Visualizing brown shirts with swastika armbands marching on Lincoln Avenue was more than they could take. Skokie citizens were glad it was over.

In the final week before the cancellation, to better facilitate communications, we moved our base of operations from our downtown office to Skokie's Village Hall. A bank of phones was installed and assigned exclusively to our agency team. From the new agency command post, we continued to answer phone calls and to speak directly with the international army of media representatives who had arrived. Working side by side with the police information officer, we developed a plan for the issuance of press passes. Large and bright in color, they would quickly identify working press and allow them free access to the demonstration site, which for security reasons was being cordoned off. We located the pressroom in a high school adjacent to the scene of the counterdemonstration. News updates were to be fed to the media each half-hour. Immediately before and after the march, we planned to make village and police officials available for interviewing.

Skokie village leaders were highly intelligent men and women, but their only media experience had been with the local Skokie paper. They were neophytes and totally naïve as to how to conduct themselves when involved in a major television or newspaper interview situation. Some guidelines and some training had to be conducted. Several specific points were made:

1. Expect to be quoted on anything you say. Be certain of your facts and remember that nothing is off the record.

2. You have no editing prerogative. Once the interview is complete, you do not have the option to review and cancel what you may have said. On rare occasions, an unusually considerate interviewer might provide an advance copy. However, requesting and/or anticipating this right is not realistic.

3. You will be briefed as to the media person's background and given any personal idiosyncrasies to be alert to. Each interview subject matter could be different, and PR counsel will provide the basis upon which the news representative was interested in conducting the interview.

4. The Skokie executive is counseled against, "No comment" or "Yes-No," one-word answers. For television, particularly news programs, avoid long answers. They usually like to use thirty-second sound bites.

5. Do not assume anything. It is your responsibility to make your points early in the interview. Do not wait for leading questions before interjecting the points we wish to make. This alleviates the problem of looking back after the interview and rationalizing why certain information was not given with, "But he never asked me the right questions."

6. Limit the interview to the exact subject matter planned and do not volunteer additional information (which may make you look more knowledgeable).

7. The PR representative will be present at the interview, but will be a quiet observer maintaining a low profile. Nevertheless, he will not hesitate to interject himself should a particularly compromising question be raised.

8. Avoid answers that have hidden or double meanings. Organize your thoughts in advance.

9. Don't bluff! Simply say that you do not have accurate information on that subject.

10. Try to eliminate personal physical mannerisms that may distract the audience. These may include twisting or cracking knuckles, pulling on one's ears or nose, wiping eyeglasses, etc.

The Skokie Spirit logo identification abounded and served as a focal point of the deep sense of pride displayed throughout the community. The resultant editorial coverage following the cancellation of the Nazi march focused heavily on the "real" rather than the originally "perceived" Skokie. As for me, it was the first and only time in my life I gave thanks for not having to implement a campaign.

CHAPTER 12

Finding a Home with Century 21_____

Six thousand brokers nationally, a $40 million advertising
budget, and zero allocation for public relations.

Chicago was growing, and we weren't just sitting there watching it happen. We were playing an active role in making the city's skyline change.

After World War II and the Korean conflict, there was a tremendous demand for moderately priced housing. Two of our clients, Winston-Muss and Centex, apparently recognized this expanding market and bought a huge piece of land in Melrose Park, Illinois. Again, it was media friends who gave me the lead. The developers actually built six model homes and erected a circus-style tent adjacent to the models as their sales office. Josh Muss knew the market was alive, but wasn't sure as to the receptivity of their models and pricing. After a modest amount of real estate page publicity and fifty phone queries from one or two ads, we all began to have more confidence.

SELLING HOMES SUPERMARKET STYLE

It was decided to try to sell supermarket style, with long tables along the perimeter of the entire tent, stocked with brochures and floor plans and attended by many members of their sales staff. For fun, we planned to have three couples come at 5 a.m. to simulate camping out enthusiasm. We had publicized that the sales office would open at 8 a.m. When our three couples arrived they found twelve families lying in sleeping bags and pup tents, waiting for the office to open. They had been out there all night.

By the time the office opened, there were fifty people waiting in line and the action began in fast and furious fashion. Each time a sale was made, a bell went off and a large numbered sign, hung dead center in the circus tent, changed to indicate the number of homes remaining. As the day went on, it was like a fever had befallen those in line. They pushed to the tables claiming to be next and couldn't wait to sign the contract. Winston-Muss offered 240 home sites and they sold every one within one weekend.

A mid-size Chicago real estate firm was anxious to communicate to its desired publics the fact that it was now a full-service company capable of handling any transaction or development on a local, regional, national, or international level.

Their interest was to upgrade the perception of Romanek-Golub & Company within the real estate, financial, and insurance communities through a broad array of communications vehicles. At the same time, they wanted to develop and implement marketing support programs for the company's four operating divisions: management, marketing, development, and investment. We then covered every possible avenue for them, from publication of a quarterly newsletter for external and internal distribution to the creation of bylined articles by key executives on current industry subjects. While publicity was deemed an important part of the overall effort, it was by no means the only dimension considered. We became immersed in all aspects of the company's communication needs, from an effective employee information program to creation of support materials, including consumer information pieces on condominium buying and financing, as well as individual property brochures.

The company grew to become one of the top three real estate firms in Chicago, with offices in other major cities and overseas. Their investment portfolio was in excess of $550 million. With Romanek-Golub, the Cushman agency helped to open and market many new downtown skyscrapers, including the Xerox Building, 444 North Michigan Avenue, and 625 North Michigan Avenue.

EARTH CITY: "DISTRESSED PROPERTY"

Earth City is St. Louis' largest industrial/commercial development today, but originally it came with a "distressed property" label. Opinion research conducted by the agency among a cross section of publics indicated the park's primary problems were negative image; unrealistic original development concept; a history of unsuccessful marketing efforts by two previous owner/developers; allegations of flooding problems; lack of new ownership awareness (Ford Motor Credit Corporation); poor identification to airport accessibility; and general lack of knowledge of Earth City compared to other industrial sites. Outside of that, everything was just perfect.

The Cushman St. Louis office developed a full communications program with these strategic targets:

1. Positioning Earth City as the leading industrial/commercial site in metropolitan St. Louis.

2. Emphasizing Ford Motor Credit Corporation as the new owner/ developers in all press releases.

3. Building Earth City's image by emphasizing its strategic location, adjacent to Lambert Field and its proximity to several major state and federal highways.

Ford created a more realistic development plan and we publicized it. As new plants and warehouses were added, we made certain the nation knew of Earth City's marketing success. Our creative staff did a complete redesign of corporate identification and a similar redesign of sales facilities. During the first full year following our retention, acreage sales increased twentyfold and seventeen times as many square feet of space were started compared to the previous year. Within eighteen months Earth City had lost its "distressed property" label.

McCLURG COURT TWIN TOWERS: A REAL CHALLENGE

Jupiter Corporation had a king-sized white elephant on their hands with the McClurg Court's twin towers. With a strong condo market in downtown Chicago, these very attractive high-rise buildings had been ignored. The towers had been open for over a year and were showing occupancy in the area of twenty-five percent. Jerry Wexler, Chairman and CEO of Jupiter, was a very unhappy man. He recruited Jack Schatz, who had been an owner of the Chez Paree, to take over management and sales. As I had mentioned earlier, Jack was both a practicing attorney and a CPA. "Dynamic" would probably best describe Jack. He had a unique way of expressing himself so that everyone he spoke with got the message. Either they got it quickly or they were gone.

Since we'd been together for ten years at the nightclub, Jack looked at me as a comfort factor. He needed to rebuild his entire sales staff and recreate a grand opening for a building that was over a year old. In a sophisticated market like Chicago, we both knew it would take some doing. Jack drove himself and his sales people unmercifully. He was the kind of man who wanted it to happen, and not tomorrow. We met often, *à la* Chez Paree days, and laid our promotional plans carefully.

Between the hard-driving staff and a lot of solid PR work, we sold out one entire building, over 140 apartments, within the first twelve months. Jack talked about developing his own skyscraper near Grand Avenue and Lake Michigan, but before he was able to obtain financing, he died suddenly. Although he seldom let up, working with Jack was a joy.

Because of our strong real estate background, I was not surprised to be invited to present to the broker board of directors of Illinois and Northern Indiana Century 21. We were one of four agencies being considered by the franchise group. The meeting was to be held in a small conference room of their River Road offices. As our team waited in a reception room, we saw the competition was leaving. We shook hands and exchanged pleasantries as often happened on such occasions.

It was Dave Arts and Wanda Gilchrist who welcomed us and guided our team into the inner sanctum where we were introduced to the seven-person board. Five men and two women looked up from their desks, giving us their best smiles. I dreaded being the last to present; you didn't have to be unusually observant to see that this was a group of tired folks who looked slightly bored. Nevertheless, our team of four spoke and showed visual samples, making a point of moving around the room. During the one-hour time limit, I stopped across from each committee member, and from a distance of about one or two feet, stared into their eyes while I covered one element. We tried desperately to keep them awake. When we finished, there were smiling faces everywhere, but I couldn't tell if they liked our material or were just glad it was over and they could go home.

At nine o'clock the next morning, Dave Arts called to invite us back for a second round. It seemed we had made the short list of two. At the conclusion of the second meeting, the board made it clear that we were their first choice. However, before our celebration got out of hand, Dave told me that the "boss man" had to put his stamp of approval on the selection before it became a *fait accompli*.

They, meaning both the board members and the staff, spoke about Lowell Stahl as if he were a fearsome god. His name was mentioned with reverence and seemingly always in hushed tones. On that day, Mr. Stahl may have been the "invisible man," but his presence was felt.

Dave took me to Mr. Stahl's office alone, and my colleagues waited back in the reception room. I didn't know what to expect. It was a happy day and I wasn't going to be concerned. After the hours the committee had put in, I couldn't see anyone overturning their decision unless I took a major pratfall or made some real *faux pas*.

Mr. Stahl was sitting at his desk when I entered. He immediately walked around to shake my hand and said, "Please let me add my congratulations." That was it. There was no inquisition, no cross-examination. It was over, and we had the account. Mr. Stahl could not have been more receptive or friendly. He invited me to join him on his couch, where we chatted for about fifteen minutes and discovered that we lived within half a block of each other. If he was overpowering, dictatorial, or frightening in any way, I certainly didn't see it. I walked out on cloud nine and whispered to myself, "I like this man."

We had lunch together a few days later at his Mid-America Club, conveniently located around the corner from our offices on Wacker Drive. It was then he explained how Century 21 was structured. It was a giant franchise organization with most regions owned by independent operators, like Lowell, and yet the parent corporation owned some geographic territories.

Every franchise operator and every broker member was charged a fee, which became the national marketing budget. With the exception of the cost of the national convention, one hundred percent of the $40 million raised annually was allocated to advertising. In fairness, it should be pointed out that the convention was done in first-class style, opening with a laser light show. After a myriad of awards, the 10,000 or more agents and brokers in a sea of gold jackets were entertained by speakers like former President Gerald Ford and NBC news anchor, Tom Brokaw. There followed top name entertainers like Barbara Mandrell. Their convention was a happening, not dissimilar to the Republican or Democratic conventions. Each state was well-represented with appropriate signage. And throughout the upbeat motivational three days, enthusiasm was sky high. People danced in the aisles to the semi-rock music beat.

GAINING AND HOLDING BROKERS IS THE NAME OF THE GAME

We spent the first five years with Century 21 gaining prestige and recognition for the Illinois and Northern Indiana franchise. Lowell had explained that this impressive image was the key to gaining and holding more brokers throughout his area.

At Lowell's request, we made appearances at all his local and regional broker and agent meetings, where we did our dog and pony show. Brokers could see how the exposure was bringing them more listings and helping to close more sales. We provided publicity support to individual brokers and wrote many people features from among those who wore the gold jackets. We built a cadre of loyal supporters within the company. The regional communications program, coupled with an aggressive staff, was what was making Lowell Stahl's franchise the most profitable within the entire national Century 21 organization. Century 21 Illinois became the talk of the country. People were asking Lowell, "How are you getting all this exposure?"

Lowell Stahl wasn't shy about telling his colleagues in other territories about Cushman. He recommended us to everyone who called, and we expanded our Century 21 relationship by picking up at least three other geographic territories. Finally, the word got to Irvine, California, and we received an invitation to come to their national headquarters and make a presentation for the whole enchilada. After five years with Lowell and attending the annual convention each year, I felt comfortable with all the national players I had met. I knew that Mr. Stahl's recommendation meant a lot, but it wasn't until some years later that I realized that he was regarded as the number-two man in the company, next to chairman and president, Dick Loughlin.

It was a tremendous opportunity, and I wanted to make sure we did our homework. We had become so familiar with the company that planning a national program came almost as second nature. Every person on my staff realized that we had a shot at our first million-dollar account, and they pitched in like never before. To keep us fresh, we decided to do our brainstorming early in the morning instead of staying late at night. I've always found that creativity seems to flourish in the morning. The tempo of our meetings seemed to pick up with each passing day, and ideas were coming fast and furious. When our management group agreed that we were ready, Tom Amberg, now in Chicago as senior vice president, and I booked a flight and headed west.

When we arrived, Dick Loughlin said hello and told me we would be presenting to Bruce Oseland, vice president of marketing, and his assistant, Monte Helm. They both seemed very receptive to each proposed idea, but, for sophisticated marketing men, their questions indicated an amazing lack of knowledge in the PR field. We were with them over two hours and, when we were finished, Bruce asked Monte for his reaction. Sitting in the same room together with us, the question placed Monte in an awkward position. My first impression of Monte was that he was a person who would hesitate to speak his mind, not a stand-alone guy. He proved me wrong when he said, "If they can do what they say they can do, I think it's great." I could have kissed him. There were a few more questions relating more to budget than to creative aspects, and then we shook hands on a deal. Bruce asked me to draw up our contract and he would sign it on behalf of the company. What he said next shook me. "I don't pretend to know anything about your business, and what's more, I don't want to know about public relations. Monte will be your in-house contact from this moment on. Call me only if you have a real problem or some kind of impasse," he said. Before taking our leave, we mutually agreed that a photo simulating the signing of the contract, and/or their putting the gold coat on me, might be an excellent way to start the program. It took place in Dick Loughlin's office with Dick signing the document while I happily peered over his shoulder.

Back home, it was party time again. We had our first seven-figure client and we were clear on our direction. Tom and I were heroes. I no sooner got my coat off than Lowell was on the phone with his congratulations. He was almost as happy for me as I was for myself. Now it was time to perform.

A NETWORK OF 6,000 BROKERS

No other real estate company could claim 6,000 brokers, and to us it was like a beacon in the night screaming for attention. As our regular campaign began to roll, we checked on the geographic spread of these brokers and their agents to be sure they represented a true picture of each city in the country. Once confirmed, we visualized a national capability to provide accurate survey information on many subjects relating to home ownership. Our information would be garnered locally by brokers and would be far superior to any national survey done by long-distance phone or mail.

Survey subjects were not hard to find. Where is the safest place to live? Which city is America's favorite retirement location? Where will you receive the most house for your money? Where will you find the best quality of life? How much house will $1 million buy in different parts of the country? Considering the cost of living, what are the twenty-five best places to live?

Where will you find the least expensive home prices? There was no shortage of survey concepts.

HITTING A HOME RUN

We took our first shot with an approach to *USA Today* with their massive circulation and hit a home run. In their January 25, 1990, edition, the publication ran two full pages in color. They used a front-page teaser and then ran a banner across the full page that read, "Putting a price tag on the American Dream." On the adjacent page, their banner read, "From starter homes to mansions, coast to coast."

The opening paragraph read, "Most reports on housing costs talk about the median price of homes sold in a given area – but most people don't buy median-priced homes. To better gauge how home prices vary across the country, Century 21 asked its brokers in twenty-four cities to price and describe houses for four categories of white-collar employees at a typical large company:

1. Young entry-level workers buying their first home or condominium.

2. Low- and mid-level managers looking for trade-up homes.

3. Upper-level managers (department heads, vice presidents) looking for executive homes.

4. Senior managers (senior vice presidents, presidents, CEO's) looking for luxury homes."

After that spread broke, we made an arrangement with *USA Today* to provide them with solid survey material once a month. It would take us that long to gather the facts from our brokers and take the necessary support photographs. In the article mentioned above, *USA Today* ran fifteen photos. Century 21 calculated what it would have cost them to buy the same space and were floored. When we were able to repeat the exposure time after time over more than a year, they couldn't believe it. It would be untrue to claim that each story carried two full pages; however, most survey stories did run almost two pages.

CENTURY 21 GOES TO THE ROSE BOWL

Early in the year, we suggested that Century 21 become involved in the annual Rose Bowl Parade, primarily for the vast network television exposure. We investigated costs versus anticipated audience and got approval for the expenditure. Millions of people around the world saw the glamorous float that was prepared. However, to ensure additional value for the company's investment, we produced a video news release, which ran for sixty seconds. It was the visual story of the actual construction of the Century 21 float. We planned its release for the weekend prior to the parade, when we felt media interest would be at its peak. The video news release was carried by 114 stations, and some showed it several times.

THE IDITAROD DOG SLED RACE

Always on the prowl for features, we discovered that a Century 21 agent was preparing to drive his dog team in the Iditarod race across Alaska. He had actually driven the race before and agreed to become the subject of another video news release. For a full month, we had a camera crew follow the preparations he was making, training his dog team and outfitting his sled. In recent years, the race has been carried by cable and syndicated television; however, in the early '90s, it was a highlight on the news. Again, we timed the distribution to hit the airwaves one week before the race began. Our man did not win the race, but he probably had more international exposure than any other driver. He wore a Century 21 logo on his earflap hat, so our credits appeared on ninety-seven stations.

Our success had encouraged other franchise operators to seek local PR counsel. Lowell asked repeatedly that we assist his associates in other markets to find the most professional PR agencies or people possible. It was a throwback to our Marriott days, with several of our staff people traveling from city to city to do interviews. Monte Helm asked if we would conduct a PR seminar at the next national convention for all of the fifteen agencies involved. We again recognized the disparity in capability and tried to build some common denominator for all agencies in the two-hour session, which thereafter became an annual seminar.

COOPERSTOWN ON WHEELS

Bill Veeck and I had kicked around an idea to put the Baseball Hall of Fame on wheels and tour it across the country. Not knowing if the hierarchy at Cooperstown would look favorably on the idea, I decided to go there and check it out. The managing director of the Hall agreed to arrange a meeting, at which I broached the idea. I promised a first class presentation, protective insurance for the artifacts and agreed to give them full control of quality. I asked how many visitors came to Cooperstown annually and was surprised when he said, "About 250,000." I explained that we anticipated spending three years on the road and would cover every top and secondary market, which would expose the mobile unit to hundreds of thousands of people; the media exposure would reach millions. I sold hard on the prospect of people seeing a smattering of what was in the Hall of Fame and wanting to see more by coming to Cooperstown. They gave me a tentative nod of approval but explained that they might have a difficult time providing enough in the way of memorabilia to make the exhibit plausible. I accepted the limitation, feeling confident after they had shown me what was available in their basement storage department.

Exciting? My God, yes! But before taking the promotional idea to any would-be sponsor, I needed to get a handle on costs. In two weeks, I had put together a reasonably accurate budget. We priced the cost of renting the longest trailer available and the purchase of a truck. We calculated operating costs such as fuel, oil changes, washing, driver and assistant, constructing interior displays, the exterior paint job showing the sponsor "Big Time," an advance PR person with attendant travel and per diem expense. We went so far as to include the retention of a retired ball player who was a member of the Hall of Fame to travel with the unit and be available for radio, TV, and press interviews. The bottom line looked to be a little over $1 million the first year.

Century 21 had to have first crack. The promotion was tailor-made for that company. Every franchise holder, every broker, and every sales agent would participate when the Baseball Hall of Fame came into their town. I saw it as a marketing bonanza, with the local brokers able to entertain their biggest customers and their families with advance free tickets given to anyone who came into a Century 21 office. Entry was free to everyone, but a VIP line was to be created.

Before flying to California, I prepared a schedule routing the unit initially in the South to capitalize on warm weather. Our plan was to have the unit on display at the World Series in the fall, so we followed the sun across the country. It would take us a good three years to hit every market city on our list. I was counting on a strong visual display painted on the outer wall of the truck with strong Century 21 credits to help sell the idea. In addition to the four-color artwork, I had the display house make a mock-up of the truck using a toy truck. With my portfolio jammed, I flew to Orange County.

I had tested the idea on Lowell and gained his support. He called Dick Loughlin and asked him to personally sit in on the discussion. As anticipated, there were numerous questions. Was I certain of the cooperation of Cooperstown officials? How sure was I of the budget size? Could the

Cooperstown On Wheels vehicle be brought to the Century 21 national convention? What was our plan for crowd control? Could we find approved parking facilities in high traffic locations? When all the questions had been satisfied, they agreed to be sponsors.

My staff spent the next nine months making things happen. We had gained approval for an initial press conference to be held in the Commissioner of Baseball's office in New York and to unveil the completed unit at the national convention in Orlando, Florida. We had all our ducks in a row when the bottom fell out. In the interim, there had been a drastic change in the real estate business. The economy took a downward turn and apparently Century 21 was feeling it. They pulled the plug on the program after spending several hundred thousand dollars. I went back to Cooperstown with my tail between my legs, told them what had happened, apologized, and quietly left. I had hoped to leave the door open for a return at some time in the future with another sponsor.

We began having our problems with Bruce. I could never understand why. Aside from the cancellation of the mobile unit, the PR program continued to produce outstanding results. Nevertheless, shortly thereafter we were notified of the company's intention to have a review of the program and to open it to competitive PR agencies. I began to see the light. The major reason for his sudden emotional change seemed to be his resentment of my close personal relationship with Lowell Stahl. In his mind, we had become a threat and we had to go. The review was a sham. We beat our brains out but it was for naught. No one was more familiar with the company, and Dick Loughlin later told me that no other agency came close with their ideas. He just could not overrule one of his vice presidents. It was over.

We continued to represent the Illinois franchise for another year, at which time Lowell had sold out and Century 21, the parent company, was acquired. It is true that we get too soon old and too late smart; however, I have learned the difference between an acquaintance and a friend. Lowell Stahl was and is my friend.

CHAPTER 13

Creativity, the Magic Elixir

Everyone claims to have it – few actually do! It's compa-
rable to public relations' continuous search for the
industry's Holy Grail.

Children are taught that the magic words in life are "please" and "thank you." For me, within the confines of the PR business, the magic word has always been "creativity." It is a never-ending search that challenges you and every member of your staff to combat the client's "What have you done for me lately?" thought process with a stream of innovative and meaningful ideas.

The search for creative people begins with the interview process. The last segment of a brief writing test that interesting prospects are asked to complete is a one-page story on a non-existent new product. Kent Frankfother got his job with us on his story introducing "solar pizza" to the world. Pizza that could be taken anywhere – the picnic, the beach, the ballpark, or the family back yard – and would cook itself simply by exposure to the sun. Impractical today, yes. But certainly a unique idea and that's exactly what I was after.

Another example of innovative thinking occurred when I received a resume from a twenty-three-year-old woman that came in an elongated box, the size that would hold a dozen long-stem roses. Inside was one rose, slightly oversized, and the petals were made from shaped pieces of paper. Each petal had a segment of her resume written on it, and all the petals were collectively tied together to replicate a rose. There was no way I could ignore such an interesting application. She got her interview and our company received a gem who grew to become a vice president.

Competing for Fortune 500 clients without a staff of hundreds and without dozens of foreign and domestic offices, the hallmark of the Cushman agency was its creative staff. It was either 1989 or 1990 when Bob Dilenschneider, the CEO of Hill & Knowlton, called to inquire if he could have a meeting with me. I hadn't the faintest idea as to what he had on his mind, but I was cordial and told him he was welcome.

A week later he flew in from New York and we met for the first time. Everyone in the industry knew Bob Dilenschneider's name and, although we had competed against his company several times, I had never met him personally. Bob was a big man physically, and the impression he gave was exactly what you would expect from the man who led the largest PR company in the world. He was confident and direct, and he didn't waste words. He asked if my company was for sale. I told him I had honestly not considered selling. Recovering from my surprise, I asked why he wanted to buy Cushman. "You have over 200 people in your Chicago office. What makes us an interesting acquisition?"

Dilenschneider answered, "We compete regularly against Dan Edelman, Young & Rubicam, J. Walter Thompson, and Carl Byior, and have won more than our share of new business in that arena. Those times when we have gone head-to-head against your company, your creative ideas have given us fits. I would like to have those creative staffers on H & K's team."

I'd be a liar if I told you the thought was not interesting. However, we had just closed out our most successful year with strong seven-figure profits, and I didn't feel ready to call it quits. A few days after our meeting, I called Bob and thanked him, but explained that at this time I just wasn't interested in selling.

BAKING COOKIES IN THE MAGIC OVEN

The Keebler Cookie Company invites everyone coming to their executive offices in Chicago's suburbia to taste an assortment of their finest cookie products. Something tells me that is one reason why there never was a shortage of volunteers when it came to a visit to that client.

I was pleased, but not surprised, to receive Keebler's invitation to a meeting with their president and CEO. Food and food by-products had been a specialty category within Cushman. Our list of credentials was extensive and included Quaker Oats for both pancakes and an employee benefits program; Con Agra in Omaha, Nebraska, for Kids Cuisine; Armour Meat Products including lower salt bacon, ham, and hot dogs; Armour Frozen Foods; Banquet Frozen Foods; Belgium Waffles; Hygrade Ball Park Franks; and Ralston Purina for cereal products, and their sponsorship of national dog and cat shows. We had founded the National Root Beer Institute and had represented Hires Root Beer, Orange Crush, and Seven-Up.

Tom Garvin, Keebler's president, was all business. He didn't waste a moment before telling me, "Although our company does over $1 billion annually, we would not be considered an industry giant. We are entering a multi-million-dollar consumer products battle, and the combatants are America's best-known bakers, and two consumer products giants, Nabisco and Procter & Gamble. The stakes are high and so are the risks. Besides, our competition has had its product on grocery store shelves for at least five months, and we have yet to make our first shipment."

Mr. Garvin went on to say, "We have made a strong effort and commitment to being a successful participant in what has become one of the most competitive markets in the U.S. food industry. This commitment includes entering the fray with a superior product line, which we believe has true market upset potential. We have been working around the clock for over a year to create 'Soft Batch.' It's an innovative cookie line with oven-fresh taste, soft and chewy inside, yet crisp outside. We believe that product superiority combined with greater variety gives Keebler an advantage over its larger competition."

He concluded by saying, "We must avoid an advertising confrontation. Realistically, we cannot compete against Nabisco and Procter & Gamble if it comes down to sheer advertising expenditures. Keebler's executive committee has searched for an alternative marketing plan and we feel that it will take an unusually creative public relations program to inform and motivate distributors and retail grocery chains to stock our product. That's why you are here." I got the message loud and clear.

Back in our office, I convened a taste panel to munch on Keebler's eight different cookie varieties. It's amazing how fast the word got around. "Hey, there are cookies in the conference room!" We had purchased quantities of competitive products to measure against, but the panel was unanimous in its decision that the Keebler product was superior and that the variety gave us a leg up on the competition. Now all we had to do was figure out a way to communicate that to Keebler's target markets, using public relations techniques and minimal advertising dollars.

For days, we searched for an idea or a key word to hang our creative hats on. It was the David versus Goliath size differential that struck the chord. Garvin had spoken about the forthcoming battle and when one of our people stumbled on the word "war," we climbed all over it. Newspaper headlines always loved to inform their readers about any war. It didn't necessarily have to be a shooting war. There had been price wars and labor wars, why not a National Cookie War?

We needed a major national placement to initiate the National Cookie War controversy and raise the bar on this $2 billion battle for market share. Knowing that the media feeds off the media, our initial newsbreak had to come from one of only a few media sources so powerful as to be unquestionable. The circulation and the integrity of the *New York Times*, *Washington Post*, or the *Wall Street Journal* made those publications our initial targets. With hat in hand and a loaded attaché case, I headed for New York and visited with the financial editor of the *New York Times*. I talked and he listened. Finally he said, "I'm sorry, but I just don't buy it." One down and two to go. The editor at the *Washington Post* had the same reaction.

Not quite so confident after being turned down twice, I walked into the *Wall Street Journal*. They liked the story idea, but asked for time to check their sources for accuracy. Two days later, they called and told us they were going with the story. Even then we weren't sure how big they would play it, so we followed the old axiom that insists you do not tell the client until you actually see the story in print. It was a pure home run! The story ran on the front-page, right-hand column. The next morning, my contact at the *New York Times* called to say he had apparently missed the boat, but they were still going to carry the story. The Associated Press put the story on their national and international wire, and it broke coast to coast. After that, the floodgates opened and every secondary market and community group of publications carried the story.

The size and impact of the National Cookie War story gave Keebler and Cushman confidence that we had successfully reached our initial target markets, i.e., distributors and retail grocery chains. Phase two had to be directed to the consumer.

Tom Garvin often referred to himself as "The Chief Elf." Everyone knows that the elves do their baking in a magic oven located in a hollow tree, rather than in customary baking facilities. Ernie Keebler is the symbolic elf featured in Keebler animated advertising, and, with his help, the agency was able to build a new product introduction that has become legend and has won Cushman national honors. Coincidentally, it helped to move product as well.

Capitalizing on the elf theme, Cushman developed what has been recognized as the most creative press kit of its day. We recreated the Keebler Magic Oven into a twenty-four-inch-high, eighteen-inch-wide, and twelve-inch-deep press kit. It was to replicate the magic oven, and on its front face was an illustration of the oven, as well as a drawer that held two oven mitts, so that when the press reached for our oven fresh cookies, they would not burn their fingers. That drawer was labeled, "Instant press conference."

We were aware that we would probably not be able to entice national consumer publications and trade media to attend a new product introduction press conference in Chicago, so we decided to bring the conference to them. A two-sided tape cassette was located in the pocket with the oven mitts. On the front side, Tom Garvin spoke about the National Cookie War and Keebler's plan to roll out the product, market by market, in their penetration effort. On the other side, Ernie Keebler spoke on behalf of the elves. Built into the kit was space to house bags of all eight cookie varieties. Our press kit went on the road literally and figuratively. Close your eyes for a moment and visualize caravans of limousines, filled to the brim with these giant press kits, rolling up Madison Avenue in New York. Our staff placed one kit with every major national magazine and newspaper editor, plus kits to every television producer and on-air anchor team.

The press kit was an instant hit, accruing national television exposure, including over four minutes on the "CBS Morning Show." In total, more than 250 individual videotapes, varying in length from three to eight minutes, poured in from cities across America. The advertising equivalent in dollar value for airtime was in excess of $3 million. Everything was based on a press kit. Incredible! The bottom line: Keebler achieved a thirty-three percent market share within the first twelve months.

LISTEN TO OUR BEDTIME STORY

The product was difficult to work with. It was large and cumbersome, inanimate, impossible to carry or move, somewhat unattractive, but never seen in any household in its naked state. Perhaps most complex of all, it rarely changed.

The Serta Mattress Company was an association of franchise manufacturers with each retaining certain geographic exclusivity. J. Allen Ferguson carried the title of Executive Director of the association, and, although there was a board of directors consisting of franchise factory owners, no one questioned "Fergie's" supreme command. He had been a fixture with the company for years and was in complete charge of marketing and all aspects of the financial structure of the organization.

It was Fergie who hired the agency. His directive was, "Establish greater acceptance for a quality product and provide increased brand name recognition." The staff showed a great deal of enthusiasm because Serta represented our initial entry into the home-furnishings field. Jean Leinhauser was a natural for the account supervisor role. In the fifty years I had been in the public relations business, there have been many outstanding people who helped establish the agency's national reputation. Although I'm hard-pressed to identify any one as being the most talented, I have always felt that Jean was clearly the most creative person we ever had. Possessing a Midwestern Iowa work ethic, Jean was almost always the first one in the office in the morning and the last one to leave at night. There was a soft-spoken calm about her, and she had a knack for treating junior people with thoughtful kindness. Jean was special and I will always be indebted to her for her contributions to the agency's growth. Half the battle is over if the client likes and respects his account supervisor and, in this case, Ferguson loved Jean.

We were so enamored with Serta that we rationalized its product publicity potential out of proportion. Since the client had never had counsel before, we decided to do a straightforward new product introduction with the Perfect Sleeper. Our initial press kit was titled, "Listen To Our Bedtime Story," and it contained the usual corporate background story and product information, coupled with several photographs. It failed miserably. However, even as my people were sometimes being forcibly extricated from media offices, they recognized that, though home-furnishings editors could care less about mattresses, they were deeply intrigued with the subject of sleep.

When we took a second and more realistic look at the product, we could not deny its shortcomings. We were convinced that the one positive feature was its ability to provide a good night's sleep. We needed to completely revamp our thinking and find a fresh new approach. Serta mattresses could not be publicized on the strength of the product alone.

THE SERTA SLEEP CENTER

Cognizant of the fact that there would be no news forthcoming from the product, it became essential that the agency find ways to make news. In addition, we felt that the board of directors was looking to the agency to convince the consumer that Serta cares beyond the initial sale of a mattress. We felt the need to develop material that would be geared to show that Serta is seriously interested in how well the family sleeps, in the special problems mothers may have with children at bedtime, and in coping with insomnia. As a result, we created the Serta Sleep Center, devoted to the dissemination of accurate, practical, useful, unusual, interesting, and entertaining information on sleep. The Center offered us unlimited potential for national publicity, but it was not merely a publicity device; it offered future marketing and merchandising potential.

Researching consumer reaction to sleep information, we conducted several consumer panels in key cities to discuss controversial subjects, from bedding guarantees to consumer complaints. To further test the efficacy of the Center, we began writing feature stories on subjects like, "How to fall asleep quickly," "Why do people snore?" and "What do dreams mean?" While not astounding, the results were encouraging. We went in search of a true sleep expert.

Valerie Moolman lived in Boston and we found her after having interviewed at least a dozen experts who professed to have the necessary credentials. Valerie had just written a book titled, *Forty Winks at the Drop of a Hat*, and the Cornerstone Library Division of Simon & Schuster published it. With individual factory sponsorship, Valerie went on a national tour. We booked her for two days in each city, where she was interviewed by media and, in most cities, she made in-store bedding department personal appearances, answering consumer questions while lying on a Serta mattress. Valerie covered thirty-two cities over a period of six months, and because she came to "their city," the impact on each factory was evident and brought them direct sales. In addition, the tour served to establish the Serta Sleep Center in the minds of both the media and the consumer.

THERE IS A MAN IN YOUR BEDROOM

One year, we introduced a bridal program. Research showed that there were over two million young women about to become brides. Most of these new brides were in the eighteen- to twenty-two-year-old age bracket, and every one of them would be buying new bedding, with half of it super-size.

Two million unquestioned prospects seemed like an excellent potential market and certainly worth going after. We could not understand why no one in the business had concentrated a portion of their marketing on this corner of the market. It was out there to be had and we wanted it all for Serta.

In the first phase of the bridal program, we wrote and published a booklet on bedding for the bride with a totally new approach. "There Is a Man in Your Bedroom" was a bright, lively, "now" booklet telling the new bride or the bride-to-be that things would soon be different. Sharing her bedroom with a man meant an end to the female frills and fancies she was accustomed to while single. The booklet gave advice to the young bride on how to decorate her new bedroom in such a way that it would be appealing and feminine enough for her, and yet not be too feminine for her husband. The four-color booklet, written by prominent decorators as consultants to Serta, had an extensive section on how to decorate problem bedrooms – rooms of awkward size, how to use super-size bedding in smaller rooms, etc.

The booklet was first offered free in Serta's ads in *Bride's* magazine. We asked *Bride's* to tell us how many booklets had been ordered and were advised that they had received over 15,000 requests. The stories and artwork in the booklet were then utilized in news releases sent to over 800 print publications. Using the coordinated marketing concept, the booklets were offered to Serta franchisees, and they ordered over 50,000 copies to give away in the bedding department of retail furniture stores.

Selling the bridal market is about ninety percent psychology. Brides fashion themselves as special people – a vanity that manufacturers do their best to cater to. Desiring to maintain brides' interest, we asked Serta to build bedding marked, "For Brides Only." It was simply the Perfect Sleeper in her choice of king- or queen-size and made with an opulent white fabric. Whether one bride's special mattress was ever purchased was irrelevant. The point was to attract the bride's attention and have her visit the Serta bedding department. Should she decide that the gold standard fabric mattress was more readily available, that was just fine. The entire bridal program became the focal point of the company's marketing for several years and was given prominent display in print and broadcast media advertising, as well as national publicity. To assist the retail stores, our agency wrote a "Retail Store Bedding Promotion Kit" and a "Sales Manager's Guide."

THE BRIDE'S BEDROOM COLORING BOOK

Susan Block, Jean's assistant, helped put together the successor to "There Is a Man in Your Bedroom" which we called, "The Bride's Bedroom Coloring Book." The booklet gave the consumer the opportunity to actually color-in our illustrations of a variety of room settings, focusing on the most popular furniture styles and super-size bedding. The booklet contained an ingenious rotatable color wheel that could be removed from the book and taken into her favorite home-furnishings store, then used as a guide for color selection. It was a decorating tool for every bride, and through it, Serta captured the bride's attention with its name and products.

The Serta Bridal Bedding Shower had the local retailer clip all engagement announcement stories that appeared in his local press and send an invitation to their Bedding Shower via direct mail. We designed and printed thousands of invitations, and inside the retail store, brides were shown a series of bridal bedroom set-ups depicting the use of super-size bedding in small rooms, how to decorate with period furniture, etc., plus the standard line of merchandise.

TOMORROW'S CONSUMER

Everything we had done up to this point was aimed at the consumer of today, i.e., the homemaker and the bride-to-be. Jean Leinhauser was excited about a program aimed at teenagers. At that time, they were the country's most powerful single buying influence. Forty percent of the population was made up of people under twenty. Teenagers were spending six and a half billion dollars of their own earnings and allowances, plus billions more through their parents' charge accounts. Within two or three years, the impact of their dollars will be felt in the home-furnishings field, as well as the major appliance and the construction industries – forty-two percent would marry within one year after high school graduation; fifty percent within two years.

The way to reach this viable market was through the home economics classroom. Ninety-five percent of the almost eleven million girls in the seventh to twelfth grades were enrolled in home economics classes. The home economics teacher was seeking ways to give her students information on the latest techniques and products. To gain the teachers' cooperation, we created valuable teaching aids, which were not blatantly commercial. There was a slide film and a video on furnishing the first bedroom titled, "The Small Space Age Bedroom." For the next three years, we continued to develop new material for teachers to utilize in the classroom.

Producing classroom teaching aids had become a big business on the part of American corporations in every field, from General Electric to the gas industry, from Clairol hair coloring to Papermate Pens, from Kroehler, a leading furniture manufacturer, furniture to Singer sewing machines to Gorham sterling silver. We made detailed surveys of 5,000 teachers and studied every piece of educational material produced by other manufacturers in every field. We found out what was being taught, why and how, and what the teachers wanted and could use in terms of teaching aids, student materials, and visual aids. We also discovered how to best work with schools – what to do and what not to do.

One of a series of promotions that Jean innovated was the "Dream Bedroom Design Contest." Each teen could pick up her design kit by visiting any Serta bedding department. She would then design her own dream bedroom and enter it in the contest. Materials provided within the kit included special graph paper with each square measuring a square foot. Serta would build the national winner an exact replica of her dream bedroom.

The second-year home economics course was called "Creative Bedrooms." It taught future homemakers how to create attractive, comfortable, and livable bedrooms that expressed their own lifestyle. It consisted of a teacher's guide, a student booklet written to inspire, motivate, and inform, and a color video.

After reading this far, you have come to expect a transition from the mundane to the ridiculous. No campaign could ever be complete without the introduction of fun elements, and yet, each of these had to play a role in achieving our clients' goals. Contrary to many of our colleagues, we just refused to take ourselves too seriously. In keeping with this mad type of thinking, we produced an audiocassette primarily for radio. We called it, "To Sleep, Perchance to Snore." It was an amalgamation of every conceivable snore, with a psychiatrist and a renowned physician analyzing each snore with appropriate comments. It was hysterically funny, and the radio DJs had a great time playing it over and over again. Of course, this element of higher education came directly from the Serta Sleep Center.

We followed that by locating a cooperative bachelor who had the proverbial pad. In this apartment, we had built wall-to-wall mattresses. That's correct, the entire floor area was covered in Serta mattresses, carrying a jaguar ticking cover. All other furnishings were built into the walls and operated via push buttons. At night, to make the bed for sleeping, you simply choose which area of the floor you wish to recline upon and out of the woodwork comes mattress pad, sheets, and blankets. Hook the linens over the edge of the bed – and there you are. In the morning, it makes up just as easily. You release each piece of linen – and zip! – it disappears back into the woodwork. The home-furnishing editors had fun with the novel idea, and we could not believe the amount of space they allocated in the press.

For television, the agency produced the world's first original unincorporated, comprehensive, international bed-making contest. There were four participants: a nurse, a bachelor, a mother of twelve, and a hotel executive. The judges were an army lieutenant and a professional housekeeping executive. Working against the clock, one would have thought that the experienced mother or the nurse had the edge. Instead, it was the hotel executive who came in first. The one-minute-and-ten-second video closed with voice-over commenting, "Ladies, from now on let your husband make the beds. Tell him it's an executive job." Distribution went to 125 stations, and results showed 84 stations used the piece.

IMPERIAL BEDROOMS

Did you know that the French kings actually held court in bed? Few people are aware that, in the days of the Roman Empire, royal beds were made of solid gold, inlaid with precious stones. The Serta Imperial Bedroom promotion was based on the theory that the bedroom is the center of every man and woman's castle. Through this project, we planned to bring to Americans a series of miniature bedrooms that were works of art in their own right. Eugene Kupjack, an internationally known artist who had produced the famous Thorne Rooms at Chicago's Art Institute, created the rooms for Serta. They covered a classic group of historical monarchs including the bedrooms of King Tut, Queen Elizabeth I, Louis XIV, Kublai Khan, Peter the Great, and Queen Isabella. These rooms were to be thoroughly researched and built with historical accuracy.

The national press preview was held at Lincoln Center in New York, under the auspices of the prestigious New York Chapter of the National Home Furnishings League. The wire services, national magazines, newspaper home-furnishings editors, and producers of popular talk shows attended, and the resultant publicity was extraordinary. At the Chicago June market, *Display World* magazine ran a two-page spread on the exhibit. And as a result, the AMC Department Store chain contacted Serta and said,

"We feel that many of our stores would like to have the privilege of showing these rooms to our customers."

Imperial Bedrooms opened the door for us to work closely with stores like Bloomingdale's, Carson, Pirie & Scott, Burdines's, Rich's, Dayton's, and Bullock's. Giant shopping centers across the country requested the six Imperial Bedrooms as a centerpiece around which to build their own traffic. Lastly, we convinced Serta management that after the Imperial Bedrooms had their run, which we estimated at about five years, the exhibit was of museum quality and could be donated for a healthy tax write-off.

Serta and Cushman had a ten-year happy relationship. When one considers the fact that there never was a new product, never was the tiniest semblance of real news about the product, it is amazing the success we had gaining brand name identification and making serious inroads toward increased market share. To my mind, because of the complexity within the product market, the Serta campaign was the most outstanding example of pure creativity our organization enjoyed during my fifty-year tenure. To this day, I tip my *chapeau* to Jean Leinhauser, Susan Block, and those other staff personnel that made it happen.

ST. PATRICK'S DAY

One more wave of the flag for creativity and fun. On this day each year, sacred to the Irish and for the wearing of the green, the agency unofficially changed its name to Erin O'Cushman & Associates. Existing letterheads had a green line slashed through the agency name and Erin O'Cushman was superimposed. A cover letter, originating in St. Louis read: "The Saints are marching in! In March, everyone's a little Irish, and we all can raise a toast to St. Patrick. We invite you to celebrate St. Patrick's Day this year, compliments of your friends at 'Erin O'Cushman & Associates' (the Gaelic spelling for one of the nation's largest independent public relations firms). This letter is redeemable at either the Top of the Sevens in Clayton or at the Press Club-Radisson Hotel downtown for two drinks. Simply present this letter to the staff when you order. To accommodate as many Irish persons as possible who might have a full day of work planned for March 17, we have arranged for this 'Luck of the Irish' to be honored after 11:30 a.m. on either Tuesday, March 16 (a St. Patrick's preview), or Wednesday, March 17. Top O' the Day." The letter was sent to media, clients, suppliers, and friends.

CHAPTER 14

The World of
Professional Sports _____

Whether participant or spectator, the field of emotions
extends from agony to ecstasy and ranges from the frenzy
of exaltation to the pit of despair.

Winning has become an American tradition. In life itself, there is more than winning or losing. Most of us have found happiness within a middle ground, somewhere between phenomenal success and abject failure. Not so in sports, and particularly not so in professional sports. There is no middle ground. No gray area. You either win or you lose, and no one remembers who came in second. My friend Bill Veeck used to say in his own inimitable fashion, "Show me a good loser, and I'll show you a loser."

There is so much money in every professional sport today that it has created an acceptable area somewhere between heroes and those who completely fizzle. A below-average professional ball player, whether in baseball, football, or basketball, can still scratch out a living at a mere $3 to $4 million per year. Albeit his career may be short-lived, but at those salary levels it is now possible to retire at age twenty-five with in excess of $10 million as a safety net – not too shabby. I make the assumption that this is a case of supply and demand rather than team owner's stupidity.

With corporate sponsorship underwriting the unbelievable prize money now being offered in golf and tennis, you have to look hard to find what used to be called golf and/or tennis bums. Tiger Woods, Pete Sampras, and Andre Agassi have set the standard in their respective sports' fields as winners, and have enjoyed the financial rewards that come with winning.

Million-dollar first prize money is no longer unusual, but it wasn't always that way. Kenny Rosewall, the great tennis champion, once told me that before the advent of open tennis, he and other name pros would play for six months and earn $20,000, $30,000, or $40,000 a year. John Newcombe, another member of the Tennis Hall of Fame, pointed to one specific day in which he played for ten minutes short of five hours for prize money that averaged $2,080 per hour. That may be a bit more than you or I will earn in comparable time, but in today's world of professional sports, it's peanuts. Industrial corporations have made the difference by underwriting prize money in major tournaments and acting as sponsors. Without this financial resource, few, if any, golf and tennis tournaments could be moneymakers for the promoters.

The size of the prize money, some colorful leadership, and a great deal of hard work lie in back of an increasing interest on the part of the media to treat tennis as a major sport. Tennis professionals and enthusiasts can thank the media for helping to build awareness. Not too long ago, such simple things as how to keep score were unknown to many. Expanded newspaper coverage and network television exposure have helped develop increased awareness and comprehension for a game that really sells itself. Going back to the "ad gap," the concept was never more viable than when analyzing marketing technique for a pro tennis tournament. Publicity is the life's blood of any successful tennis tournament. There simply is not sufficient advertising budget to reach the vast numbers of prospective spectators. Despite the most astute utilization of promotional dollars, the practical aspects are that without editorial support and publicity in all media, it is economically not feasible to communicate to the market. Most market cities offer limited seating in their arenas and, therefore, gate receipts alone cannot cover expenses.

Sports have always been a major part of my non-business life. Being able to partake of softball, basketball, handball, golf, and tennis have been one of life's joys, and it has helped to keep me physically and mentally fit. Within the agency public relations realm, every practitioner has his or her favorite fields and mine have always been travel and sports. When the Cushman agency got involved with the White Sox, I was beside myself. Over the years we have been blessed to represent teams in professional basketball (Chicago Bulls), professional soccer (Chicago Sting), World Championship Tennis, World Cup Polo, Arlington Park, Washington Park and Hawthorne Thoroughbred and trotting racetracks, a Grand Prix Formula

One auto race in Ontario, California, several USAAC racing teams, and an attempt to break the world land speed record on the Utah salt flats. Add to that a Latin American Soccer Association Program, several builders of the world's finest and largest yachts up to 125 feet, the Denver Bronco's Orange Crush Super Bowl team, The National Sports Show, Wilson Sporting Goods Company's introduction of colored golf balls, Spalding Sporting Goods Company, The Chicago Marathon, The American Fishing Tackle Manufacturers Association, and a series of high school and college sports events sponsored by McDonald's.

ALL-STAR TENNIS, INC.

Only rarely do you meet someone like Asher Birnbaum. Asher may be small in stature, but he is an intellectual giant. This quiet man has more drive, more desire to win, than anyone I have ever met. Asher and I had met on the tennis court before I knew he was editor and publisher of *Tennis* magazine. Asher and his wife, Irene, had founded the magazine and struggled with it for years until it gained its rightful place in national prominence. During those early difficult years, Asher's prestige and reputation grew within the world of tennis, and the players developed a sincere fondness for him. He knew everyone in tennis – equipment manufacturers, USTA officials, umpires, linesmen and women, and both male and female professional players.

Despite my lifelong reluctance toward partnerships, the melding of our two areas of specialization was so perfect that we agreed to form All-Star Tennis, Inc., for the promotion of professional tennis in Chicago and Milwaukee. With Asher's tennis connections and savvy, and my sports media contacts and promotional experience, we became a team. It was the best move I ever made outside of my family. We were together for ten years, during which time we profitably promoted twelve tournaments. Much more important than any monetary return are the many years of a cherished, cohesive friendship that continues to this day.

Lamar Hunt was in the throes of building World Championship Tennis into a series of twenty interrelated one-week tournaments with a total of $1 million in prize money. Asher and I flew to Dallas and met with Mr. Hunt, requesting the franchise rights for Chicago and Milwaukee. The only question from Mr. Hunt and his tournament director Michael Davies related to our financial stability. Once convinced that we had both the capability and financial wherewithal, the agreement was sealed, and we became geographic partners. Back in Chicago, Asher and I began to put our first tournament into actuality. We checked out every conceivable facility, searching to find one that offered at least 8,000 seats and a location that gave us the best chance for success. Northwestern University's McGaw Hall in Evanston was the perfect site. It was dead center in the area that had built more indoor courts than any other in Chicagoland. Ticketron would handle tickets electronically, and the Northwestern box office would sell to walk-ins.

Asher began making arrangements for playing surface, additional lights, nets, balls, and the recruitment of name players. He also tracked down USTA officials who led him to qualified umpires, linesmen and women. Frank Parker, a member of the Tennis Hall of Fame, a personal friend, and a Chicago resident, agreed to act as our chief umpire. Tony Trabert, another Hall of Famer, became our public address and broadcast voice. I was in the midst of ordering tickets, posters, brochures, and fliers, and establishing a minuscule media-advertising budget, a direct mail program, and a full-scale public relations campaign. We were on our way.

There remained only one insignificant problem. We needed a sponsor. Asher and I talked it over, and before contacting any of our prospects, we needed to place all our ducks in a row. A sponsor required a *quid pro quo* in the form of exposure to justify sponsorship cash outlay, and the best way to provide it was via television. We met with the general manager of WBBM-TV, the CBS network affiliate in Chicago. They agreed to do highlights through the preliminary matches and to televise live action of the semis and finals over the weekend. With that contract in hand, we quickly sold Planter's Peanuts on becoming our first sponsor.

Don Pierson of the *Chicago Tribune* called our Planter's WCT Classic "the richest and biggest pro tennis tournament Chicago had ever had." Total prize money was $50,000. Don could never have imagined that thirty years later, Grand Slam tennis events would announce prize money somewhere between $2 million and $4 million.

With only one court to work with, play continued for twelve hours for the first four days. Quarterfinals and semifinals were played in the evenings on Friday and Saturday, and the finals were held on Sunday afternoon. Asher and Mike Davies had recruited a cadre of the world's outstanding players, including Rod Laver, John Newcombe, Ken Rosewall, Tony Roche, Marty Reissen, Arthur Ashe, Pancho Gonzales, Roy Emerson, Dennis Ralston, and Cliff Drysdale. The thirty-two-man draw also included Stan

Smith, Bob Lutz, Fred Stolle, Tom Okker, Nikki Pilic, and Charles Pasarell, with the balance being the best European and Australian players to be found.

I was able to stop traffic on Michigan Avenue at noon for about ten minutes. It was just long enough for Asher and me to stretch a portable net across the width of the street, right in front of the *Chicago Tribune*, and have Frank Parker and the Illinois State champion tennis player, Alan Schwartz, bang the ball back and forth. Photographers and television cameras were on hand to record the event for the next day's paper and the 10 p.m. television news. The following year, we duplicated the stunt with some slight revisions. Using the same two players, we had them posted on two different yachts parked across from each other in the Chicago River right at the Michigan Avenue Bridge. Tennis balls were batted back and forth across the water, with hundreds of spectators watching from atop the bridge and a plethora of media to cover. The sportswriters went way beyond the call of duty, and I couldn't help feeling that although the tournament did provide a legitimate news story, the guys that I had known and worked with for so many years were coming through partially because they knew I had my own money on the line. I reflected upon "building positive press relations."

The first two days had meager attendance, but when we announced that the weekend was a complete sell-out, the crowds poured in on Wednesday and Thursday.

When it was over, we had a justifiably unhappy sponsor. They were pleased with the television coverage, but unhappy with the press because too many "holier than thou" editors used their blue pencils excessively to eliminate the credit to the sponsor. Politically, my first stop had to be the sports editor. I explained that we were grateful for the volume of coverage, but questioned the judgment in deleting the sponsor's name. "I do not question your right to cover or not to cover a given story, but when you do allocate pages of written and photographic material on the tournament to your readers, I believe the sponsor, the people who make it possible for the event to be here, deserve some consideration," I added.

He smiled and said, "Aaron, I'm sorry, but those are management's rules and the only person who can change them is the managing editor." I knew that my meeting with the sports editor was just going through the motions to maintain goodwill. Eventually it had to go upstairs and that's where I went.

The managing editor listened and happily concurred. The new rule that came down allowed at least one sponsor credit per story and/or caption. In a way, it was a major victory for fairness, and that media attitude has not changed over the years. Other tournaments in other sports have become the beneficiaries of the action I took.

At the Kemper International in Chicago, the fifteenth leg of the 1972 World Championship of Tennis, Arthur Ashe sat on a bench in the cluttered locker room underneath Northwestern University's McGaw Hall, looking at nothing in particular, thinking quietly. I sat next to him as he picked up a can of thirst quencher, flipped off the lid and took a couple of gulps. "The best I ever tasted," he said. That was a typical reaction. As I came to know him through our tournaments, I found that Arthur delighted in little pleasures, and when he liked something, he said so. His enthusiasm made dining with him a pleasure. "I just love paella," he said at Spanish restaurants. "I just love prosciutto," he said at Italian places. "I just love hard-boiled eggs," he said at the hospitality room where hard-boiled eggs were served. Arthur was very easy to please.

What was not typical, as he sat thinking and sipping, was his despondence. He had just lost the final of the $50,000 Kemper International to Tom Okker 4-6, 6-2, 6-3, and he was upset. He didn't look it – he never does – but he was rather disturbed. "Damn it," he said, about to slam a locker before thinking better of it. "I can't stop thinking about that match. A set and a break-up, and I blew it. I'll think about that all day and all night. You don't have that many chances to win one of our tournaments and when you get to a final and have it all wrapped up, you don't let it get away. All I had to do was hold my serve four times, against a guy I usually beat with ease. And this happening on my favorite surface. That doesn't seem so tough. But I couldn't do it. Why? How do you explain it?"

Ashe's whippy serve, usually a great weapon on the quick Sportface carpet, lost its effectiveness in his second set tailspin. He couldn't control it. "If he had been a pitcher or a quarterback," *Chicago Tribune* writer Bill Jauss reported, "he would have been yanked for a relief man."

I said, "Arthur, it was a tough match, but you never looked disappointed or emotional out there."

He responded, "I never do, so don't let that fool you."

The first night of that tournament was nearly snowed out. A blizzard swept into Chicago dropping ten inches of snow, and as Asher and I drove to the matches, all we heard on the car radio were hazardous driving warnings. "Stay home, it's treacherous weather for traveling," they advised.

Meetings and events all over the area were cancelled, but the tennis went on. All the players, and even a few hundred spectators, made it to the matches. On the third day of the tournament, most of the snow was washed away by a thunderstorm. "It was," someone said, "just a normal weather week in Chicago."

MARTY REISSEN SAVES THE DAY

The U.S. Open Grand Slam Tournament was being played at Forest Hills in New York. There had been consistent rain for several days and the matches were backed up. Instead of ending on Sunday afternoon, they announced that the quarters, semis, and finals would be played on Monday and Tuesday. That's great, except it put us out of business in Chicago. Traditionally, our tournament began the day after the U.S. Open, but of the sixteen players scheduled to appear in Chicago, eight were still to play in New York. There could be no comparison between the prestige and prize money winning a Grand Slam event afforded and playing in our tournament. It looked like we would have to scrub at least two nights of the Chicago event with refunds to the advance ticket purchasers. Sunday night was another sleepless night for Asher and myself.

Looking for a small-sized miracle, Asher decided to call Marty Reissen, whom we knew was scheduled to play two matches that Monday in New York. He was playing semifinal matches in men's doubles and in mixed doubles. We had him scheduled to play the first singles match of the evening to open our tournament. I mentioned that Asher had drive and determination; I neglected to mention that he had a ton of guts. (Some call it *chutzpah*!) He got Marty on the phone and pleaded our case. When you are asking for the moon, you hold your breath waiting for a response. Marty was quiet for a moment and then told Asher that he would catch the earliest plane he could following his matches. Marty asked if we could meet his plane with a car to rush him to Northwestern and have the car stand by to take him back to O'Hare Airport immediately after he played. He planned to return to New York, assuming he would be playing a finals match there the next day.

Marty Reissen graduated from Northwestern and was willing to do anything to help the Chicago WCT event. In New York, he lost the men's doubles semifinal match and won the mixed doubles semi with Margaret Court and did have to return to Forest Hills to play the finals on Tuesday. A near-exhausted Reissen got off the plane in Chicago at 6 p.m. Monday night. He dashed to McGaw Hall to play Tom Okker in a best-of-three set match starting at 7 p.m. Amazingly, Marty won the match. He knew he had saved our skin and that we would be forever grateful. The next day in New York, he won the mixed doubles championship. No one will ever convince me that all pro athletes only care about the money. I will always point to Marty Reissen and whisper a prayer of thanks.

The next day, Rod Laver and Roy Emerson, and John Newcombe and Tony Roche, the number one and two seeds in the U.S. Open doubles, defaulted their semifinal matches and flew to Chicago to play for Asher and me. It was a big-time gesture, and the appearance of those four really made the remainder of our tournament successful.

That weekend was to be a benefit for the Olin Parks family. Olin was a much-beloved member of Wilson Sporting Goods Company, of whom the players thought the world, and he had passed away suddenly. On Friday night, both Doris and Irene were in the box office working feverishly to handle a mile-long line of customers anxious to get inside. It was clear they were being overrun. Without asking, both Jack Kramer and Tony Trabert appeared out of nowhere and insisted on staffing another box office window to help expedite our gate rush. Here were two of the most famous American tennis heroes, both members of the Tennis Hall of Fame, taking cash and making change for patrons because they knew we needed help.

It was easy to understand the press's interest in locker room dialogue. Catching the players either relaxed or worn out, but usually off-guard, sportswriters have uncovered some of their juiciest stories hanging around after a close match. Pierre Barthes, a handsome and charming Frenchman, covered with dripping perspiration following his three-set semifinal match with John Newcombe, sat in front of his locker with his head in his hands. In their third set, Pierre had hit a lob so high that it struck one of the giant lights atop the court and knocked it out. There was a thirty-minute delay before maintenance could make the replacement. Once the action began again, Pierre intentionally blew the next point as a form of apology to John. That gentlemanly gesture cost Pierre the match. He saw me standing next to him, when he lifted his head and softly said in broken English, "I never do that again."

PLAYERS REVOLT IN NEW ORLEANS

The ten years of tournaments came and went so quickly. It was hard work, but both Asher and I were doing what we loved and tended to forget the gut-wrenching experiences that accompanied the good times. There was the tournament in New Orleans when we faced a revolution among the players. Tennis was to be played at Tulane University gymnasium with a capacity of 5,500 starting at 9 a.m. Monday morning. We had thirty-two players in the new Marriott Hotel, and at 9 p.m. Sunday night, a delegation of about fifteen players came to us in the hotel lobby, announcing their intention not to play the next morning. The problem revolved around their claim that we were not providing sufficient space in back of the baseline. WCT regulations require twenty-one feet between the baseline and the first row of spectator seats. The delegation had gone over to the gym, measured the space and found it lacking by three feet. Of course, they were correct. We reminded them that they had played under similar circumstances at DePaul University in Chicago and no one had said one word. Why the fuss now, the night before opening?

Either we pull three rows of the best pre-sold seats out, or they refused to play. No amount of cajoling was working. The group, led mostly by European players, turned a deaf ear to our explanation. The two unquestioned leaders among the players were Stan Smith and John Newcombe. Both men were out on the town, and we simply had to bide our time waiting for them to return. The entire situation was ridiculous. The players involved were venting their spleen over something that had happened in a previous city where we had not been involved. They were acting irrationally, but their action was a clear threat to our tournament.

Smith and Newcombe returned about midnight, and we grabbed them the moment they came through the revolving door. John grimaced when we explained what was going on and beckoned Asher and me to follow him upstairs. The entire group of recalcitrants was gathered in one room, boisterously expressing their views when Stan and John walked in. By the clock, the conversation didn't last more than sixty seconds. John started by saying, "What is this crap about not playing tomorrow?" Suddenly the room went deathly quiet. John continued, "Any player that doesn't show for his morning match tomorrow can forget about the rest of the WCT tour." The revolution was over.

On another occasion, Bob Lutz, Stan Smith's doubles partner, was missing. With twenty minutes left before they were to take the court, Lutz was nowhere to be found. He casually sauntered in with five minutes to spare, and, smiling, said, "What were you worried about? I told you I would be here, and I always keep my word."

Ken Rosewall won one of our tournaments, and while feted with his winner's check, Miss Whatchamacallit gave him a big kiss. Asher ran the picture in the next edition of *Tennis* magazine, and Kenny was furious. His wife saw the photo and was quite disturbed. Then there was the Sportface carpet-playing surface that kept coming up during play. Matches had to be stopped periodically for repairs. It finally got so bad that we insisted a Sportface Corporation executive and maintenance man stand by throughout the tournament. The overall experience was so worthwhile, even though there were many nights when Asher and I took a swig of Maalox before retiring.

Just about the time Jimmy Connors and John McEnroe were coming into prominence, we decided to forego future tennis promotions. Prize money had reached $300,000 and, without network television guarantees, selling sponsors became almost impossible. We banked our profits and quietly folded our tent. All-Star Tennis, Inc., had had its day.

MEMO TO THE PLAYERS

To the players, I always wanted to say that to sustain the current monetary rewards being offered, outstanding play on the court is not enough. There is evidence that purchasers of tickets are unhappy with childlike deportment, histrionics, racquet throwing, and fits of temper. They expect a top level of play regardless of the player's emotional stresses. Tournament tennis is partly show business, and lackluster play will be successful only in keeping audiences to a minimum. Fans come to the matches expecting to view overall expertise. In addition, they are searching for charisma, the magic spark that makes a player exciting to watch. It's the ingredient that brings a legion of loyal fans to stare at men like Arnold Palmer, Jack Nicklaus, Tiger Woods, Andre Agassi, and Pete Sampras.

There should be a comprehension by the players of the tremendous value of publicity and an enthusiasm on their part to participate in building attendance, to want to help justify the prize money. Some players do. Some players recognize their key role and are anxious to take advantage of the news media's interest in the sport. I am happy to see that the USTA has made it mandatory that players participate in their post-match press briefing.

WORLD CUP OF POLO

Emperors of the T'ang Dynasty tapped their treasuries to pay for the ponies imported from beyond the Great Wall. They played polo at night by the light of a thousand candles and conferred imperial favor upon palace high goalers. Polo then, as now, was a game of speed, beauty, and danger. It also was as expensive then as now. Leaders of the polo fraternity agree that while low-goal polo was flourishing in this country, costs of the high-goal international game were soaring faster and higher. Maharajas, kings, and other such traditional sponsors find exorbitant polo costs no longer fashionable, and, prior to the relatively recent bull market surge, even Texas oil barons pulled back. There have been two exceptions; they are William Ylvisaker, Chicago industrialist, and Carlton Beal, a Texas oilman.

Both men believed that commercial sponsorship alone could rescue the game and restore it to the high-goal heyday of the '20s and '30s, when Tommy Hitchcock, Jr., and Cecil Smith were nationally known polo players.

A polo player since his undergraduate days at Yale, Ylvisaker was chairman and CEO of Gould, Inc., a giant electrical manufacturer heavy in government contracts. He was also captain of the Yale tennis team. Gould's vice president of marketing was Del Fuller, another enthusiastic tennis player. Del and I had played together several times with not even the tiniest reference to what either of us did for a living. On one occasion, he had invited me to his club for a doubles game, and Bill Ylvisaker turned out to be his partner. To my surprise, Ylvisaker seemed to be aware of the success Asher and I had had in promoting men's professional tennis. He told me that he had hopes that polo could gain the kind of sponsors who had backed pro tennis in recent years. Were this to happen, he envisioned a new golden era for the sport, including national television coverage. It was all casual conversation over a cool beer following our doubles match, and I didn't give it a second thought.

Del and I played often and wore each other out regularly. Dripping wet after our combat, Del asked me to meet with Bill Ylvisaker at his office to discuss a public relations matter. I was pleased at the invitation, and actually thought we were going to discuss Gould, Inc. I was in for a rude awakening. Mr. Ylvisaker wanted to talk about polo. He explained that, although he only carried a three to five handicap, he was driven to find a way to reclaim the former fame and prestige of the game here in the United States. He was determined to bring the World Cup of Polo back to the U.S., but needed someone to help promote the event and bring a large, attentive audience to watch the world's foremost players in action. I told him I thought the idea had merit, but couldn't figure out what he wanted of me. It didn't take long to catch the drift, and I quickly responded, "Whoa, Bill. I don't know diddly about polo. I have never seen a polo match. I don't even know how they keep score, or what a chukker is. I don't know one damn thing about polo. There is no way I could handle the publicity."

Ylvisaker never struck me as a man who laughs easily, but he burst out laughing. "There's no bullshit about you, is there?" he said.

"Bill," I stammered, "the last thing I want to do is turn business down. As an agency, we're growing and we are hungry. Working with you and Del would be a client situation that I would take great pride in. However, if I were to take the account telling you how expert I was in polo promotion, it would be scandalously dishonest."

Bill laughed again and told me, "There is no one in the Chicago market that is experienced in polo promotion. You and your organization have proven yourself over and over again with your success with the White Sox, and with tennis. If I am to pull this World Cup together, I need your help." And so, a new page in the public relations book was turned.

It took the staff team six weeks to absorb every word that had ever been written about polo, and to start feeling comfortable with the idea. Bill's brainchild was a $150,000 event titled the Gould World Cup, and it was to be held at the Butler polo grounds in Oak Brook, Illinois. Invitations went out to countries all over the world known to have top-ranked professional polo teams. Three teams from the United States were recruited, and one each from Mexico, India, England, and two from Argentina. As the event began to take shape, it didn't take long to see a total lack of interest on the part of the news media. We were cranking out material on the various international players coming to Chicago as fast as our fingers could press the keys on our computers. Nothing was breaking. It was as though we were about to play a pickup softball game in a schoolyard.

I reread every line that the staff had written and found the material informative and legitimate news for the Chicago market, perhaps of interest to the wire services. We were butting our heads against a concrete wall. There was an occasional tiny one-column story about one inch deep, but nothing more. Del and I talked it over several times, and we both felt something was wrong. Either the media didn't understand the magnitude of the Gould World Cup, or they felt that it was not major news and no one really cared about polo. In either case, it was time for some head-to-head confrontation, and I was elected to carry the ball.

The sports editors at the *Sun-Times* and *Tribune* both said, "Who cares?" Dick Hackenburg, sports editor of the *Sun-Times*, told me he felt that polo was strictly a rich man's sport and that his readers couldn't relate. He said, "Our readers do not own horses and, except for an occasional fling at the Thoroughbred racetracks, couldn't care less."

Now I knew Dick to be one of the most open-minded newsmen in Chicago, and he had been more than fair to me through innumerable ventures. He had always been very approachable with ideas and I felt this was a critical conversation. Had I left without changing his mind regarding polo coverage, there was no way the World Cup could hope to draw the kind of crowds we were counting on. So I took a deep breath and came back at him with, "Dick, how many people attend the Indianapolis 500? Is that not the largest sports draw in the country? What about the Daytona race, and practically every Grand Prix automobile race, wherever it is held? Isn't it true that auto racing holds the all-time record for attendance? If the answer to those questions is 'yes,' then how many people in America can afford to own a racing car? Is automobile racing considered a rich man's sport? You know it's not and that, if anything, it has become a blue-collar sport. Is that any different from polo? The problem really is that most people have not been exposed to top-level polo and don't understand how beautiful and thrilling and dangerous it can be. Dick, they are the best in the world, and by not permitting our stories to appear, you are preventing Chicagoans from ever learning about polo and perhaps enjoying the spectator aspects of the game."

He said, "That's enough. One more minute and you'll have me in tears. We will try to do better for your World Cup and see if it can draw." I thanked him and hit the road. Someone had once told me that when you've made the sale, know when to shut up.

I've seen more accounts lost because the presenter didn't know when to stop. On a high, I repeated my spiel at the *Tribune* and came away with a promise to give us a full-color, front sports page feature on opening day. Shortly thereafter, the publicity gates opened wide and, surprise, surprise, tickets began to move.

Persistent rain nearly caused cancellation of the opening game. The field was so soaked that it presented a dangerous situation for both horse and rider. In desperation, we brought in helicopters to fly five feet above the ground with their whirling propellers, which would create wind drafts to help dry the ground faster. The cost was astronomical, but it worked. Mrs. Jorie Ford Butler, the driving force of Oak Brook, was a diminutive powerhouse before and during the tournament. The World Cup would not have been possible without her. She was everywhere and always at the right time. She kept track of more than fifty players from the various countries, cantered out to inspect the various practice fields, served as best pony judge at the big games, settled disputes, and soothed the ruffled feathers of Mexican players, who felt they needed more practice field time. She even served as hostess with Mrs. Ylvisaker at parties for the players, wives, and officials.

The world seemed to know, and we quickly learned, that the Argentineans were the finest polo players. There are only five 10-goal players in the world, all Argentineans. Three of them were on the current team, including Alfredo Harriott, Alberto Heguy, and Gonzalo Tanoira. The fourth member of the Argentine team was Juan Carlos Alberdi, a mere 8 handicapper. Combined, they represented 38 goals. Their closest competition came from an American team that featured Tommy Wayman (9 handicap), Joe Barry (9 handicap), Charles Smith (7 handicap), and Red Armour (8 handicap).

Looking like motion picture stars, the Argentine team gathered before the match to plan their strategy. Although I stood nearby, my Spanish was so poor that I could grasp a few words at a time. Each man was dark, handsome, and dressed to kill, with what appeared to me to be a devil-may-care attitude. The American team came from the West and Southwest and, with one exception, appeared to be cowboys. U.S. high-goalers were nearly all professionals who raised and sold ponies. On the other side, the Argentine high-goalers were wealthy ranchers who considered themselves amateurs, because being a professional is frowned upon. To make the Gould World Cup enticing to the teams from Argentina, the Americans agreed to buy ponies sight unseen. As a result, the Argentine team came in from Buenos Aires, played with their ponies, and then turned them over to the Americans. The Americans then held an auction and sold the ponies.

The polo world was a new adventure for our public relations team. Oak Brook comes alive at first light, and to gather the background color for feature stories, we agreed that it was necessary to be there at that time. Country music played on transistor radios, which hung from stall doors. Strange smells were in the air, combining liniment with manure. Although it was barely dawn, the polo players had already gathered with mugs of hot coffee, wearing their cowboy hats and blue jeans. They sat on bales of hay and watched the female grooms hose down their Thoroughbred ponies. Nearby in a tack room, dozens of mallets were neatly stacked and ready for action. I stood there, thinking that scene was just one more reason why I loved that crazy business. It has never been the same. In the public relations business, at least as I have practiced it, you can never become bored.

WEST PALM BEACH, FLORIDA

As expected, the Argentine team won. For the uninitiated Cushman team, watching the speed and daring of the players, and the amazing dexterity of both riders and horses, was a revelation. The polo bug had bitten us. When it was over, receipts showed that the World Cup had drawn about 5,000 paying patrons. Not a smashing success for all the time and money that had been invested, but enough to indicate there was a solid base upon which to build. However, Bill Ylvisaker and his polo leadership colleagues were shaken with the Chicago weather, which had almost ruined the international competition. They definitely wanted to continue, but were going to move the second Gould Polo World Cup to West Palm Beach, Florida. Del asked if we would be interested in handling the next go-around and now, considering ourselves quite expert in polo machinations, I told him yes.

This time, things would be considerably different. We would not have the luxury of working in our familiar back yard, with easy access to friendly media. We would be living in hotel rooms, removed from our homes and families for lengthy periods of time, with no Jorie Butler watching every detail. Ylvisaker wanted me to be responsible for everything from ticket sales, parking, signage, security, VIP accommodations, press credentials and conferences, souvenir purchasing and selling, food concessions and catering to the VIP lounge. This, in addition to promotion, advertising and publicity. It seemed like he was asking me to climb Mt. Everest. Had we learned enough in the Chicago tournament? This was clearly more than promotion. It was management from start to finish. The only element we would not be responsible for was the recruitment of international teams and providing facilities for their ponies. Happily, Mrs. Ylvisaker agreed to host the social functions. Could we do it successfully? Was the risk of falling on our respective faces worth the promised fee? You're damn right it was!

This time, we had almost a year, and we needed every single minute. The constant reminder that we still had one of the largest independent public relations firms in the country to operate gave me cause to hesitate. The Cushman team would have to be a very committed group, and I felt they needed to volunteer for this assignment. They had to be people who really wanted to go. Everyone I asked was ready. They made it easy for me. I found an unexpected bonanza with Nancy Quinn, who was my administrative assistant. In fifty years, there have only been four secretaries. Nancy came from Denver following an unhappy marriage and provided references. After testing her secretarial skills, I asked her to wait in the reception room while I called her former employer. The conversation went like this: he said, "Is Nancy still there? If she is, lock the door and don't let her get away." What I didn't know was that in her recent past, she had handled tickets for several important events in Denver. She took over control of ticket printing, reserved seating, and banking. I relegated myself to making periodic trips to Florida, and otherwise watched my staff work wonders.

We did make a pitch to ESPN for national coverage of the final match. They had all the doubts we had heard before, but finally agreed to tape delay the presentation. To make it happen, Ylvisaker agreed to underwrite some aspects of the cost.

As the polo matches began, I found our biggest problem was handling the crowds and the parking. Historically, polo in West Palm Beach attracted a few hundred die-hard fans, most of them very social. They were accustomed to coming to the Sunday matches, parking next to the stadium, casually lunching with friends before and during the matches, and generally "ooing" and "ahing" the horses and riders. With several thousand folks attending each day's games, there was a drastic change awaiting these polo regulars.

My introduction to these well-meaning, but somewhat pompous, people came opening day. Using walkie-talkies to communicate, I heard a plea from the parking director, "Would you please come down and help me with an unhappy customer?" Wearing slacks and a T-shirt in the ninety-degree heat, I flew down the stairs and into the parking lot.

Of course, it was a Rolls Royce and the driver was a lovely senior lady. "Young man," she started, "for years I have been parking my car exactly at the front stairs to the grandstand, and this gentleman tells me that I cannot do that today because all the spaces are taken."

I could see she was quite upset and tried to explain that the World Cup had attracted many more people than she was accustomed to seeing on a normal Sunday afternoon. She was having none of it. Becoming somewhat boisterous, she said, "Do you know who I am?"

I apologized and said, "No, ma'am, I don't."

"Well, sonny, I am Mrs. Got Rocks," or something to that effect, "and if I can't have my regular parking place, someone will hear about this."

It was not the only problem, but typical of what we ran into. We had invaded their private, comfortable domain, and "they" didn't appreciate it.

Despite these rare occurrences, the Gould World Cup matches were a great success. Yes, the Argentineans won again. Crowds were excellent, and everyone left with that wonderful feeling of winning.

THE ORANGE CRUSH DEFENSE

Increasingly, the corporate world seeks an accurate measurement for their investment in public relations. To me, the marketing side of public relations results can best be addressed by examining the bottom line. More often than not, looking hard at sales, comparing advertising expenditures and results prior to the advent of public relations techniques and after, can tell a lot. Admittedly, it does not tell the whole story, because other elements must be considered, such as production, distribution, warehousing, etc.

One such situation I had previously described was the introduction of Keebler Cookie Company's Soft Batch brand. They achieved more than a thirty percent share of market, a good portion of which was attributed to the public relations effort. Another bottom line building program revolved around the Denver Bronco professional football team and their Orange Crush defense.

In 1977, the Denver Broncos enjoyed one of their finest seasons, buoyed by a defensive unit nicknamed "The Orange Crush." Dick Stahler and I had just returned from the Utah Salt Flats and an unsuccessful try at breaking the world's land speed record. Dick, an agency senior vice president and long-time colleague, was creative director of the agency. A little rough around the edges, but a tremendous creative talent, Dick had been responsible for many of the agency's meaningful ideas in producing bottom line sales impact for several clients. He wasn't much on tact, and fiercely defended his direct approach, but I respected his ability and loved him personally. He was my kind of guy.

On a cool and breezy Sunday afternoon, the two of us were high up in the bleachers watching the Broncos play. When we first sat down and saw the sea of orange worn by Bronco fans, Dick and I looked at each other. We had been representing Crush International, Inc., bottlers of Orange Crush soft drink. It was two minds with a single thought. On that fateful day, neither Dick nor I could tell you who won the game because we didn't stay in our seats long enough to watch. We beat a path to the promotional office of the team, and before we left, had cut a deal directly tying the soft drink to the Bronco defense.

Because of the instant fan recognition for the product, "Orange Crush Fever" swept Denver, and then the nation, as the Broncos went all the way to the Super Bowl. This groundswell of enthusiasm was managed and nurtured by the agency via a number of creative and perfectly timed publicity-generating activities.

From the time the agency involvement began, through Super Bowl Sunday, sales of Orange Crush rose fifty-four percent nationally, and more than two hundred percent in Colorado and adjacent states. This sales spurt took place during a time of the year (winter) when orange drink demand is usually soft. Interesting aside: the promotion didn't cost Crush International one penny in licensing or rights fees. There were two amazing facts: first, all Bronco print collateral and support T-shirt type products featured the actual Crush logo exactly as it appeared on the Crush product; secondly, over $2 million of television time was obtained during the Super Bowl telecast on behalf of Orange Crush, at no cost to our client.

It was the one and only time I had ever been to the Super Bowl. Dick Stahler and I had the time of our lives watching those cases of Orange Crush being unloaded from charter aircraft, seeing the sea of Orange Crush logos on shirts worn by almost 50,000 screaming fans, and watching the network television program pick up our client's material.

CHAPTER 15

Cushman's Top 20 Tips
for Public Relations _____

Any PR person, regardless of level, who takes advantage
of these Top 20 Tips is destined to succeed.

As the year's pass, the public relations business will undoubtedly take many twists and turns as it continues to grow and gain management respect. Opportunities can be found within a myriad of specialties including marketing, finance, internal and international relations, hospital/medical, politics, and government.

In the hope that some element of what I have learned through five decades of experience may be helpful to today's practitioners, as well as to students with an eye toward a future in public relations, here is a list of my Top 20 Tips for success.

1. Maintain your integrity. In the eyes of your client/management, you are a public relations counselor, not a hired copywriter or secretary. Your responsibility to your client/management means you have to advise suggest, counsel, and recommend. If you believe in something, or are firmly opposed, it is your responsibility to stand up and support your position. Never be afraid to tell management when, in your professional judgment, they are wrong. Show PR leadership. You are the expert. Be confident. Don't *ask* your client, *tell* him or her. This evidence of confidence will gain their respect, and you will be maintaining your integrity without being antagonistic.

2. Be pro-active. Have a nose for news. Initiate news and feature stories, promotions, and special events. Don't wait for the client or management to suggest them.

3. Write for media acceptance, not client approval. Build a reputation for accurate and quality material. In his newsletter, Jack O'Dwyer reported, "Clients Air Gripes About PR Firms." Some of these gripes were, "They want well-edited copy" and "Too much material comes from agencies with misspellings, typos, and grammatical flaws."

4. You cannot bury a negative story, so play it straight with the media. The story will run its course, and hopefully you will have built sufficient positive media relations to help soften their approach. Counsel client or management against hiding during trying times… and *never* lie.

5. There is no such thing as off the record. Today, as reporters madly surge to win a Pulitzer, most media people are trustworthy, despite the temptation to stretch the truth and occasionally spin. Nevertheless, the frequency of violating a promise not to publish is so flagrant that any PR practitioner, attempting to protect his or her client, must advise the interviewee that if they don't want to see it in print or on television, they simply shouldn't say it.

6. Be solid business people. Talk the client's language. Discuss distribution channels, warehousing, competition, pricing policies, marketing techniques, production, research, inventory, and shipping, not column inches and double trucks. Confirm important decisions and conversations in writing.

7. Maintain a daily "to do" sheet, and update it regularly. PR is a business of detail. To avoid errors or overlooking a key element, keep your to-do sheet current. Use normal working hours (8 a.m. to 5 p.m.) for implementation. Do preparation and planning when the media are in quiet time.

8. Protect your reputation for fairness. Rotate your key announcements between a.m. and p.m. media. Understand and respect media deadlines. Avoid sending "For immediate release" material to magazines and non-daily newspapers.

9. Research your media targets. Before submitting written material or making a phone contact, research each columnist's or broadcaster's style and subject matter interest. Don't waste your time, media time, or your client's money by submitting improper or uninteresting stories to the wrong people.

10. Research your client's or company's market. Know whom you are attempting to reach. Study their demographics: age level, income, education, marital status, working or retired, gender, culture, and geographic limitations. Make a concentrated effort to learn the client's industry: its history, growth, problems, and chief competitors.

11. Think creatively. Challenge yourself to develop ideas that will make news. The recognized father of the public relations business, Edward Bernays, said, "Make news, not news releases."

12. Spend your client's money like it's your own. Maintain meticulous budgetary control to avoid running out of funds before the campaign is complete.

13. Programming: The Art of Thinking Ahead. Work from a written program that is understood and accepted by management or client. Some new accounts come equipped with a basic PR program that was included in your initial presentation. In most cases, the client has received only general ideas and rudimentary guidelines, so a program of specific activities and clearly established direction must be developed. Always maintain a certain amount of flexibility to take advantage of targets of opportunity.

14. Be a good listener. I have sold more major business by letting the prospect talk himself into accepting our proposal. Remember that "please" and "thank you" are the ABC's of the PR business.

15. Become an insider. To service any client satisfactorily, you must establish a close working relationship – become an "insider." Early in your employment, there is a necessity to gain their respect and confidence. To properly fulfill your obligations, there needs to be access to all client/ management information. As a counselor, your position should be a part of management. Remember, you are never offstage. Regardless of the circumstances, whenever you are in the presence of the client or management, whether social or business, you can never relax and "let your hair down." You are constantly being scrutinized. Unsuccessful PR persons will always be relegated to the "back of the bus."

16. Nothing takes the place of persistence and determination. Remove the phrase "It can't be done" from your lexicon and fight to avoid accepting any "no." Almost always, there is a way to succeed, if one remains determined. Be persistent, but maintain dignity. Never ask media for favors.

17. Measure impact not output. In a lean economy, results matter. Every dollar expended counts. More than before, corporate executives are demanding bottom line results. PR practitioners are expected to produce more tangible results with fewer budgetary dollars. The writing and distribution of information, no matter how carefully thought out and prepared, is not the measure of success. You are in the publicity and public relations business, and, unless a meaningful placement is made, the entire effort is wasted. Depending upon the subject matter, whether financial, internal relations, or marketing, the measure of success is the market's reaction or the impact to your placement. Was the market affected? Did your story placement assuage a potential employee problem? Did your placement result in the movement of product off the shelves? Be prepared to statistically prove the effectiveness of your campaign.

18. Use innovation in marketing. Let PR add another dimension to the marketing mix. Be strong in merchandising the results of your publicity efforts to the point of sale and in creating marketing-oriented promotions and special events.

19. Keep your promises. That thought is so simplistic that no further explanation is needed. Keep in mind that following through on your promises applies to both media and management.

20. Don't be an ostrich. Everyone in PR hopes it never happens, but sometimes your program, in spite of your best efforts, just doesn't work out, leaving you with no results to show management or client. During such crisis conditions, it is not unusual to run scared and be afraid either to see or talk to the client. We justify this approach to ourselves with the rationale that something is bound to break soon, at which time we will again magically appear in the client's office. Don't hide from the client! He has the right to know what is going on. He will respect your honesty if you come forward. If you have done your preparatory work in client education, the client should know that every story will not pull and that every promotion may not be a rousing success. Candidly explain that the campaign direction has not been bringing in the desired results and that you are suggesting a change in approach. Take the initiative and things will work out better than if you bury your head or kick the problem under the rug.

Admittedly, these Top 20 Tips are not individually earthshaking. They are, however, a practical compilation of genuine thoughts and ideas learned over more than fifty years of practicing public relations. Any PR person, regardless of level, who takes advantage of these Top 20 Tips, is destined to succeed.

Looking through the rear window, I realize how fortunate I have been to participate in five careers thus far in my life: military, entertainment, corporate, professional, and family. Through it all, I have carried a passion for winning. I have found that philosophy applicable to each career, and have tried to implant that positive attitude into every person that ever worked in the Cushman agency, as well as within my children and grandchildren.

How rare to find a vocation within which to spend your life and never regret a single day! How truly fortunate to be compensated for doing what you actually enjoy. To those thousands of men and women who have selected public relations for their life's work, it is my sincere wish that, recognizing all the pressures and frustrations in our business, you will feel as I do: I love the PR business.

Acknowledgements

I am indebted to Amy Wilton, Steve and Wilma Davidson, and Steve Moore for their computer expertise. To David Whitaker for his early encouragement. To Judy Tabacik, John Birnbaum, Audri Adams, and Sherman Wolf for their research assistance. To my dear friend, Alan Bell, one of our nation's most prominent PR practitioners; and to Jack Ryan, my agent, confidant, and good friend. To Ralph Yearick and Lighthouse Point Press for their confidence.

Some of the early people who helped build the Cushman agency were Eddie Gettelman, Helen LeSieur, Audri Adams, Susan Edwards, Lee Gottleib, Lee Block, Sherman Wolf, Richard Stahler, Cher Patric Cox, Jean Leinhauser, Sue Block, Janet Blair, Dennis Cline, Karen Thompson, Dawn Plambeck, Cindy Kurman, Megan Vincenzo Bueschel, Bob Lunn, Sherry Bail, Rich Brill, Steve Knipstein, Chris Hills, Joanie Stat, Peggy Reinhert, Nick Bridges, Phil Hoffman, Sherwood Wallace, Chuck Shriver, Jay Kelly, Sharon Lang, Jan Johns, Holly Bligh Kravitz, Gilda Moss, Elaine Katz, Ralph Banghart, Herb Baum, Beverly Winkey, Tom Simons, Edward Wade, Enid Stenn, Loretto Bavaro, Val Savic, Kathy Wingo Grambauer, Virginia Carroll, and Dorothy Delasso.

On the business side, there was Tina Horwitz, Avis Rudner, and Rose Kasman. In the fifty years I was in the PR business, I was fortunate to have exceptional secretaries, or more accurately, administrative assistants. There were only four, and each was a super lady, including Joan Beckert, Nancy Quinn, Francine Podegraz, and wonderful Judy Tabacik.

To each of the above, the writer of this book is deeply grateful.